UNITED STATES FOREIGN
CAMBODIA, 1977–92

GW01451734

CONTEMPORARY HISTORY IN CONTEXT
Published in association with the Institute of Contemporary British History

General Editor: Peter Catterall, Director, Institute of Contemporary British History

Titles include:

Oliver Bange
THE EEC CRISIS OF 1963: Macmillan, de Gaulle, Adenauer and Kennedy in Conflict

Christopher Brady
UNITED STATES FOREIGN POLICY TOWARDS CAMBODIA, 1977–92

Peter Catterall and Sean McDougall (*editors*)
THE NORTHERN IRELAND QUESTION IN BRITISH POLITICS

Helen Fawcett and Rodney Lowe (*editors*)
WELFARE POLICY IN BRITAIN: The Road from 1945

Harriet Jones and Michael Kandiah (*editors*)
THE MYTH OF CONSENSUS: New Views on British History, 1945–64

Wolfram Kaiser
USING EUROPE, ABUSING THE EUROPEANS: Britain and European Integration, 1945–63

Spencer Mawby
CONTAINING GERMANY: Britain and the Arming of the Federal Republic

Jeffrey Pickering
BRITAIN'S WITHDRAWAL FROM EAST OF SUEZ: The Politics of Retrenchment

L. V. Scott
MACMILLAN, KENNEDY AND THE CUBAN MISSILE CRISIS: Political, Military and Intelligence Aspects

Paul Sharp
THATCHER'S DIPLOMACY: The Revival of British Foreign Policy

Contemporary History in Context
Series Standing Order ISBN 978-0-333-71470-6
(*outside North America only*)

You can receive future titles in this series as they are published by placing a standing order. Please contact your bookseller or, in case of difficulty, write to us at the address below with your name and address, the title of the series and the ISBN quoted above.

Customer Services Department, Macmillan Distribution Ltd
Houndmills, Basingstoke, Hampshire RG21 6XS, England

United States Foreign Policy towards Cambodia, 1977–92

A Question of Realities

Christopher Brady
Lecturer in Decision-Making Theory and Systems
City University Business School
London

in association with
PALGRAVE MACMILLAN

ICBH

First published in Great Britain 1999 by
MACMILLAN PRESS LTD
Houndmills, Basingstoke, Hampshire RG21 6XS and London
Companies and representatives throughout the world

A catalogue record for this book is available from the British Library.

ISBN 978-1-349-14847-9   ISBN 978-1-349-14845-5 (eBook)
DOI 10.1007/978-1-349-14845-5

First published in the United States of America 1999 by
ST. MARTIN'S PRESS, INC.,
Scholarly and Reference Division,
175 Fifth Avenue, New York, N.Y. 10010

ISBN 978-0-312-22021-1

Library of Congress Cataloging-in-Publication Data
Brady, Christopher, 1947–
United States foreign policy towards Cambodia, 1977–92 : a
question of realities / Christopher Brady.
p.   cm. — (Contemporary history in context series)
Includes bibliographical references and index.
ISBN 978-0-312-22021-1 (cloth)
1. United States—Foreign relations—Cambodia.   2. Cambodia–
–Foreign relations—United States.   3. United States—Foreign
relations—1977–1981.   4. United States—Foreign
relations—1981–1989.   5. United States—Foreign
relations—1989–1993.   I. Title.   II. Series.
E183.8.C15B73   1999
327.730596—dc21

98–48284
CIP

© Christopher Brady 1999
Foreword © Peter Catterall 1999
Softcover reprint of the hardcover 1st edition 1999

All rights reserved. No reproduction, copy or transmission of this publication may be made
without written permission.

No paragraph of this publication may be reproduced, copied or transmitted save with
written permission or in accordance with the provisions of the Copyright, Designs and
Patents Act 1988, or under the terms of any licence permitting limited copying issued by
the Copyright Licensing Agency, 90 Tottenham Court Road, London W1P 9HE.

Any person who does any unauthorised act in relation to this publication may be liable to
criminal prosecution and civil claims for damages.

The author has asserted his right to be identified as the author of this work in accordance
with the Copyright, Designs and Patents Act 1988.

10   9   8   7   6   5   4   3   2   1
08   07   06   05   04   03   02   01   00   99

For Tara, Ellie and Patrick

Contents

General Editor's Foreword

Palmerston famously argued that states do not have permanent allies, only permanent interests. But how are these permanent interests calculated and pursued? The answer offered in Chris Brady's case-study of US policy towards Cambodia 1977–92 is that the prime factor is the explicit or implicit understandings on which policy-makers proceed. In other words, policy is based on how those who make it construct reality. Policy-making is thus directed at managing or changing (depending on priorities) that constructed reality. That reality is not necessarily singular. As Brady shows, policy-making may be the end-product of a bureaucratic process in which a number of different realities, both of the situation in Cambodia and how it relates to US interests, compete.

This could result in apparently contradictory outcomes. For instance, the over-arching rhetoric of the Carter administration, the absolute commitment to human rights invoked in his first inaugural in 1977, seems dramatically at odds with subsequent policy towards Cambodia under Pol Pot. The Khmer Rouge may have been international pariahs as far as Congressional critics were concerned. But successive administrations constructed their policy towards Cambodia within a rather different context. The prism through which they viewed Cambodia was not distinctive to Cambodia itself. Nor was it the human rights agenda which the Carter administration had overtly set itself which determined how it was viewed. Rather, policy towards Cambodia was constructed in a setting in which the Cold War was the dominant reality. The pursuit of human rights, as Brady shows in his account of the conflict between Vance and Brzezinski under Carter, was to prove subordinate to this over-arching theme. Cambodia, therefore, despite the significance it might have been expected to have had, was no more than a minor actor in the Cold War. Policy towards Cambodia was thus determined by an environment in which opposition to Vietnam, particularly as a Soviet ally, was more significant than abhorrence of the Khmer Rouge. Admittedly US policy-makers would probably have preferred a more palatable choice than one between Vietnam and the Khmer Rouge, but much of the time there were, in practice, only the most limited alternatives.

One of the main reasons why US alternatives were so limited was

ix

because of a subordinate, but nevertheless influential reality which impinged significantly on its options. This was the apparent lesson of the Vietnam War. As Brady shows, there was considerable debate about what these lessons were for policy-makers in the period under review. George Bush, in the end, was to revise these lessons. However, this did not seem to undermine the significance of the key lesson as far as policy towards Cambodia was concerned. This was the need to avoid any further entanglements such as the Vietnam War. Therefore, whilst human rights might be on the agenda, there were strict limits to how these might be pursued, particularly in a situation where none of the possible alternatives, whether Sihanouk, the KR or the Vietnamese to take some examples, seemed both feasible and desirable. The result was that US policy towards Cambodia tended to be reactive. Instead, the US sought to align its policy with that of ASEAN, as the relevant regional actor. Insofar as it had a Cambodian policy, as distinct from the way in which the Cold War impinged upon its policy towards Cambodia, it reflected this constructed reality that the best way to pursue it was in association with and through the agency of ASEAN.

This remained true with the end of the Cold War. In a sense the unravelling of the Soviet Union created opportunities for a shift in policy towards Cambodia, by removing the prime determinant of that policy hitherto. Indeed, policy was to shift during the Bush administration, because one of the major elements in the construction of the policy-makers' reality had gone. However, the lessons of Vietnam were nevertheless still there. Chris Brady thus shows us that the construction of reality not only drives foreign policy-making, it also constrains it.

PETER CATTERALL

Acknowledgement

Anita Brady, for all her help.

List of Abbreviations

ANS	Armée Nationale Sihanounkiste
ASEAN	Association of South East Asian Nations
CGDK	Coalition Government of Democratic Kampuchea
DK	Democratic Kampuchea
DRV	Democratic Republic of Vietnam (N. Viet)
FUNCINPEC	United Front for an Independent, Neutral, Peaceful and Co-operative Cambodia
FUNK	Khmer National United Front
GRUNK	Royal Government of National Unification of Kampuchea
ICK	International Conference on Kampuchea
ICP	Indochinese Communist Party
IFMC	Indochinese Foreign Ministers Conference
IMC	Informal Meeting on Cambodia
JIM	Jakarta Informal Meeting
KCP	Kampuchean Communist Party
KPNLA	Kampuchean People's National Liberation Army
KPNLF	Khmer People's National Liberation Front
KPP	Khmer People's Party, also known as Khmer People's Revolutionary Party (KPRP)
KR	Khmer Rouge
MMWG	Mixed Military Working Group
MOULINAKA	Mouvement pour la Liberation Nationale du Kampuchea
NADK	National Army of Democratic Kampuchea
NCR	Non-Communist Resistance
P5	Permanent 5 members of the UN Security Council
PFLANK	Khmer People's National Liberation Armed Forces
PRC	People's Republic of China
PRK	People's Republic of Kampuchea
RAK	Revolutionary Army of Kampuchea
SCR	Security Council Resolution

SNC	Supreme National Council
SOC	State of Cambodia
SRV	Socialist Republic of Vietnam
UN	United Nations
UNAMIC	United Nations Advanced Mission in Cambodia
UNGA	United Nations General Assembly
UNSC	United Nations Security Council
UNTAC	United Nations Transitional Authority for Cambodia
VC	Viet Cong
WPK	Workers' Party of Kampuchea

Chronology

	1863	King Norodom accepts French protectorate.
April 25	1941	Norodom Sihanouk, aged 18, crowned king by French.
March 12	1945	Under Japanese Occupation, Sihanouk declares independence from France.
May	1945	Son Ngoc Thanh returns from refuge in Japan.
June	1945	Son Ngoc Thanh becomes foreign minister.
August	1945	Son Ngoc Thanh becomes prime minister.
October	1945	British and French troops occupy Cambodia; Son Ngoc Thanh deported for treason.
November 11	1945	Indochina Communist Party (ICP), originally formed by Ho Chi Minh in 1930, dissolves itself.
	1946	Democratic Party win healthy majority in Assembly election; Party President Son Sann becomes Prime Minister.
September	1949	Sihanouk dissolves Assembly.
	1949	The Paris Group, including Saloth Sar (Pol Pot), Ieng Sary and Khieu Samphan meet.
November 8	1949	French grant limited independence to Cambodia with Franco-Cambodian Treaty; Cambodia becomes an Associate state in the French Union. Sihanouk includes Lon Nol in cabinet.
September 30	1951	Vietnamese reorganise remnants of ICP into three national parties, forming and dominating the Khmer People's Party (KPP).
October	1951	Son Ngoc Thanh returns to Cambodia at request of the Democratic Party but is quickly forced back into exile with Khmer Serei.
Summer	1953	King Norodom Sihanouk briefly exiled in

		Thailand; launches 'Royal Crusade for Independence' from France.
November 9	1953	French grant complete independence to Cambodia.
May 7	1954	Dien Bien Phu falls.
May 8	1954	Geneva Conference on Indochina convenes under British and Soviet chairmanship.
July 21	1954	Geneva ends, orders free elections for Cambodia and Vietnam, plus a pullout of Viet Minh forces in Cambodia; KPP pulls out with Viet Minh, goes to Hanoi, to return in 1968 and 1970; a few KPP cadres stay to fight, some to form Pracheachon or 'People's Party' (political wing of KPRP) to contest elections
November	1954	Son Ngoc Thanh exiled to Thailand.
December 31	1954	United States announces aid to Cambodia, South Vietnam and Laos to combat communism.
March 2	1955	Sihanouk abdicates to father (Norodom Suramarit) and forms Sangkum Reastr Niyum; he remains head of this central political institution until 1970.
September 11	1955	National election returns 83% for Sihanouk's Sangkum, 13% for Liberal Democrat Party and 3% for communist Pracheachon Party.
February 13	1956	Sihanouk signs Sino-Cambodian Friendship Treaty.
Spring	1956	CIA begins funding anti-Sihanouk rightist group, Khmer Serei, led by Son Ngoc Thanh.
February 21	1959	Cambodian General Dap Chhuon secessionist attempt with Thai, South Vietnamese, Laotian, and US involvement is discovered and crushed by Sihanouk.
August 31	1959	Assassination attempt on king, queen and prince.
April 3	1960	King Suramarit dies, succession crisis follows.
June 20	1960	Prince Norodom Sihanouk becomes head of state.

September 30 1960	Second KPP congress, later renamed first congress of the Kampuchean Communist Party (KCP), convenes secretly in Phnom Penh and founds the Worker's Party of Kampuchea (WPK). Pol Pot, Nuon Chea and Touch Samouth are ruling truimvirate.
February 1963	Second WPK congress elects Pol Pot as Secretary General only seven months after mysterious disappearance of Touch Samouth, the previous SG.
May 1963	WPK changes name to Kampuchean Communist Party (KCP), sends 90% of leadership personnel underground for infrastructural work; Solath Sar confirmed as General Secretary; he and Leng Sary go to northeast and later visit China.
August 1963	Sihanouk severs relations with South Vietnam, renounces US military assistance.
December 1963	PRC begins delivery of military aid to Cambodia.
August 2 1964	Gulf of Tonkin incident.
March 8 1965	US marines land at Da Nang, Vietnam.
May 1 1965	US airstrikes in Cambodia's Parrot's Beak region.
May 3 1965	Sihanouk breaks diplomatic relations with US.
September 1965	Khieu Thirith and Khieu Ponnary (two sisters who became KCP Central Commitee members and wives of Leng Sary and Saloth Sar) go underground.
November 1965	Sihanouk sends General Lon Nol on aid-seeking mission to Peking; he returns with arms for 20 000.
September 11 1966	First election in Cambodia without pre-selection of candidates by Sihanouk.
October 22 1966	Rightist-dominated government emerges; Lon Nol is elected premier.
April 1967	Peasant uprising in Battambang province is viciously suppressed by Lon Nol at an estimated cost of 10 000 lives.
April 22 1967	Sihanouk accuses Khieu Samphan and

others of responsibility for uprising; Khieu Samphan flees and rejoins KCP.

April 30	1967	Sihanouk removes Lon Nol; Son Sann appointed as new Prime Minister.
May 2	1967	15 000 students demonstrate in Phnom Penh over assumed liquidation of Khieu Samphan by Sihanouk security forces.
January 8–12	1968	US Ambassador to India, Chester Bowles, visits Cambodia to explore resumption of relations with United States.
January 17	1968	KCP's newly founded Revolutionary Army of Kampuchea (RAK) begins guerrilla operations in 17 of 19 provinces.
January 27	1968	Sihanouk decares war on KCP and refers to them as the Khmer Rouge (KR).
January 29–30	1968	Sihanouk names 'Government of the last chance': Penn Nouth is Prime Minister, Son Sann his deputy.
March 17	1969	Nixon approves request for airstrikes in Cambodia.
June 11	1969	After hard-won progress by KR, Sihanouk re-establishes relations with the US.
August 1	1969	Penn Nouth resigns as Prime Minister.
August 12	1969	Lon Nol regains the Prime Ministry.
September	1969	Lon Nol returns banking and foreign trade to private sector. Sirik Matak becomes acting Prime Minister.
January 7	1970	Sihanouk goes to French Riviera for annual rest cure.
March 18	1970	National Assembly pass vote of no-confidence on Sihanouk by 83–3.
March 23	1970	Sihanouk announces formation of Khmer National United Front (FUNK); Khmer People's National Liberation Armed Forces (PFLANK) also formed.
March 26	1970	Khieu Samphan joins FUNK.
May 5	1970	Sihanouk's FUNK forms Royal Government of National Unification of Kampuchea (GRUNK); Sihanouk is the Chief of State; Khieu Samphan is vice premier and Minister of Defence. Penn

		Nouth is Prime Minister. DRV and PRC immediately recognise government in exile; PRC breaks relations with Lon Nol regime.
July 5	1970	Military tribunal sentences Sihanouk to death.
July 20	1970	Son Ngoc Thanh returns to Phnom Penh and joins Lon Nol regime.
October 9	1970	Lon Nol proclaims republic: Khmer Republic born.
December 31	1970	FUNK claims liberation of 70% of Cambodia.
April 21	1971	Lon Nol is proclaimed Marshal of the republic.
October 18	1971	Lon Nol dissolves National Assembly.
October 20	1971	Lon Nol declares state of emergency.
December 17	1971	Lon Nol revokes civil liberties and political rights in Khmer Republic.
March 11	1972	Lon Nol declares himself President of Khmer Republic, commander in chief of FANK and President of the Council of Ministers; Sirik Matak, Prime Minister.
March 13	1972	Sirik Matak is dismissed; Lon Nol takes the post of Prime Minister, later appoints Son Ngoc Thanh to Cabinet.
June 4	1972	Lon Nol is elected President of the republic, with 55% of the vote.
October 22	1972	Henry Kissinger goes to Phnom Penh to confer with Lon Nol.
November 11	1972	Sihanouk rejects Lon Nol ceasefire offer.
December 4	1972	PFLANK attacks Phnom Penh harbour.
December 9	1972	Khieu Samphan rejects Lon Nol call for talks.
January 27	1973	Paris Peace accords signed.
March 3	1973	PFLANK shells Phnom Penh.
March 21	1973	Sihanouk begins tour of liberated zones of Kampuchea.
June 3–4	1973	Nixon rejects Sihanouk negotiation offer.
August 1	1973	PFLANK tightens siege on Phnom Penh.
November 21	1973	Nixon pledges 'all out support' for Lon Nol.
March 28	1974	Khieu Samphan leads delegation including Sihanouk on tour of socialist and non-aligned nations.

August 9	1974	Richard Nixon resigns.
January 1	1975	GRUNK/FUNK/PFLANK/KCP launch final offensive, known as the 'Mekong River Offensive'.
April 1	1975	Lon Nol flees Phnom Penh.
April 17	1975	Khmer Rouge march into Phnom Penh.
September 9	1975	Sihanouk returns to Phnom Penh as head of state, at Khieu Samphan's request.
November 15	1975	Sihanouk goes on an eleven-nation tour on behalf of emergent state.
December 31	1975	Sihanouk returns to Kampuchea.
January 5	1976	Democratic Kampuchea comes into existence.
March 20	1976	Pol Pot elected to National Assembly.
April 4	1976	Sihanouk resigns as head of state and placed under house-arrest; Khieu Samphan new head of state.
April 14	1976	Internal shake-up in Democratic Kampuchea leadership; Pol Pot becomes Prime Minister.
September 27	1976	Nuon Chea replaces Pol Pot as Prime Minister.
October 15	1976	Pol Pot regains Prime Minister's portfolio.
January 20	1977	Jimmy Carter sworn in as 39th US president.
April 30	1977	DK launch large-scale attacks on Vietnamese border regions.
May	1977	Fierce Vietnamese-Kampuchean border battles.
June 30	1977	US formally ends membership of SEATO (after 23 years).
July 18	1977	Vietnam and Laos sign 25-year Treaty of Mutual Friendship and Co-operation.
August	1977	Abortive coup against KR (possibly Hanoi sponsored).
August 21–25	1977	Vance visits China.
September	1977	DK engage in border attacks. Vietnam retaliates with incursions along the entire border length.
November 1	1977	US confirm no aid for Cambodia, Laos or Vietnam.

November	1977	Vietnam's 9th Division invades border regions with 20 000 men; fierce resistance. Heavy clashes between Vietnamese and KR forces in Parrot's Beak area.
December	1977	Formal visits to DK by Burma, China, Laos and Malaysia.
December 16	1977	Further Vietnamese incursions to relieve 9th Division (up to 50 000 troops).
December 19	1977	US resume Paris peace talks with Vietnam.
December 31	1977	DK breaks diplomatic relations with Hanoi.
January	1978	Vietnamese and DK forces finely balanced in Takeo and Kampot provinces.
January 3	1978	Prince Sihanouk condemns aggression by Vietnamese.
February 5	1978	Vietnam proposes negotiations, withdrawal of troops and neutral surveillance of border-Phnom Penh rejects proposition.
April	1978	Vietnamese leaders begin visits to Moscow. Hun Sen defects from KR to Vietnamese.
May	1978	Unsuccessful insurrection in Eastern Zone led by Heng Samrin. He escapes subsequent purges.
May 20	1978	Brzezinski begins 3-day visit to China.
June 21	1978	Radio Hanoi accuses DK of 'systematic genocide'.
June 28	1978	Vietnamese offensive (60 000 troops) begins.
July 3	1978	Beijing suspends aid to Hanoi.
August 21	1978	George McGovern, before Senate Foreign Relations Commitee, calls for international force to destroy Pol Pot regime.
August (late)	1978	Switzerland, Japan and Indonesia establish diplomatic relations with DK.
September 30	1978	DK lift Sihanouk's 2-year house-arrest.
November 3	1978	25-year Russo-Vietnamese Friendship Treaty signed.
December 3	1978	Khmer National United Front for National Salvation (KNUFNS) formed.
December 22	1978	Major Vietnamese offensive launched.
January 1	1979	US and China re-establish diplomatic relations.

January 7	1979	Phnom Penh falls. Pol Pot flees and re-establishes guerrilla war.
January 8	1979	Heng Samrin heads new government of People's Republic of Kampuchea (PRK). Hun Sen is Foreign Minister.
January 28	1979	Deng Xiaoping visits Washington.
February 17	1979	China launches limited, punitive offensive against Vietnam.
February 18	1979	Vietnam and Cambodia sign Friendship Treaty.
March 9	1979	China ends punitive action.
March 19	1979	Sihanouk (from Beijing) breaks tie with KR.
March 23	1979	PRK and Laos sign Friendship Treaty.
August 25	1979	US Vice-President Mondale visits China.
September 5	1979	Non-aligned nations conference in Havana. Cambodian seat left vacant.
September	1979	DK secures UN seat.
October 9	1979	Son Sann forms anti-communist Khmer People's National Liberation Front (KPNLF). Located near the Thai border.
December	1979	Pol Pot steps down as Prime Minister of DK in favour of Khieu Samphan.
January 5	1980	Harold Brown (US Secretary of Defence) visits Beijing. He calls for 'complementary action to counter Soviet expansionism'.
January 5	1980	First Indochinese Foreign Ministers Conference (IFMC) held in Phnom Penh.
March	1980	Khieu Samphan in Beijing – talks of 'Soviet expansionism'. Son Sann meets with Sihanouk in Washington.
May 17	1980	Vietnam's Nguyen Co Thach calls situation in Cambodia 'irreversible' during talks in Bangkok.
June 27	1980	SoS Muskie meets with ASEAN foreign ministers and pledges military aid to Thailand to resist Vietnamese and Cambodian incursions.
July	1980	Second IFMC held in Vientiane.
September	1980	Move to declare Cambodian UN seat vacant is defeated 75–35.

January 4	1981	Solarz reports after visit to Indochina that the Vietnamese would not participate in the ICK.
January 20	1981	Reagan inauguration.
January 20	1981	Schanberg's article 'The Death and Life of Dith Pran' appears in *New York Times* magazine.
January 27	1981	IFMC – Ho Chi Minh City.
February 9	1981	Non-aligned conference in New Delhi approves resolution calling for Vietnamese withdrawal.
February 14	1981	Australia withdraw recognition of DK.
April 26	1981	Son Sann meets SoS Haig in Washington DC.
May	1981	Continuing Sino-Vietnamese skirmishes.
June 14	1981	SoS Haig visits Beijing.
June 15	1981	IFMC – Ho Chi Minh City.
June 19	1981	New Zealand withdraw reconition of DK.
July 13	1981	ICK convened in New York (Vietnam, USSR and PRK boycott conference).
September 4	1981	Sihanouk, Son Sann, Khieu Samphan meet in Singapore and agree in principle to form a 'united front'.
September 18	1981	UN approves DK credentials 77–37–31.
October 21	1981	UNGA approve ASEAN sponsored resolution (36/5) demanding that ICK be reconvened (100–25–19).
November 1	1981	Son Sann dissociates himself from coalition discussions.
November 10	1981	ASEAN decides not to supply arms to resistance groups, although Singapore and Malaysia decide to continue to do so.
November 28	1981	Son Sann and Sihanouk agree to 'loose coalition'. KR request two months' 'thinking time'.
December 4	1981	Son Sann visits US requesting military aid for KPNLF.
December 7	1981	Kampuchean Communist Party (KCP) dissolves itself.
December 9	1981	Open letter from a group of 130 interested parties (congressmen, religious leaders,

		entertainers etc.) urges Reagan not to support DK credentials.
December 10	1981	ASEAN foreign ministers meeting endorses 'loose coalition' concept.
February 3	1982	Thailand refuses to host further meetings of resistance groups.
February 16	1982	IFMC – Vientiane.
February 18	1982	Sihanouk visits Deng Xiaoping in Beijing.
February 21	1982	Sihanouk and Khieu Samphan meet in Beijing – Son Sann refuses to join them.
June 22	1982	Kuala Lumpur declaration of formation of Coalition Government of Democratic Kampuchea (CGDK). Sihanouk (President), Khieu Samphan (VP), Son Sann (PM).
July 6	1982	IFMC – Ho Chi Minh City.
July 7	1982	Vietnam announce significant troop reductions. Dismissed as 'troop rotation'.
September 30	1982	Sihanouk addresses UNGA as head of CGDK.
October 6–8	1982	Sihanouk and Son Sann meet VP George Bush who pledged moral and political support for the CGDK.
October 25	1982	UNGA approve DK's credentials 90–29–26.
October 28	1982	UNGA votes 105–23–20 for Vietnamese withdrawal.
November 13	1982	Heng Samrin visits Moscow for Brezhnev's funeral.
February 2–4	1983	SoS Shultz meets Sihanouk and Deng Xiaoping in Beijing.
February 23	1983	IFMC – Vientiane.
March 7	1983	CGDK not invited to non-aligned meeting in New Delhi. Kampuchean seat left vacant.
March 23	1983	ASEAN foreign ministers meeting.
April (early)	1983	Fighting between Vietnamese and CGDK (mostly KR) spreads all along Thai–Kampuchean border.
April 17	1983	China/Vietnam border clashes (Yunon province).
June 1	1983	Sihanouk threatens to resign from CGDK.
September 26	1984	CGDK attack Vietnamese bases in Pailin.

October 12	1984	UNGA approves DK credentials for fifth successive year.
Dry season	1984–85	Vietnamese forces over-run resistance group camps and drive inhabitants into Thailand.
March	1985	Gorbachev assumes power in Soviet Union.
August	1985	IFMC announces withdrawal of all Vietnamese forces by end of 1990.
July	1986	Gorbachev's Vladivostok speech advocates *rapprochement* with China.
December	1987	Sihanouk and Hun Sen in secret talks.
July (late)	1988	First Jakarta Informal Meeting (JIM-I) includes four Cambodian parties plus Vietnam, Laos and the ASEAN states. Reaches consensus to link Vietnamese withdrawal with cessation of external aid to all Cambodian parties.
January 25	1989	Hun Sen visits Thailand.
February 17	1989	IFMC announces all remaining Vietnamese troops out of Cambodia no later than end September 1989.
February	1989	JIM-II re-affirms JIM-I consensus.
April	1989	Vietnam announces complete troop withdrawal by end of September.
May 2–3	1989	More talks between Sihanouk and Hun Sen at which Hun Sen proposes a four-party leadership council, headed by Sihanouk to organise elections.
May 5	1989	PRK changes name to State of Cambodia (SOC).
May 31	1989	Bush administration approves covert aid to Non-Communist Resistance (NCR).
July 30– August 30	1989	International Conference on Kampuchea (ICK) opens with 19 participants: these were the P5, the ASEAN states, the four Cambodian factions, Laos, Vietnam, Australia, Canada, India, Japan and Zimbabwe (chair of the Non-Aligned Movement).
September 26	1989	Vietnamese withdrawal completed.
November	1989	Soviet Union tell Vietnam that military

		assistance will be drastically reduced.
November	1989	Australia Peace Proposal launched by Foreign Minister Gareth Evans.
January	1990	Permanent Five (P5) members of the Security Council meet in Paris and agree on 'enhanced role' for UN.
February 6–28	1990	JIM participants meet in Jakarta for Informal Meeting on Cambodia (IMC) at which Australian proposal is presented as the 'Red Book'.
June 4–5	1990	Tokyo Conference on Cambodia.
July 18	1990	SoS James Baker meets with Soviet Foreign Minister Edvard Shevardnadze and announces that the US would end support for CGDK seat at UN. US also to open direct talks with Vietnam.
August	1990	P5 transform Australian plan into a comprehensive 'framework document'.
September	1990	Final Jakarta meeting accepts 'framework documents'.
September 20	1990	Security Council accepts 'framework documents'.
September	1990	Cambodian factions form an all-party Supreme National Council (SNC).
October 15	1990	General Assembly accepts 'framework documents'.
February	1991	Fierce conflict resumes.
May 1	1991	UN sponsored ceasefire comes into effect.
June 24–26	1991	SNC meets in Thailand, agrees unlimited ceasefire and invites diplomatic representation to the SNC: Australia and ASEAN states take up offer.
October 16	1991	UN Advanced Mission in Cambodia (UNAMIC) approved by Security Council.
October 21–23	1991	Peace Conference in Paris; Peace Accords signed.
November 9	1991	UNAMIC formally established in Phnom Penh.
November	1991	Hun Sen government announce Cambodia would be a multi-party state.
November 20	1991	Sihanouk recognised as the head of state.

January	1992	Anti-corruption riots.
February 28	1992	UN Transitional Authority in Cambodia (UNTAC) created by Security Council.
March 15	1992	Yasushi Akashi, head of UNTAC, arrives in Phnom Penh.

Prologue

Foreign policy cannot be analysed in an historical vacuum, particularly in this case where so many of the significant *dramatis personae* played roles before, during and after the period under scrutiny. Consequently this prologue serves as an aid to those readers unfamiliar with the intricate history of postwar Cambodia.

In 1863 the new king, Norodom, accepted French protectorate status and Cambodia as we know it came into existence. 'Cambodge', as the French named it, remained under colonial rule until Norodom Sihanouk, who had been crowned king by the French in 1941, declared Cambodian independence in March 1945. He and his Prime Minister Son Ngoc Thanh, co-operated with the Japanese until their eventual defeat in August 1945 when the French returned as part of de Gaulle's attempt to rebuild French imperial ambitions in Indochina. During the brief period of independence Sihanouk had appointed the previously exiled Son Ngoc Thanh to positions as both foreign and prime minister; with the return of the French, Son Ngoc Thanh was tried for treason, for collaborating with the Japanese, and deported to France in October 1945. Sihanouk, by contrast, was not deported and although only 22 years old was already beginning to exhibit the attributes of the consummate survivor.

In November 1949, two months after dissolving the National Assembly, Sihanouk signed a Franco-Cambodian treaty which recognised Cambodia as an Associate State in the French Union. During this period of semi-independence (1949–53) Sihanouk engineered the demise of the Democratic Party under the Presidency of Son Sann, taking over the functions of Prime Minister himself and reinforcing his position by including anti-Communists such as Lon Nol in his cabinets. Son Ngoc Thanh returned to Cambodia in October 1951 at the request of the Democratic Party only to be forced back into exile operating from the Thai border.

By early 1953 France was nearing defeat in Vietnam and recognised the inevitability of withdrawal from Indochina. Sihanouk stepped up his campaign and launched his 'royal crusade for independence'. On 8 November 1953 he returned to Phnom Penh, from a brief exile in Thailand, and the next day formally took command of the Cambodian Army. It is acknowledged that Cambodian independence is marked

1

from that day, 9 November 1953. On 7 May 1954, Dien Bien Phu fell and the next day the Geneva Conference on Indochina was convened which eventually recommended free elections in Cambodia.

Sihanouk immediately began positioning himself for the forthcoming elections. In December 1954 he declared Cambodian neutrality and in February 1955 received a massive endorsement for his declaration in a referendum. A month later he abdicated in favour of his father and formed a political party, the Sangkum Reastr Niyum (Popular (or People's) Socialist Community). In the September elections Sihanouk won a handsome victory when the Sangkum gained 83 per cent of the vote compared to the Democrats' 13 per cent. This further defeat, and its margin, doomed the Democrat Party which by 1958 ceased to exist. Unfortunately, the US, not for the last time, had backed the wrong horse by supporting the Democrats. With the collapse of the Democrats, Son Ngoc Thanh became leader of the Khmer Serei, an anti-Sihanoukist right-wing group purportedly 'financ[ed], train[ed] and arm[ed]' by the CIA.[1]

After the election Sihanouk began to develop alliances with Asian communists, most notably the People's Republic of China (PRC). In February 1956 he signed the Sino-Cambodian Friendship Treaty in Beijing only seven months after he had signed an agreement for military aid with the United States. In June 1956 Cambodia became the first non-communist state to receive PRC aid (some $22m), possibly as a counterbalance to the CIA aid being received by the Khmer Serei.

Between 1955 and 1966 Sihanouk *was* the State. He actually became Head of State in June 1960 after surviving a plot in early 1959 and an assassination attempt in late 1959 which had originated, according to Sihanouk, 'from an American military base in South Vietnam'.[2] The plot, led by General Dap Chhuon, the Governor of Siem Reap province, was, at the least, tacitly supported by the CIA. More substantially it was backed by Thailand who were alleged not only to have tried to link Sam Sary and Son Ngoc Thanh in an anti-Sihanoukist alliance but to have actively encouraged the idea that the northern provinces of Cambodia could be annexed and 'with the southern provinces of Laos ... form a new secessionist state which would have been immediately recognised by the USA'.[3]

Unsurprisingly, the Dap Chhuon plot confirmed Sihanouk's anti-Americanism. Dap Chhuon himself was killed in the coup while Sam Sary fled to Thailand to join Son Ngoc Thanh as deputy leader of the Khmer Serei. Sihanouk's Prime Minister at the time, Son Sann, survived the 'lacquer-box attentat', as the attempt was called, and continued to serve loyally until the 1970 coup. As a result of the failed plots Sihanouk forged even stronger links with external communist groups while continuing his domestic attacks on both the left and right. This policy led to the severing of relations with South Vietnam (August 1963), the cessation of the US military aid programme (November 1963) and inevitably to the final break with the US in May 1965 after they had violated Cambodian airspace and bombed the Svay Rieng (Parrot's Beak) area of the Cambodia/South Vietnam border.

As ties with the US weakened so those with the PRC strengthened. Unfortunately, in economic terms the PRC were unable to fill the void left by the Americans and the Cambodian economy began to disintegrate. As a result 1966 saw the beginnings of one of Sihanouk's ends. He had by this time completely allied himself to the North Vietnamese cause having long since lost faith in the United States' ability to defeat them. In trying to keep out of the Vietnam War by breaking with the US he had finally and reluctantly become embroiled in it.

On 11 September 1966 the first election since 1951 without pre-selected candidates took place. From that election a rightist-dominated government led by Sihanouk's previous ally Lon Nol emerged. Sihanouk remained Head of State but power had shifted. In April 1967 there was a large peasant uprising at Samlaut in the Battambang. Sihanouk appeared genuinely surprised at this turn of events and permitted Lon Nol to viciously suppress the revolt at the cost of an estimated 10 000 lives. During the aftermath, Sihanouk accused Khieu Samphan, among others, of instigating the revolt and Khieu Samphan was forced to leave the government and return to the communist resistance to which Sihanouk would eventually apply the generic term 'Khmer Rouge' (KR).

Sihanouk was exhausted and Lon Nol increasingly 'managed' the political machine. The situation worsened when the Kampuchean Communist Party (KCP) launched an 'armed struggle' against Sihanouk. His policies became more and more reactive and he sought *rapprochement* with the US as his fear of the left grew. The US was only partially interested, mistakenly according to Kissinger who subsequently insisted that, 'Cambodia was misperceived in America as a separate "war" that we must avoid'.[4] Nevertheless, in January 1968 Sihanouk declared war on the Khmer Rouge at the same time as the United States announced its policy of 'hot pursuit' which was simply an extension and formalisation of OP SALEM HOUSE[5] which had started in May 1967. Simultaneously the PRC continued to supply arms, including MIGs, to Lon Nol. Cambodia had become the archetypal Cold War crucible.

By early 1969 Sihanouk was committed to re-establishing links with the US, reasoning that the Cambodian economy could not be revitalised without foreign aid and that meant *American* aid. Politically he believed that an American presence would achieve two objectives; firstly, it would counterbalance the growing influence of the Soviets and Chinese and secondly, it would act as a warning to both internal and external communists that he had powerful external support. However, his about-face with the US only succeeded in undermining his position by confirming right-wing suspicions that the original break had been a fatal error of judgement. Sihanouk's fate was sealed once he had finally re-established diplomatic relations with the United States on 11 June 1969. By August Lon Nol had become Prime Minister, with Sirik Matak as his deputy.

On 7 January 1970 Sihanouk and his entourage left for Grasse on the French Riviera for his regular rest cure. He had failed to rally any real support at the 28th National Congress (27–29 Dec. 1969) and was physically, mentally and emotionally drained by the effort to do so. Sihanouk's demonisation of the Vietnamese backfired when, during Sihanouk's absence, Lon Nol co-opted the tactic and organised demonstrations which culminated in the sacking of the North Vietnamese (DRV) and Provisional Revolutionary Government (PRG) embassies on 11 March 1970. This was followed on 13 March 1970 by Lon Nol issuing an edict instructing all Vietnamese troops to withdraw from Cambodia by dawn on 15 March 1970. Lon Nol had naively assumed almost instantaneous US backing and assistance, but it was not forthcoming. Notwithstanding, Lon Nol moved ahead on a wave of anti-Vietnamese hysteria and manoeuvred the National Assembly into an 83–3 vote of no confidence which deposed Sihanouk on 18 March 1970. Lon Nol and Sirik Matak retained their positions as Prime Minister and Deputy Prime Minister and were later joined by the returning Son Ngoc Thanh. Five days later, from Peking, Sihanouk issued an appeal for the formation of a resistance movement, the Khmer National United Front (FUNK), and also announced his alliance with the DRV and Laos against the Lon Nol regime.

Events moved quickly from this moment. At the end of March the DRV launched an invasion of the Cambodian territories bordering the NVA and Viet Cong sanctuaries. The lack of resistance encouraged them to continue deeper into Cambodia. By mid-April they controlled virtually all of the North Eastern provinces. As a result of these successes Sihanouk initiated a Summit Conference of Indochinese Peoples which was held in Southern China and chaired by Zhou Enlai. The final text of the conference pledged 'mutual support for [the] three peoples' struggle against American imperialism for the liberation and independence of [the] respective countries'.[6] Three days later US and South Vietnamese forces invaded Cambodia, ostensibly in further 'hot pursuit' operations. Within a week Sihanouk announced the formation of a government in exile, the Royal Government of National Unification of Kampuchea (GRUNK) of which he was head of state and Khieu Samphan (his recent enemy) was vice premier. The DRV, PRC and Laos recognised the new government and PRC broke with the Lon Nol government as did North Korea. Lon Nol re-established Cambodian links with Saigon and Bangkok. In anticipating a high level of US support Lon Nol had failed to recognise the hardening of US public opinion against the Vietnam War and the debilitating effect this had upon their government's ability to act in the region.

By late 1971 Lon Nol had initiated two counter-offensives against the rebels, both of which were dismal failures. He had also dissolved the National Assembly and declared a state of emergency. In the space of eighteen months the Lon Nol government had turned overwhelming popular support into terminal decline. A year later Lon Nol controlled Phnom Penh and Battambang, but little else. His government was reduced to seeking ceasefires with Sihanouk and Khieu Samphan, both of which were rejected because by that stage the Khmer Rouge were taking greater responsibility for their own war and, more to the point, they were winning it. The North Vietnamese felt able to withdraw in late 1972 because 'the back of the Lon Nol army had already been broken by Hanoi regulars'.[7]

However, it was the political manoeuvring of the first half of 1973 which might be said to have finally doomed Cambodia to the 'killing fields' of the late 1970s. By early 1973 there had been a convergence of US and Chinese interests. The Chinese were beginning to realise that while a Vietnamese victory over the US would represent an ideological victory, it could also be a defeat in the regional geostrategic arena by elevating Vietnam's regional importance. For the United States extrication from Indochina was the imperative. The Americans reasoned that Sihanouk's return, at the head of some sort of coalition, would serve their purposes, and the Chinese agreed. The problem was that by that time Sihanouk was firmly under Khmer Rouge control, he had even toured the 'liberated' areas of Cambodia in early April, and the KR were winning and did not need to negotiate. A Kissinger note to Beijing at the time captures the *realpolitik* atmosphere:

> With respect to Cambodia, we are prepared to work with you to bring about some coalition structure ... We are not committed to any particular personality.... Our objective in Southeast Asia seems to us not totally dissimilar to yours. We want to prevent a security system extending in South and Southeast Asia controlled by one unit and one outside power.[8]

By this time the infamous Cambodian bombing campaign had moved imperceptibly from attacks on 'sanctuaried' Viet Cong to support for Lon Nol's troops.[9] Although the bombing did help Lon Nol in the short term – it was crucial in staving off the KR's first attempt to take Phnom Penh in early August 1973 – it only really delayed the inevitable. Due mainly to an erosion of Nixon's presidential authority the bombing had to be halted later in August, and it forced a hardening of positions. Both the US and China believed that the effective withdrawal of US support enhanced the inevitability of a Khmer Rouge victory. Kissinger argued that 'our inability to maintain domestic support ... doom[ed] ... Cambodia'.[10] It also compromised Zhou Enlai with the result that China 'place[d] all their bets on the Khmer Rouge'.[11]

With victory in sight Sihanouk became irrelevant to the KR for anything other than PR purposes. Sihanouk himself is reported to have said in August 1973, 'I understand very well that when I shall no longer be useful to [the Khmer Rouge], they'll spit me out like a cherry pip'.[12] During the 1973/74 dry season the communists shelled Phnom Penh to great psychological effect and came very close to actually taking the city. Somehow FUNK survived for another year. However, on 1 January 1975 the combined forces of GRUNK and the KR launched the final offensive during which they cut off all access to Phnom Penh. The US embassy closed on 12 April having previously witnessed the flight of Lon Nol on April Fools day. On 17 April 1975 the Khmer Rouge peasant army solemnly entered Phnom Penh – and was generally welcomed.

Very soon after the KR victory it became clear that they would not abide by Cold War protocol and did not consider themselves to be obliged to any patron. As Nayan Chanda pointed out, 'history and nationalism – not ideology – shape the future of this volatile region. Whatever may be the appearance, it is very hard to find real puppets in Indochina.'[13] Peking and Hanoi quickly came to recognise this unpalatable truth. Both were appalled by the ruthless purity of the KR's agrarian revolution in which the collective farm became the only operational unit in the country. The Chinese were also incredulous to find that virtually none of a $20m aid package had been spent by the Pol Pot government despite the fact that it was non-refundable; such a favour was designed to have given China some measure of control.

Nevertheless, despite their discomfort with the virulence of the Cambodian revolution, the Chinese remained supportive. The Vietnamese victory over America and consequent decline of US influence in Indochina had fuelled China's worst nightmares of 'a strong, unified Vietnam challenging China from the south in cahoots with China's bitter enemy in the north'.[14] The continuance of a KR and Chinese alliance was probably inevitable given their common fears of Vietnamese hegemony coupled with Soviet expansionism. The Vietnamese, for their part, were never able to co-exist easily with the xenophobic Pol Pot regime.

Although the Khmer Rouge did not accept the usual geopolitical niceties, they were cognizant of the need to consider, and even appease, world opinion. They despatched Sihanouk (who had returned to Phnom Penh in September 1975) to the United Nations (UN) in order to lay claim to Cambodia's seat. On completion of that duty Sihanouk embarked on a eleven-nation tour, to promote the new state, before returning to Phnom Penh on the last day of 1975. By April 1976 he was under house arrest and had literally become a figurehead to be produced for both foreign and domestic consumption. Sihanouk would remain a KR 'prisoner' until 1979. In the two years between Sihanouk's return and Jimmy Carter's inauguration in January 1977, Cambodia disappeared from the agenda as far as the outside world was concerned. *Internally* it was a different matter where a power struggle within the KR saw Pol Pot gain the leadership, lose it, and regain it; a situation which continued until July 1997.

Jimmy Carter became President, against this background of shifting alliances and crude *realpolitik*, with a commitment to an ethical foreign policy. He was soon to realise how difficult it would be to deliver such a policy, not least towards Cambodia.

Introduction

The human mind, unable to encompass a vast, complex, and largely unknown reality, substitutes simple mythological views, to which foreign policy then addresses itself.

Louis Halle[1]

This book analyses United States foreign policy towards Cambodia from 1977 to 1992 by focusing on the 'simple mythological views', or 'realities', created by the decision-making elites. It investigates the realities those elites inhabit and the role they play in the development and implementation of foreign policy. It combines assumptions drawn from theories of foreign policy analysis, linguistics and sociology and concentrates on public statements as its primary units of analysis accepting that the parameters of linguistic environments effectively create reality.[2]

United States foreign policy towards Cambodia was chosen as a case study because previous American involvement in Indochina suggested it would be a significant issue for United States' foreign policy-makers. In particular, Cambodia carries echoes of Vietnam, which clearly *is* a central issue in US politics. The importance of the 'Vietnam syndrome' is oft-cited but rarely agreed upon; it generates great passion and many 'lessons'. Early in Jimmy Carter's presidency, for example, he said:

> Vietnam has impressed on the American people deeply, and I hope permanently, the danger of our country resorting to military means in a distant place on Earth where our security is not being threatened.[3]

That statement represented *Carter*'s lesson from the Vietnam experience. Vietnam is so deep in the American psyche that everybody has their own lesson. In the 1984 presidential campaign Gary Hart argued that Walter Mondale did not understand the crisis in Central America because he had 'not learned the lesson of Vietnam'.[4] Mondale responded that 'Hart ha[d] learned the wrong lesson from Vietnam'.[5] George Bush provided a revisionist interpretation in his inaugural speech which was itself derived from that which had been developed during the Reagan era. Given that Vietnam clearly had a unique place in American political life, and since it was the Vietnamese who invaded Cambodia during the Carter administration, occupied it through both Reagan administrations, and withdrew from it during the Bush administration, it seemed reasonable that Cambodia would provide an excellent lens through which to view US foreign policy.

Concentrating on the decision-making elite is not new;[6] Roger Hilsman, for example, described the group of immediate, trusted, personal advisers which operates at the heart of US foreign policy as a 'principate'[7] and Schlesinger referred to a 'presidential court'.[8] The fact that others[9] have argued that the president has little real power to actually command, and is thus forced to persuade and cajole, both in the legislative and executive arms of government, fails to recognise that it is *only* the president that possesses both the carrots and sticks with which to engage in the persuasion and cajoling. Even Morton Halperin, who in his original work on bureaucratic politics did not accord the president any special status,[10] later revised his views and admitted that 'the President is qualitatively different – not simply a very powerful player among less powerful players'.[11] President Johnson explained the situation in this way:

> There are many, many, who can recommend, advise and sometimes a few of them consent, but there is only one that has been chosen by the American people to decide.[12]

Using the 'principate' as a *primary* focus for analysis has been under-utilised in recent years, possibly as a result of the perception of a diffusion and limitation of presidential power. Even if this were true in general, it is certainly not true in foreign affairs, where 'presidents have indeed reigned supreme'.[13] In fact, in the 'field of foreign affairs ... presidents have fewer limits on their power'[14] than in any other sphere for which they have responsibility.

Jerel Rosati provides further evidence for the pre-eminent role of the president when he argues that presidential dominance is a function of the criticality of current events.[15] The more critical an issue, he contends, the higher will be presidential dominance and the lower group or bureaucratic dominance. Analysis completed by Margaret and Charles Hermann on 5185 decision-making events, in twenty-five separate countries, showed that in 3256 (63 per cent) instances the decision was taken by the 'predominant leader', and 1680 (32 per cent) by a 'single group'.[16] In their study, therefore, the presidential court accounts for 95 per cent of particular decision-making events. There is no reason to suspect the situation has changed very much since the research in 1989, despite tighter congressional controls. Although there might be debates about the actual or potential limits upon presidential power there is, nevertheless, sufficient agreement concerning the significance of the president and his immediate entourage to justify concentrating on them in order to explain foreign policy.

Given that it is reasonable to accept the notion that a principate exists and exerts significant influence over foreign policy, how best is that influence analysed and assessed? The intention here is to examine the realities of the principal actors and groups of actors through an analysis of their public utterances. The term 'reality' is used in a generic sense to define the way in which an individual or group of decision makers interpret their significant world, what has been called 'a set of ideas about how the physical and social environment works'.[17] There is an extensive literature on 'realities', 'belief systems', 'mindsets' and 'weltanschaung' and their relationship with foreign policy analysis. As early as 1918, for example, Joseph Jastrow argued that man is essentially a 'belief seeker' rather than a 'fact seeker' and that individuals cannot operate merely on the basis of an interpretation of facts.[18] Man constructs 'beliefs' which act as filters for otherwise dissociated facts. Many contemporary analysts have extended and refined Jastrow's thesis and agree that the notion of constructed realities, by whatever name, *does* have a relevance in policy analysis and is 'central to the descriptively detailed analysis of decision-making'.[19] Just as important is the recognition by the actors themselves of the notion of realities. Both George Shultz[20] and Ed Muskie,[21] for example, wrote of 'new realities' and there are many other instances where decision-makers refer, by implication, to the existence of separate realities.

How, then, can these 'realities' be identified or inferred? The method chosen here is a form of 'content analysis' which has been described as a 'diagnostic tool for making specific inferences about some aspect of the speaker's purposive behavior'.[22] It is *not* a quantitative version, being aware of Jervis's warning not to be

> seduced by the existence of numbers, mathematical manipulations, and tests of statistical significance into believing that results are automatically 'harder' and more significant than those produced by less quantitative methods.[23]

The form of content analysis used in this book heeds Jervis's words of caution and relies on what Hedley Bull called 'the exercise of judgement'.[24] A content analysis of the significant public utterances made by members of the 'principate' enables inferences to be drawn regarding their 'realities'. Although identifying individually constructed realities from public utterances is relatively straightforward, 'assessing the conviction with which they are held' *can* present difficulties.[25] However, these difficulties are not insurmountable since beliefs inferred from public statements can actually *become* accurate because public statements and policy will eventually fuse. Logically, therefore, such statements *can* be relied upon as accurate indicators. Larson goes so far as to argue that inadvertent or misinterpreted public statements can actually *become* policy.[26] Similarly, Coral Bell's notion that 'words *are* deeds'[27] indicates the importance of public utterances because it accords rhetoric two simultaneous functions, that of defining reality and of *being* reality. Thus even a lack of veracity does not diminish the value of the insights that can be gained by concentrating on public statements.

Analysts from other disciplines also recognise the importance of rhetoric in the identification and analysis of constructed realities. Berger and Luckmann, for example,[28] presented a theory of society as a dialectical process between objective and subjective realities, between the indisputable and the contentious. They argued that everyday life is only a reality interpreted by men and understood and constructed by means of shared linguistic environments. For them human reality can *only* be understood as socially constructed reality.

Linguistics also has a strong history of theorists supporting the notion of created realities. Whorf, for example, observed that '[s]peech is the best show man puts on ... it is the window to his thought processes and thus the reality that he both creates and inhabits'.[29] More recently George Grace argued that since language is the 'one essential tool which makes a social construction of reality possible', we should be talking about the '*linguistic* construction of reality'.[30]

It is proposed in this book to accept the notion of constructed realities, which can be inferred by studying relevant public utterances, and to make those inferences using interpretative content analysis. The data for this non-quantitative variant of content analysis has been gleaned from a variety of sources but ultimately it is what Roxanne Doty has described as an 'ensemble of data found in the documents surrounding [a] particular site of United States foreign policy'.[31] In this instance the site is the decision-making staff within and surrounding the 'principate'. The data recognised as suitable for inclusion was not determined *a priori* but *during* a thorough investigation of the 'ensemble'.

The book is structured firstly to distinguish the *levels* of influence within the principate of each administration.[32] Secondly it identifies *conflicts* between the levels and then examines the underlying *foreign policy* tenets of each administration. From an analysis of the content of relevant public utterances, contained in sources such as congressional hearings, newspapers, journals, presidential papers and biographies, an *administration's reality* will be inferred.[33] *Alternative realities*, with which the administration's version was forced to interact and against which it was often judged, are also identified. Finally, an *amalgam of realities* is constructed in order to enhance the explanation of US foreign policy towards Cambodia. Naturally such an amalgam is influenced by the reality the author inhabits, although an awareness of the phenomenon will hopefully limit its effect. The book involves a content analysis of the public utterances of significant actors within the presidential decision-making elite.[34]

1 The Carter Administration, 1977–81

Our commitment to human rights must be absolute.... We will not behave in foreign places so as to violate our rules and standards here at home, for we know that the trust which our Nation earns is essential to our strength.

Inaugural Address of President Jimmy Carter, 20 January 1977

Jimmy Carter entered office with high expectations of significantly changing US foreign policy-making. He was committed, at least rhetorically, to a foreign policy which reflected and promoted America's domestic values. Given such a predisposition towards human rights issues it might have been reasonable to assume that Cambodia would be high on his agenda for action. It was also reasonable to assume that when President Carter made his inaugural address he believed it would be possible to sustain his ideals in the face of the challenges he would undoubtedly encounter. Inevitably inaugurals are only ever a very basic statement of United States foreign policy but they do provide at least a guide to the ambitions of the administration, to the reality in which they intend to operate, and Carter had chosen a particularly perilous reality.

Throughout Carter's presidency there was a philosophical tension which coloured foreign policy decisions, nowhere more demonstrably than in those affecting Indochina. This tension might best be described as a 'principled pragmatism', or in Brzezinski's words, as a struggle between 'power and principle',[1] or sometimes more prosaically as a battle between idealism and realism. Notwithstanding the tension, the commitment of the administration to human rights and a more avowedly moral stance remained at the heart of foreign policy from the electoral campaign throughout the entire presidency – again rhetorically. The qualification inherent in the use of the word 'rhetorical' fundamentally summarises the central concerns about US foreign policy during this period. In other words, did the rhetoric match the action, did the exercise of power match the statement of principle? Foreign policy was clearly of central importance in defining the Carter administration since the President seemed to genuinely

13

believe that America had a 'commitment to human rights' which could and *should* be exported. He also had a very clear vision which he was not afraid to enunciate and as such he invited judgement. There was no shortage of commentators prepared to pass that judgement.

THE ADMINISTRATION

The 'Court' of President Carter, as it related to foreign policy decision-making, worked on three basic levels. The President occupied level one; the National Security Adviser (NSA), Zbigniew Brzezinski and the Secretary of State (SoS), Cyrus Vance, level two; the Vice-President, Walter 'Fritz' Mondale, the Secretary of Defense (SoD), Harold Brown, Warren Christopher (Assistant SoS), Hamilton Jordan (Assistant to the President and White House Chief of Staff) and Richard Holbrooke (the Assistant SoS for East Asian and Pacific Affairs), level three. Although it has been argued that Harold Brown was an equal player with Vance and Brzezinski at the second level that assessment was made on the basis of formal rank.[2] It is true that Brown worked very closely with Brzezinski and Vance in what Brzezinski described as a 'triangular relationship'[3] but Brown's role was closer to that of a floating voter. Brzezinski recalls, for example, that 'Brown's gradual shift to a harder line made for a subtle but important change of balance'.[4] In the 'triangular relationship' Brown was the movable third point to the fixed Vance/Brzezinski base. The bias provided by the skewed positioning of that third point often provided a decisive influence and was, therefore, extremely important. Nevertheless, it is difficult to accord equal status to Brown's role in comparison to those of Vance and Brzezinski.

On level three the actors all had a degree of influence but naturally less than those at the higher levels. Their influence was also issue-specific in that clearly the Secretary of Defense was more powerful than Assistant Secretaries of State but he was happy to defer that power on the Cambodian issue. Thus at this level Richard Holbrooke was pre-eminent by virtue of his specialist expertise. His advice on Indochina was considered invaluable and consequently his influence was enhanced accordingly. He was also an old friend of Cyrus Vance and an acknowledged Vietnam specialist who believed in the opportunities that normalisation provided.

Levels one and two, which consisted of the small coterie of President, NSA and SoS, were the foreign policy elite which Carter had actually been keen to avoid. He had deliberately appointed *nine* assistants of more or less equal status, with a set of specific responsibilities, in an attempt to garner a wealth of information from which he could select the most appropriate course. Carter believed that he should 'be personally involved so that [he could] know the thought processes that go into final decisions'.[5] Unfortunately the simple mechanics of government often mean that avoiding the formation of an elite becomes virtually impossible. Once the elite has formed, factors such as status, personality and the force of character of the participants combine to affect the direction of policy.

LEVEL ONE

As President, Jimmy Carter was said to have been comfortable with what is described as a 'multiple advocacy' style of decision-making.[6] This approach envisages the ultimate decision-maker sifting through a variety of advice before settling on a particular option. Additionally, there is another important element of multiple advocacy: the need to foster 'competition among the advisers for the adoption of their preferred options'.[7] Carter may have been competent at fostering the competition, but he seemed unable, perhaps unwilling, to control it. He *wanted* to control foreign policy from the White House, to be an 'active-positive' president,[8] but adopting such an approach means that, when necessary, firm and positive decisions must be made. The criticism of Carter was that he could not be decisive.[9] In the desire to peruse *all* the data he failed to recognise the moments when sufficient information was available. Carter admitted as much when he said, '[i]n making the final decisions on foreign policy, I needed to weigh as many points of view as possible'.[10] He made this point when discussing his appointments of Brzezinski and Vance. It was they who would head the competition that it was argued Carter later failed to control. He believed, it seems incorrectly, that the process of competition and consultation would effectively generate its own decisions.

Despite his apparent indecisiveness it seems unlikely that he could have risen to the presidency without a cutting edge somewhere in his armoury. It may have been the case that he was able to be decisive on structural matters, that is, in deciding on procedures which he then assumed would operate untended. He was very clear on the way in which he wished his administration to run and speedily enacted the necessary changes. This behaviour fits with descriptions of him prior to becoming President. Late in the election campaign, for example, he was described in the following way, '[w]hen a decision is made, it will be his decision. He listens to many people but when it is time for a decision, he doesn't take a vote.'[11] It is possible that the bureaucratic and personality battles which are part of any administration were too much for a man who assumed that consensual Cabinet responsibility would be the norm.

It is argued that as early as the inauguration speech Carter was demonstrating a passivity which would at 'a later point in his tenure ... be called weakness and would be blamed on his actions, or lack of actions'.[12] This seems less than fair since Carter had merely provided the American people with what they needed, a reaffirmation of what they believed themselves to be. As one commentator explained, '[i]n a sense [they] voted for themselves'.[13] Carter might have exhibited passivity but this was most likely the result of his belief that he needed to be all things to all people. As Charles Mohr put it, 'Mr Carter is as conservative – or as liberal – as he needs to be at any moment or in any political situation.'[14]

Carter was a deliberator; for him each decision was taken in turn but there was little evidence of an overall strategy designed to implement his vision. Lacking a strategy meant the vision could only be promoted by the use of convincing rhetoric. Unfortunately, in an attempt to provide such rhetoric, Carter could resort to the use of superlatives and absolutes as his way of demonstrating passion and involvement. Probably because it was not a natural posture for him, it could backfire disastrously, most infamously when he described the Soviet invasion of Afghanistan as 'the most serious threat to peace since the Second World War' (State of the Union Address, 1980). Edward Kennedy pounced on this indiscretion by asking, quite legitimately, whether Berlin, Korea, Hungary, Czechoslovakia, Cuba or Vietnam might not have posed a 'greater threat' and damagingly added that '[e]xaggeration and hyperbole are the enemies of sensible foreign policy'.[15] This was Carter's personal dilemma: he had a genuinely powerful vision of a better world but all the 'components of [his] style – feeling, tone, language, voice and physical aspects – contributed to the perception of Carter as a weak man, a weak president'.[16] Carter did appear to wilt, under the strain of the presidency, more than most. During the latter stages of his term, which coincided with the interminable Tehran hostage crisis, he looked a beaten man.

LEVEL TWO

The appointment of Brzezinski and Vance, as National Security Adviser (NSA) and Secretary of State respectively, was an indicator not only of Carter's multiple advocacy approach but also of the idealist/pragmatist, power/principle tensions inherent in the President himself. The contrasting personalities of Brzezinski and Vance mirrored the contradiction which existed within Carter. In Hamilton Jordan's terms they were the 'deliberate Vance and [the] feisty Brzezinski'.[17]

If Vance was deliberate it was not necessarily a fault. He provided a constancy of vision that supported Carter, and he provided it because he believed it was achievable. In December 1980 Harold Brown was quoted in the *New York Times* (*NYT*) as saying that 'Secretary Vance was persuaded that anything that involved the risk of force was a mistake.'[18] This was meant as a criticism of a perceived lack of resolve but in the structure envisaged by Carter it was a necessary counterbalance to the brinkmanship of Brzezinski. Like Brown, Brzezinski himself also had serious reservations about Vance's unwillingness to resort to force, and he wrote that, '[Vance's] deep aversion to the use of force was a most significant limitation on his stewardship in an age in which American power was being threatened on a very broad front.'[19] He felt this aversion stemmed, in part, from the fact that Vance was a 'representative of an elite [the WASP elite] that was no longer dominant either in the world or in America'.[20] But Vance believed that conflict and confrontation should not be the first and were rarely the most suitable responses. On the contrary, he believed that managing foreign policy

> requires that we be idealistic, not ideological, and that we be unafraid to admit past mistakes and take prudent chances. It compels us to recognise that it is not a sign of weakness to negotiate compromises that are in our interest, and that in trying to achieve too much too fast, the best can become the enemy of the good.[21]

Such sentiments reflect the antithesis of the Brzezinski approach. Vance was not *afraid* of the use of force, he distrusted it.

Brzezinski had no such reservations. A comment he made about Vance illustrates both his view of Vance and his belief in himself. He said that as a consequence of Vance's WASP-ness he 'had a different estimate of the proper balance between power and principle in our age'.[22] The significant word here is 'proper'. Vance's opinion was not just 'different', it was improper, only Brzezinski was able to correctly assess the 'proper' balance between power and principle – and the whole tone of his book *Power and Principle* conveys this same self-belief. Nowhere in his book is it specifically stated but the impression is that Brzezinski was never comfortable with a 'collegial' approach; he suffered it rather than embraced it.

Nowhere is Brzezinski's character better defined than in a particularly illuminating Hamilton Jordan anecdote. He describes how he and Brzezinski often played tennis together and recalled how he had once said to Brzezinski, "'Zbig, you play tennis like you conduct foreign policy." Brzezinski replied, "You must mean that every shot is well-planned, crisply hit, low and hard." "Yes" said [Jordan] "and usually out".'[23] Jordan may have jokingly denigrated Brzezinski in that anecdote but elsewhere he described Brzezinski, perhaps more accurately, as 'a good athlete [who] played a hard, intense game – without subtlety.'[24]

Clearly Brzezinski *was* a hard-nosed manipulator with his own view of the way in which idealism and pragmatism interacted. He was given Cabinet status, the first and to date last time this happened to an NSA, and he revelled in the power of such a position. He also viewed himself as the 'hard-man', the pragmatist of the administration. He wrote, as early as 11 January 1977, that he would 'try to sensitize [Carter] to the need to have somewhat more tough-minded a group' in the Cabinet.[25] He also took easily to the competitive element of the multiple advocacy approach and began working for *his* position very quickly. He was, for example,

> uneasy even in [the] early days about the policy orientation of some of Carter's foreign policy appointments. [He] feared that [Carter] would not be obtaining, especially from the State Department, the kind of realistic and hard-nosed advice which should balance his more idealistic views.[26]

Brzezinski's most enduring problem was that the image he cultivated had its drawbacks, it encouraged a wariness bordering on distrust as well as a fierce loyalty. It was said that he had an 'intelligence [which] was intense and raw, and when [this was] added to his tough-guy image, it made many people uncomfortable.'[27] To his friends he was direct, to his enemies Machiavellian. Vance and Brzezinski could have made a formidable level two team had it been possible for them to work together, and it was reasonable for Carter to have assumed that it would be possible – unfortunately it was not.

LEVEL THREE

At this third level Hamilton Jordan, as the President's aide, had an important if not a key role. Carter effectively acted as his own Chief of Staff and Jordan was, therefore, more of a confidante and a manager. He was well respected for his ability in both roles, and his views were constantly sought by the President as part of his data collection exercises. However, in the bureaucratic power play concerning foreign policy Jordan's influence was marginal and, therefore, he does not demand serious attention in this analysis.

The same was true of both Warren Christopher and Walter Mondale. Mondale was Carter's *domestic* touchstone and as such he tended to approach foreign policy issues with an eye firmly on their domestic implications. As Brzezinski said, 'He was a vital political barometer for the President.'[28] Carter called him 'the best public servant I ever knew'.[29] He was discreet, loyal, a painstaking negotiator, and quietly efficient. Warren Christopher was not a political street-fighter either and '[i]f red meat is your taste in foreign policy-making, Warren Christopher is not your man.'[30] At the level on which he operated within the Carter administration this was not really a drawback. However, it became more of an issue when he finally assumed the mantle of Secretary of State in the first Clinton administration.

As previously mentioned Harold Brown is located at this level because in foreign policy terms his influence was as a catalyst rather than an initiator. Carter himself implied as much when he said that, '[i]n making the final decisions on foreign policy, I needed to weigh as many points of view as possible. When Brzezinski and Vance were joined by Fritz Mondale and Harold Brown ... they comprised a good team.'[31] Brown resembled Carter more than anyone else in the administration. He was 'a superb analyst ... [who] tended ... to dissect the problem and then to examine alternative responses'.[32] His reputation was high and his integrity well respected by Carter, so that when he began to favour the Brzezinski stance later in the term it was a crucial factor but again only in shifting emphasis.

Probably the most significant member of level three was Richard Holbrooke. His importance lay in his expertise in Indochinese matters and especially in his particular views regarding normalisation with Vietnam, which he considered an absolute priority. He argued that it was the 'Far East where America ha[d] had its great problems over the last thirty years. Our last three wars have started out there, and we've had the greatest domestic battles over who lost China and Korea, Vietnam and Cambodia.'[33] He also believed that it was essential to cut Vietnam off from the Soviet Union in order to drive it into the waiting arms of the Association of South East Asian Nations (ASEAN), and possibly to become the US's main regional ally. Such a standpoint was important because it could be argued that it was both correct and ignored. Holbrooke is also worthy of attention because he was required to represent the administration at congressional hearings and, given his views on South East Asia, the language he used at the hearings to protect the administration was both ingenious and illuminating.

CONFLICT

While the interaction between individuals and between levels was important in a general sense in the Carter administration, the interaction between Vance and Brzezinski was specifically so, not least because it involved everybody else, directly or indirectly. The importance of the Brzezinski/Vance schism cannot be over-emphasised. As mentioned above, Carter *wanted* the competition. The problem was that the antipathy between the two men needed little encouragement and the situation became particularly difficult for Carter in that he counted 'Vance, and his wife, Gay, [as] the closest personal friends to Rosalyn and [himself]'.[34]

Carter's idea was not that the two should compete on each issue but that they should generate new ideas and once he (Carter) had decided the way forward Brzezinski would provide policy direction and Vance would implement it: 'The roles were clear to [Carter]. Zbig would be the thinker, Cy would be the doer.'[35] Unfortunately for Carter this arrangement never materialised. Instead the battle lines were drawn across several boundaries – structural, personal and status. In structural terms the relationship between the new Policy Review Committee and the Special Coordination Committee was an early bone of contention. The Policy Review Committee had responsibility for foreign policy issues, defence policy issues and economic issues and was formally chaired by either the SoS or the SoD (although in the majority of instances it was Vance), and the Special Coordination Committee (SCC) was responsible for international policy issues, arms control (e.g. SALT) and crisis management; it was chaired by the NSA. Vance believed that crisis management and in particular

SALT, should be the responsibility of the SoS given that SALT was the high status issue of the moment.

Additionally the new structure involved Brzezinski at the earliest stage. He was required to prepare Presidential Review Memoranda (PRM) which would form the basis of discussion at the Friday Foreign Policy Breakfasts (FFPB), at which Carter, Brzezinski, Vance, Mondale, Brown and Jordan were present. Naturally the drafter has an advantage denied to the others and neither Brzezinski nor Vance would have been unaware of such an opportunity. Incidentally an interesting bureaucratic footnote to the FFPB was that gradually Vance, Brzezinski and Brown began to meet for Thursday lunch to iron out differences before the main meeting. These were known as the VBB lunches.

In personal terms Vance and Brzezinski were simply different people – temperamentally, intellectually, culturally, in fact, on almost every level. A comment by Jimmy Carter illustrates how their personal qualities also spilled over into issues of status. Carter explained that he had been warned that the controversial, outspoken Brzezinski 'might not be adequately deferential to a secretary of state'.[36] There is no doubt that such deference *was* lacking and this further fuelled Vance's irritation regarding matters of status.

One thing that needs to be said about the Vance/Brzezinski battle for supremacy is that, according to all the participants, the disagreements between the two men 'were greatly exaggerated'.[37] However, a considerable body of evidence suggests otherwise. There were two critical issues which indicate the Vance/Brzezinski split was very real. The first was who spoke on foreign policy and the second was which man's staff controlled which 'turf' – and the two issues were mutually infectious. For example, according to Brzezinski at least some of the resentment between himself and Vance was the 'turf-consciousness' of their respective subordinates. Characteristically he added that this phenomenon was more pronounced in the State Department than in the NSC because of 'the more *insecure* State Department bureaucracy'[38] (emphasis added). However, others lay the blame more firmly on the NSC staff whom they even accused of deliberately leaking 'highly classified' communications to the *New York Times* in an effort to embarrass the State Department, which it did.[39] One of the results of these efforts was that a 'Brzezinski factor' developed – and it was the undue influence exerted by Brzezinski on foreign policy matters which really aggravated Vance.

Vance's disquiet is clearly illustrated in the following extract:

I supported the collegial approach with one critical reservation. Only the president and his secretary of state were to have the responsibility for defining the administration's foreign policy publicly. As time went on, there developed an increasingly serious breach of this understanding. Despite his stated acceptance of this principle, and in spite of repeated instructions, Brzezinski would attempt increasingly to take on the role of policy spokesman ... [this] practice became a serious impediment to the conduct of our foreign policy.[40]

Vance found it difficult to come to terms with this issue. He later opposed a Brzezinski trip to China for several reasons but most importantly was his 'concern that such a highly publicised trip would bring into sharp relief the question of who spoke for the administration on foreign policy'.[41] Thus of all the obstacles to the China visit it could be argued that internal bureaucratic status was the most serious. Vance 'felt very strongly that there could only be two spokesmen, the president and the secretary of state'.[42] In hindsight it appears that Vance had reason to be concerned. He could see the vision of a collegial approach to decision-making being lost to the machinations of a pragmatist. Vance had embraced the collegial idea and acted accordingly. Brzezinski had not and Carter eventually allowed himself to be swayed by him. The idealist can often be persuaded by the bravura and confidence of the pragmatist, self-censorship becomes pervasive and the pragmatist flourishes in an indecisive environment.

Brzezinski admitted as much when he said that as a consequence of Vance's reticence in the public arena he 'was pushed by the White House ... to go on the tube more often, to give more interviews, to explain the position of the administration'.[43] Thus he filled the vacuum Vance created by his reluctance to engage the media. Carter liked to believe that Vance could be a restraining influence on both himself and Brzezinski but this was not the view of most observers. Averell Harriman, for example, said that the 'perception is that there are two voices on foreign policy – and that is hurting the President. There can only be one spokesman on Foreign Policy – and that spokesman has to be the Secretary of State.'[44] While both Vance and Brzezinski have since argued that the conflict was insignificant, the *perception* in Washington was the reverse, and perceptions count even if they are not true, and these probably were.

It is likely that neither man actually believed the other to be disloyal but it *is* true that Brzezinski was not convinced that Vance's subordinates were that loyal and later argued that a Kennedy-style purge of second-level personnel might have been warranted.[45] The tension between the two camps meant that it was inconceivable that foreign policy would not have been affected to some extent by the level of conflict and this is evident in the discussion of Foreign Policy below.

FOREIGN POLICY

From the outset there was an evangelical tone to the statements of both Carter and Vance on foreign policy with Brzezinski always remaining more cautious. In Carter's first major presidential statement on foreign policy at Notre Dame on 22 May 1977 he said that:

> Our policy is based on an historical vision of America's role. Our policy is rooted in our moral values, which never change ... Our policy is designed to serve mankind.

The speech as a whole promoted the notion of a foreign policy founded on moral imperatives; it was also a speech based on a 43-page foreign policy booklet developed by Brzezinski (written in collaboration with Henry Owen, Richard Gardner and Professor Huntington) which he had hoped would be the administration's 'blueprint'. It contained ten major goals and Brzezinski left human rights floundering in ninth position. Although Carter's tone was idealistic the base document for his speech was realistic, and provided by Brzezinski.

Carter's own rhetoric was naturally much closer to that of Vance. They both admired the idealism of Jefferson and Wilson and the humanitarian drive of Harry Truman. Carter had even announced his candidature for the presidency by stating that the United States should 'set a standard within the community of nations of courage, compassion, integrity, and dedication to basic human rights and freedoms'.[46] He had, he continued, been 'deeply troubled by the lies our people had been told'.[47] He seemed genuinely to believe that the values America held domestically could provide the basis for those exhibited by the US internationally: 'Our country has been strongest and most effective when morality and commitment to freedom and democracy have been most clearly emphasised in our foreign policy.'[48] Carter believed that such a foreign policy would result in America being seen as symbolically decent, honest, compassionate and strong.

Vance had a similar vision and a similar tone. In a memo drafted on 24 October 1976 he set down 'specific goals and priorities for a Carter foreign policy should he be elected'.[49] Among such goals as the lessening of the dominance of US/Soviet issues and a new awareness of relationships between the industrialised and non-industrialised world Vance made a revealing commitment for an

> unwavering stand in favour of the rights of free men and, without unrealistically inserting itself into the internal operations of other governments, to give important weight to those considerations in selecting foreign policy.[50]

The qualification, 'without unrealistically', perhaps deliberately detracts from the strength of the statement and provides an effective escape clause. The implicit acceptance that human rights are perceived differently around the world later exposed the administration to charges of double standards when foreign policy decisions appeared to ignore human rights issues. It was a charge well made since it struck at the heart of Carter's idealism/realism dilemma. For Brzezinski no such moral dilemma really existed. For him US foreign policy needed to embody a process which recognised 'an unstable world organised almost entirely on the principle of national sovereignty and yet increasingly interdependent socially and economically'[51] – Brzezinski's dilemma was of practice not principle, it was a dilemma of management.

In contrast, Carter and Vance believed that the 'political context', in Vance's phrase, engendered certain foreign policy 'rules'. For example, the US would no longer link its national interest with any right-wing regime, even those under threat from internal Marxist opponents. Neither would it overlook human rights violations simply because governments were Cold War 'friends'. It would no longer ostracise left-wing governments *per se* and would treat Third World regimes as equals. It would be left to Brzezinski to dirty his hands with the management of the philosophers' rules.

US foreign policy, as determined by the Carter elite, was essentially the resultant of two forces. The first was a reaction to Kissinger's 'lone ranger' approach which concentrated primarily on power and relegated principle and the second, a determination 'to demonstrate the primacy of the moral dimension in foreign policy'.[52] Unfortunately the task of fulfilling the philosophical vision was placed in the hands of the pragmatist. Although the President and his two principal 'courtiers' were initially in general agreement there gradually developed irreconcilable differences. These stemmed from fundamentally different views of the world which were most clearly manifested in the perception of the Soviet threat. To Vance the USSR was a declining power; for Brzezinski if there was a decline it was definitely not significant enough to warrant a radical shift in policy. The invasion of Afghanistan in conjunction with the hostage crisis persuaded Carter that Brzezinski was right. Both fell away from their original belief in 'constructive global engagement' and settled for the tenth goal in Brzezinski's blueprint: 'To maintain a defense posture capable of deterring the Soviet Union, both on the strategic and the conventional level, from hostile acts and from political pressure'.[53] Effectively, this confirmation of the balance of power philosophy coloured a good deal of Carter's foreign policy. The Carter administration's foreign policy can be seen as the resultant of the contesting world-views of the three key players in the court and eventually that contest was resolved in favour of the Brzezinski version of *realpolitik*.

THE ADMINISTRATION'S REALITY

The administration's reality is so clearly demonstrated by reference to its foreign policy towards Cambodia because it involves the central dilemma that Carter himself described, that of idealism versus realism. He said:

> I was familiar with the widely accepted arguments that we had to choose between idealism and realism, or between morality and the exertion of power; but I rejected these claims. To me, the demonstration of American idealism was a practical and realistic approach to foreign affairs, and moral principles were the best foundation for the exertion of American power and influence.[54]

Given that early in his term Carter also described Pol Pot as 'the worst violator of human rights in the world today',[55] it was reasonable to assume that Cambodia would be an important issue for the administration – that does not appear to have been the case. In purely statistical terms, for example, Cambodia does not figure very prominently. There were only 51 mentions in the congressional records during the entire Carter term. The number of mentions in the Public Papers of the President was even lower. In the 1977 publication (vols. I and II) there were *no* mentions at all; in 1978 there were two mentions, the first dealt with a condemnation of human rights abuses and the second was a brief reference in a letter to the Speaker regarding the *Trading with the Enemy Act*; in 1979 (vol. I) there were only two statements but in 1979 (vol. II) this jumped to 23, mostly concerned with humanitarian aid; the three books published for 1980 contained only nine statements in all. The largest number, in 1979, probably resulted from the perceived need to respond in some way to the Vietnamese invasion of Cambodia.

The real interest in the above statements is not their paucity but their timing. On 13 November 1979, for example, President Carter said that, 'It's a rare occasion in human memory when there has been the possibility of holocaust ... [but it is happening] now among the people of Cambodia.'[56] This was almost a year *after* the overthrow of Pol Pot by the Vietnamese and three years after the first reports of Khmer Rouge atrocities had begun to filter out of Cambodia. Less than a month later the inconsistency was even more apparent when the President stated that 'as many as two million Cambodians may have died under the brutal Pol Pot regime'.[57] The reference here to a 'holocaust' is particularly interesting. Holocaust, genocide, Hitler, etc. were terms used by all sides and they were possibly used by the Carter administration to legitimise responses which may equally have been generated by statist imperatives. On 24 October 1979, for example, again some time *after* Pol Pot's overthrow, Carter made an appeal for 'aid for the Kampucheans', which included this opening plea:

> Thirty-seven years ago, a holocaust began that was to take the lives of more than six million human beings. The world stood by silently, in a moral lapse whose enormity still numbs the human mind. We now face, once again, the threat of avoidable death and suffering for literally millions of people, and this time we must act swiftly.[58]

Acting swiftly turned out to mean that the US would continue to strangle Vietnam and its 'puppet' regime in Cambodia with rigid trade embargoes. It also meant continuing the development of contacts with China which had been gathering momentum since formal diplomatic relations had been established on 1 January 1979. The same China, that is, which had supported both morally and materially the same Khmer Rouge who were the 'worst human rights violators' and had instigated the 'holocaust' against which the US would 'act swiftly'.

The Carter administration worked hard to rhetorically create a reality which was almost immediately at odds with their actions. Pol

Pot was nearly two years into his reign when Carter was elected and should have provided a perfect target for a human rights activist. The problem was that Cambodia did not seem to matter. Richard Holbrooke once confided that he did not believe 'that Carter had the slightest feeling on the issue [of Indochina]'[59] other than for the symbolic usefulness that Vietnam carried. He could not have been very optimistic, therefore, when making the following statement before the Sub-Committee on Asian and Pacific Affairs on 17 October 1979:

> I don't see how the United States could maintain its credibility and be consistent with all the rhetoric we state about our continued role in Asia and the Pacific and our continued commitment to our own values and principles without a substantial participation.... in these [aid] efforts. And it is absolutely vital. The consequences of a failure to do so would haunt us for years to come.[60]

To be fair, the Carter administration did have a reasonable record on humanitarian aid and the admission of refugees but there was always the suspicion that most aid, particularly food, went to feed the combatants. Holbrooke countered such charges by admitting that although some may have reached 'soldiers of either side ... I certainly don't think small diversions should lead to a suspension of our involvement in these efforts'.[61]

The importance of Asia to the Carter administration was always relative to superpower issues. In 1978, for example, Carter wrote in his diary (16 May 1978) that the administration 'all agreed that a better relationship with the People's Republic of China would help ... with SALT'.[62] The relative merits of the relationships with the other major powers was a constant factor and Indochina only became important when it affected that balance. As Carter himself said after China's punitive action against Vietnam: 'for us to terminate bilateral relationships because a major country, the Soviets or the Chinese, do something contrary to our desires would certainly be counterproductive'.[63]

However, while these sentiments might always have been part of the administration's world-view it was less evident in the early days. Throughout 1977, for example, interdependence and global community were to be the watchwords in a pluralist world-view. Even Brzezinski admitted the need for flexibility when he said that, 'We did not wish the world to be this complex; but we must deal with it in all its complexity.'[64] These views echoed an earlier Carter speech (21 July 1977) in Charleston where he argued that '[a]s Americans we cannot overlook the way that our fate is bound to that of other nations. This interdependence stretches from the health of our economy through war and peace, to the security of our own energy supplies.'[65]

Both views were, perhaps, an expression of early term optimism. Statements later in the presidency illustrated the shift in world-view from optimism to caution. The references to human rights and morality – 'human rights is an idea whose historic time has come' (Brzezinski, 1977);[66] 'we have now found our way back [from intellectual and moral poverty], to our own principles and values, and we have regained our lost confidence' (Carter, 1977)[67] – were replaced by references to geopolitical considerations. Thus Brzezinski's only reaction to the early 1978 Vietnam/Cambodian border clashes was that '[he found] it very interesting, primarily as the first case of a proxy war between China and the Soviet Union',[68] and Hodding Carter III, a State Department spokesman, told the *Washington Post* that 'while the United States takes great exception to the human rights record of the government of Kampuchea, we as a matter of principle do not feel that unilateral intervention against the regime of any third power is justified'.[69]

As 1979 progressed, governmental statements continued to delineate its affiliations. In March, Richard Holbrooke testified at a Congressional hearing as follows:

We have opposed the Vietnamese invasion of Kampuchea strongly and firmly.... We have worked actively ... to make sure that the Vietnamese puppet regime in Phnom Penh is not recognized.... On that point, I might add, our views are identical with that of our ASEAN neighbours, our friends and, I think, very similar to those of the People's Republic.[70]

In this one statement he defined the US position on Vietnam, the puppet regime, ASEAN, and the PRC. The only protagonists not mentioned were the Soviet Union and Thailand. By October Carter had covered the Thai position, 'the Thai government had performed nobly in preparing and permitting a haven for the starving Kampucheans'.[71] He soon also established the position of the USSR:

The Soviets have shown a consistent inclination to extend their own influence, through violence, into other areas of the world. They've done this primarily through surrogates. In Vietnam now, they are encouraging the Vietnamese to invade and to subjugate and to destroy the fabric of the nation of Kampuchea.[72]

Carter was inhabiting a reality and he perceived it as 'a new reality of the world today [in which] Moscow exploits unrest ... to satisfy its imperial objectives'.[73]

The Soviet Union had been reinstated as the sole enemy and Vietnam, as its acolyte, was no longer a candidate for normalisation despite the fact that Vance had argued that re-establishing normal relations with Vietnam 'would give the US an opportunity to have more influence with a nation which will obviously play an important part in the future development of Southeast Asia'.[74] Such a view was no longer acceptable in the deteriorating Cold War environment of the late 1970s and early 1980s. Progress towards normalisation was suspended and was to remain so for many years. Vance was forced to announce that the process 'had been halted by Hanoi's attack on Cambodia and could not proceed under existing circumstances'.[75]

Despite the administration's about-turn Vance tried to remain reasonably constant throughout the presidency. His was not a dissenting voice, other than in the battles with Brzezinski, it was more a voice of moderation. As early as 1976, for example, Vance had outlined the 'political context' he believed would unfold in South East Asia. He did not foresee an 'expansive foreign policy' for the Chinese, he did expect continuing progress in US/China relations and also envisioned a 'Southeast Asia ... still embroiled in the aftermath of the Vietnam war ... [in which the US] should anticipate a number of local problems, increased progress towards Southeast Asia regionalism, and a continuing competition between the Soviets and China for influence in the area'.[76] Within such a context the US, he believed, should strive to balance the two other superpowers and normalise with Vietnam as quickly as possible so that it could remain relatively neutral. Additionally, and perhaps primarily, the US 'must ensure that our foreign and defense policies abroad measure up to American values and beliefs, rather than measuring them only in terms of our most narrowly defined national interests'.[77] By the end of the Carter term Vance's vision had been seriously compromised.

However, the issue which highlighted Vance's constancy of vision was, ironically, the issue on which he buckled under realist pressure and finally acted against his stated principles. In attempting to explain his actions he merely demonstrated the validity of his original views. The issue concerned the opposing claims for the acceptance of credentials for the UN seat by the People's Republic of Kampuchea (PRK), the Soviet-backed Vietnamese-installed Heng Samrin government, and by the Government of Democratic Kampuchea

(DK), the Chinese-backed Khmer Rouge-led government in exile. Both camps saw the issuing of credentials by the UN as the most visible, and thus significant, indicator of legitimacy. Vance chose to back the DK claim, implicitly siding with the Khmer Rouge. He professed abhorrence at this position but arguably need not have taken it. He said, in the appropriately titled *Hard Choices*, that '[t]here are times when your obligations as a senior government official force you to take a position which, although essential for our national interests, is at the same time extremely distasteful'.[78] The UN seat debate was just such a time in Vance's opinion and the crucial variable in the statist equation turned out to be the perceived need to support ASEAN[79] which was vehemently opposed to the Vietnamese position.

Under Carter the US had developed close links with ASEAN in contrast to its previous policy of a series of bilateral arrangements with the original five members. The first US/ASEAN talks had taken place in August 1978, chaired by Vance. The reason for this interest was clear, ASEAN had become one of the highest economic growth regions in the world and as SEATO had been disbanded in July 1977 ASEAN became the focus of the US's South East Asian regional policy. Charles Percy, the Chairman of the Sub-Committee on East Asian and Pacific Affairs, commented that the US's relationship with 'our ASEAN friends ... [is] rapidly becoming a cornerstone of US policy in the area'.[80] It was an ASEAN sponsored resolution before the General Assembly (GA) which the US supported in calling for the withdrawal of 'all foreign forces' from Cambodia and at the 34th GA Credentials Committee 'the Assembly settled the issue of representation by accepting the credentials of the Pol Pot regime ... [and the] United States supported this decision'.[81] In essence the US support for ASEAN, with its enormous trade potential, was unconditional and, therefore, the ASEAN principle of non-intervention, coupled with its anti-Vietnamese stance, meant that implicit support for the Khmer Rouge, by the United States, was inevitable.

Vance admitted that the decision to 'support' Pol Pot was primarily the result of ASEAN lobbying:

> there were compelling reasons to consider the vote carefully. ASEAN had the full support of Japan, Australia, New Zealand, and China.... A majority of the European Community (EC), including both France and the United Kingdom was prepared to back ASEAN unless we broke ranks.[82]

Vance concluded that:

> unpleasant as it was to contemplate voting, even implicitly, for the Khmer Rouge, we could not afford the far-reaching consequences of a vote that would isolate us from all of ASEAN, Japan, China, our ANZUS treaty partners and most of our European allies, and put us in a *losing* minority with Moscow, Hanoi and Havana.[83]

The entire content of those two statements can be viewed as either morally debased or tactically naive, or both. Terms such as 'losing' (which Vance himself emphasised), 'unless we broke ranks', and 'could not afford', miss the point of leadership. It should not be in the language of the leader to suggest being led. If the leader breaks ranks then the assumption should be that the others will follow; the meek acceptance of the ASEAN proposal suggests a lack of any real leadership, and consequently any commitment to human rights. Vance argued that the vote for the Khmer Rouge was 'the only decision consistent with our overall national interests'[84] and yet less than six months later he was making the following statement before the Senate Foreign Relations Committee (27 March 1980):

> I strongly reject the idea that there is a fundamental incompatibility between the pursuit of human rights and the pursuit of self-interest.[85]

It seems that although Vance's vision remained constant his resolve did not, and essentially the reality which the administration's rhetoric constructed was infused with the same contradiction. Throughout the Carter presidential term there was a perception that a foreign policy which sought to dominate a world which refused to be dominated was inadequate. The solution was for the US to be the leading voice in a co-operative venture, the 'global community'. This attempt to throw off the yoke of the 'inordinate fear of communism' mentioned in the Notre Dame speech of May 1977 was gradually submerged in a reluctant acceptance that statist imperatives were irresistible. That view became the administration's benchmark for foreign policy decision-making; it became its reality.

Further indicators of the administration's world-view were provided in two speeches to the General Assembly, given by separate US Secretaries of State. On 27 September 1979 Cyrus Vance reserved just 46 words for Cambodia when asking the international community to restore peace to the region[86] and on 22 September 1980 his successor, Edmund Muskie, used less than 100 words which included the information that 'no progress whatsoever had been made towards securing the withdrawal of occupying Vietnamese forces'.[87] The platitudes of Vance and Muskie's preoccupation with Vietnam highlight the relative insignificance of Indochina as a foreign policy issue and thus its location at the periphery of its political reality. On that, at least, everybody came to agree.

ALTERNATIVE REALITIES

In opposition to the ultimately homogeneous reality of the Carter administration were those created by protagonists both inside and outside the administration. They are evident in the various statements made at the United Nations, especially in the debates conducted after the Vietnamese invasion of Cambodia. They can be loosely grouped in the following manner – Democratic Kampuchea (DK), with Sihanouk as its titular head, in conjunction with China formed one axis; the USSR, Vietnam and the PRK another; the ASEAN states a third; one or two significant others a fourth; and, perhaps most significantly for the Carter elite, a congressional group formed a fifth.

From 11–15 January 1979 the Security Council considered a complaint by DK that there had been consistent Vietnamese aggression culminating in the Christmas invasion. Interestingly the DK was represented by Norodom Sihanouk, a fact which lent some legitimacy and credibility to their cause. The meeting was convened as a result of a telegram sent to the Security Council on 3 January by Ieng Sary (Deputy PM) which stated that 'Vietnam was intensifying its war of aggression against Democratic Kampuchea and requested an urgent meeting of the Security Council to condemn Vietnamese aggression'.[88] The telegram referred to a previous message which had warned of 'serious threats to peace, security, independence and stability in South-East Asia which Vietnam and the USSR were creating by their aggression against Democratic Kampuchea'.[89] During the debate each state defined its own reality, in a very public way, with the exception, that is, of the Heng Samrin regime which was not permitted to send a delegate. *Democratic Kampuchea*, in the person of Sihanouk, argued that Vietnam, encouraged by its 'de facto military alliance with the USSR ... [had] launched an all-out attack with all the power of its Hitlerite armed forces for the conquest of Kampuchea'. The rhetoric continued with similarly emotive terms such as 'Rommel-style blitzkrieg' and Sihanouk also likened the re-established guerrilla war to that of de Gaulle who 'had to retreat to London after the temporary loss of Paris to the Hitlerite invaders'.[90] In one brief speech there were innumerable Nazi references calculated to garner continued recognition for the DK. Of course, the same Nazi terminology (holocaust, genocide, etc.) had also been used by the Carter administration in *its* descriptions of the Cambodian situation. Sihanouk further embellished the oppressed minnow mentality with a reference to Vietnamese 'regional hegemonism unilaterally and unjustly unleashed by Vietnam against little Kampuchea'.[91]

The *Chinese* delegate (Chen Chu) supported the Sihanouk position and asserted that 'Vietnam had long ago become the Cuba of Asia, an agent of Soviet imperialism'.[92] In response the *Vietnamese* delegate (Ha Van Lan), having first regretted the absence of a PRK representative, argued that a clear distinction needed to be made between 'the border war started by the Pol Pot-Ieng Sary clique against Vietnam ... and the revolutionary war of the Kampuchean people against the dictatorial rule of that clique which was an instrument of the reactionary ruling circles of Peking'.[93] The Vietnamese continued to insist that their intervention was the result of an invitation from the National United Front for National Salvation of Kampuchea (Heng Samrin's PRK) who had, on 7 January 1979, overthrown the DK and taken 'full control over the territory of Kampuchea. De facto and de jure, the government of so-called Democratic Kampuchea no longer existed.'[94] He also took the opportunity to utilise Nazi terminology when he spoke of the Pol Pot-Ieng Sary clique turning Cambodia into 'an immense concentration camp. The society of Kampuchea became unique in the world and in history. It became a living hell.'[95]

Naturally Oleg Troyanovsky (*USSR*) supported Vietnam, simultaneously attacking China and, by implication, the US. Interestingly Troyanovsky asserted that for the Security Council (SC) even to discuss the DK telegram was an 'intervention in the internal affairs of Kampuchea, a Member State'.[96] Of course the State to which he referred was the PRK. He argued, in effect, that what should have been Cambodian liberation in 1975 was still-born because the movement was usurped by Pol Pot who, in turn, had only survived as 'a puppet in the hands of outside forces pursuing a policy of hegemonism, great-power chauvinism and expansionism in Indochina and in Asia as a whole'.[97] The USSR was not alone in pushing the non-interventionist case. A variety of strange bed-fellows agreed with their position including France and the ASEAN countries. Jacques Leprette, the French delegate, summed up the fears of many

Members when he stated that 'France could not condone occupation of a sovereign country by a foreign power.... The notion that, because a regime [is] detestable, foreign intervention [is] justified and forcible overthrow [is] legitimate, [is] extremely dangerous'. If ever the state-centric version of reality was encapsulated in one statement surely that was it. If confirmation were needed it was provided by the President of the SC when he lamented that he had drafted four working papers in the hope of achieving a consensus but the threat of the veto had 'shot them all down in flames'.[98] The use of the veto demonstrated a *practical* manifestation of statist *realpolitik*.

Further UN debates during the remainder of 1979 and all of 1980 merely confirmed the positions and attitudes of the various protagonists. China and the USSR both, for example, sought to break the link between the Vietnamese invasion of Cambodia and the Chinese of Vietnam.[99] Supporters of the credentials of the DK argued that such support 'did not imply approval of the policies followed by that government'.[100] However, those who abstained, including France, did not accept this view and 'could not accept a government established by foreign invasion ... if it had voted against the amendment, it would have been a vote in support of the Pol Pot regime'.[101]

Effectively, then, there were four external alternative views of the Cambodian reality; *first*, the *ASEAN* version which viewed Soviet expansionism and Vietnamese regional hegemonism as the foremost dangers while remaining cognizant of the human rights abuses of the DK government, this view was also clearly in line with the US version; *second*, the *Chinese/DK* view which was also concerned with Soviet expansionism but probably viewed Vietnamese hegemonic ambitions as more important owing to Khmer Rouge xenophobia; *third*, the *Soviet/Vietnam/PRK* view that Chinese expansionism and hegemonism in conjunction with Khmer Rouge ideological puritanism were the major threats; and *finally*, a position taken by the *French* and the *Nordic* countries which while being avowedly non-interventionist was also vehemently opposed to any stance which might even suggest support for the Khmer Rouge. As an example they favoured an empty seat policy for Cambodia at the UN.

In addition to the alternative realities of *ex*ternal states the Carter administration's reality was also under considerable threat from within the US. The basis of this threat was quite simply the moral dilemma implicit in contemporaneous US policy, what Michael Haas referred to as the 'Faustian pact'. Haas argued that 'geostrategic considerations outweighed human rights regarding Cambodia'.[102]

Henry Kamm in the *New York Times* magazine (4 February 1979) agreed with Haas, claiming that 'the Carter administration, which has made human rights a keystone of American foreign policy, decided...that the violation of Cambodia's sovereignty was a greater enormity than the Cambodian regime's violations of human rights'.

One specific hearing before the Sub-Committee on International Organizations on 3 May 1977 is especially interesting because it precedes the Vietnamese invasion and yet poses questions that the actuality of the invasion would later allow the administration to side-step. During this hearing Congressman Stephen Solarz (D, NY) enunciated the moral position and was outraged by any suggestions which sought, in his opinion, to justify any of DK's actions. It is worth quoting him at length not least because he was later to serve as the Chairman of the Sub-Committee on Asian and Pacific Affairs. Solarz opened his statement thus:

> To me, the holocaust in which 6 million Jews lost their lives at the hands of Hitler is the central existential fact not only of our time, but of human history, because it provides an indication of the depths of depravity to which the human spirit can sink. And I might have hoped that, after Hitler, the world would have finally learned its lesson on genocide, and that holocausts would have been something of the past. Obviously it hasn't.[103]

There followed a series of vitriolic exchanges between Solarz and two academics, Gareth Porter and David Chandler, which ended when Solarz made the following statement:

> I am not simply talking about making statements so that we can wallow in our own sense of virtue. I am talking about doing something which can bring a criminal regime to its senses and can prevent a repetition or a continuation of what has happened.[104]

Although Solarz agreed with Porter and Chandler that what the US did in Cambodia was contemptible he nevertheless argued that 'there are certain situations which are objectively so horrendous that they obligate all people of good will and decency, however sullied their credentials may be, to attempt to do something to correct a very terrible wrong'.[105] Solarz's dilemma, anger and genuine concern were echoed in an exchange between Senator McGovern and Deputy Assistant Secretary Robert Oakley. McGovern asked:

> is any thought being given either by our government or at the United Nations or anywhere in the international community of

sending in a force to show this government [DK] out of power, just on humanitarian grounds ... It would seem to me that if there were ever a case where the international community has good reason to ask itself, 'Do we sit on the sidelines and watch an entire people slaughtered, or do we marshal military forces and move in quickly to put an end to it?' ... I just wondered if that is an option we just rule out because of the bitterness of our experience in war, or is it one that is discussed in the international community and discussed in our own government?[106]

Mr Oakley replied that 'so far as the administration [was] concerned [he didn't] believe that [it was] an option being studied anywhere'.[107] Both the Solarz statement and the McGovern question highlight the disquiet in the American political establishment over the hypocrisy which seemed to be pervading the Carter administration. The Oakley reply merely appeared to confirm that the administration was prepared to ignore that disquiet.

Further evidence of the administration's hope that this issue would go away was supplied in a hearing on 1 October 1980 in which the government replied to a letter sent by members of the committee on Foreign Affairs. The letter expressed their 'deep concern about present US policy supporting the seating of the Pol Pot regime in the UN General Assembly' and suggested that an alternative might be to support the notion of a vacant seat.[108] Such a position, they argued, could only 'enhance the credibility of our human rights policy'.[109] The reply from the State Department indicated that support for the government of DK was on 'technical grounds' alone. Those grounds apparently included the fact that there was still no superior claimant and that it demonstrated 'solidarity with ASEAN countries'.[110]

The congressional concerns of this period were never sufficient to alter the administration's view of its responsibility in Indochina because its perception remained that *any* level of acceptance of the PRK regime would have reduced the incentive for Vietnam to negotiate a peaceful settlement. Alternative views that any vote for Pol Pot, irrespective of its technical nature, effectively discredited the US commitment to human rights were considered irrelevant during the increasingly pragmatic days late in the presidential term. Cambodia had been relatively unimportant throughout the Carter years and by September 1980 a discredited Indochinese policy would have been the least of its worries; Carter had long since been persuaded into the realist camp, reluctantly perhaps, but irrevocably.

While the members of Congress questioned the administration's reality they did not create a sufficiently coherent reality of their own, although they did raise serious doubts as to the efficiency and efficacy of government policy, but with very little real impact. Each alternative reality, those enunciated in the UN as well as in the Congress, was only as powerful as it was allowed to be during interaction with other realities. As a result US foreign policy must be judged by its strength in resisting the pressures imposed upon it by both external and internal realities. By that criterion it should probably be judged a success since it managed to resist all efforts to alter it.

AMALGAM OF REALITIES

When Jimmy Carter was inaugurated in January 1977 the die was, to large extent, already cast in Indochina. The administration's view of a complex, interdependent world held that no *single* nation dominated across all spheres of the international system, and that the Soviet Union did not dominate in any, be it moral, political, economic or military. In fact at the outset of the Carter term the USSR was considered relatively unimportant in South East Asia. The two most important issues were economic concerns and normalisation. On both issues China and Asia were considered significantly more important than others and in the economic arena China was even more important than Western Europe and Japan. In terms of its importance to the US, concern over Soviet expansionism was negligible during the period 1977–79 and only registered any significance in 1980 (post-Afghanistan) when its importance rocketed to almost 70 per cent in the public's perception.

During the years 1977 and 1978 the Soviet Union was not generally perceived as posing any real threat in Indochina. It was consequently argued that US policy towards Vietnam should be generated only by regional considerations. However, Brzezinski disagreed, believing that to be a flawed appreciation. He retained the view that the USSR *did* represent an expansionist threat and as a consequence saw China as the natural counter-weight (the 'China card'). Vance resisted such a view and favoured equal treatment for both powers and saw a competitive, strategic triangle model as inappropriate. However, as long as there existed even the semblance of a Soviet threat Vance's analysis was ignored and Indochina largely remained a non-issue.

There was still a strong rhetorical regard for human rights issues and a residual antipathy towards Vietnam but very little else.

Within Indochina, however, there was naturally greater concern. Vietnam, for example, had always favoured an Indochinese socialist bloc consisting of itself, Cambodia and Laos (the old Indochina Federation). The bloc would be led, of course, by Vietnam. Vietnam and Laos had already signed a Friendship Treaty in July 1977 which allowed Vietnamese troops to be stationed in Laos in numbers which actually exceeded the host country's forces and also remained on a par with those in Cambodia throughout the 1980s. The next stage in the Vietnamese plan was to involve Cambodia, but the chances of the DK allying with Vietnam were almost non-existent. In January of 1977 the DK launched attacks on villages in the Vietnamese provinces of Long An, Kien Giang, Tay Ninh, Dac Loc and Dong Thap. These were followed in late April by larger-scale incursions at Chau Doc and Ha Tien which forced thousands to flee into the Vietnamese interior, and threatened to destabilise Vietnam's new economic zones. Ha Tien was hit again in May causing further evacuation. As a result of these attacks the Central Committee of the Vietnamese Communist Party (VCP), in an attempt at conciliation, proposed negotiations with its Cambodian counterpart (CPK) but these were rejected.

Shortly after the impasse between the two parties there was an abortive coup against the KR, reportedly supported by Hanoi, which was ruthlessly suppressed, and quickly followed by a series of purges. Once confirmed in power the DK stepped up their border campaign against the Vietnamese and in September 1977 bombarded Quan Phu Quoc island and attacked the province of Dong Thap, again with large civilian casualties. Also during this same period, a delegation from the CPK was visiting China in an attempt to secure their continued support. In late October/early November, the Vietnamese counter-attacked, eventually sending their 9th Division into the Parrot's Beak region, with heavy artillery and air support, where they met severe resistance. In order to support the 9th, the Vietnamese launched a fourteen-division attack on 16 December which comprised some 58 000 men, again encountering fierce resistance. On 31 December 1977 the DK broke with Vietnam, an action which the Vietnamese interpreted as a pincer movement with the Chinese who they accused of using 'the reactionary and genocidal Pol Pot-Ieng Sary fascist gang to make war, nibbling at the south-western border of our homeland hoping to squeeze us in a vice'.[111]

Until this point most analyses are fairly consistent and paint a picture of DK as the aggressor. However, from the beginning of 1978 accounts begin to diverge. On 8 January 1978, Brzezinski, appearing on *Face the Nation*, described the events in South East Asia as a 'proxy war', the first of its kind. Perhaps it would have been more accurate to say that neither superpower instigated the war and, in fact, both were keen to end it. However, it is also true that both felt obliged to 'assist' their own particular 'friend' in what could be described as a local quarrel fanned by ideological rivalry. The battle lines had been drawn and allegiances confirmed. Throughout the remainder of 1978 the rhetoric of all sides continued to confirm contending realities.

The Vietnamese and DK forces were finely balanced along the border with in excess of 150 000 combat troops involved. By this stage it was becoming apparent that the situation was careering out of control. The PRC, while still supplying material support, urged the DK to reopen talks with Vietnam, but they were ignored. In early February Hanoi also made an attempt to cool the situation by proposing negotiations, mutual withdrawal of troops and international surveillance of the frontier zones – Phnom Penh rejected the initiative. It might be argued that such an offer was evidence that Hanoi's prime concern was the safety of its border, although the popular interpretation saw conspiracy in every Vietnamese move. Also at this time the PRC was actually encouraging the US to pursue *rapprochement* with the Vietnamese since that seemed to China the only way to keep Vietnam away from complete reliance on the Soviet Union. Ironically the ever-present 'Vietnam Syndrome' generated the opposite conclusion so that when Brzezinski visited China in May 1978 he encouraged an anti-Vietnamese policy tilt by stating that the United States 'recognizes and shares, China's resolve to resist the efforts of any nation which seeks to establish global or regional hegemony'.[112]

Of course anti-Vietnamese sentiment needed little encouragement in the US even though it did run contrary to the Vance position which held that the restoration of diplomatic relations with Hanoi would 'increase [US] influence with Vietnam and offer it alternatives to excessive military dependence on the Soviet Union *or* China' (emphasis added).[113] The problem was that Brzezinski considered Vietnam to be of limited importance. The Brzezinski view tended to hold sway and the 'predominant reaction among US ... policymakers to the newest Indochina conflict [was] one of relief at American non-involvement'.[114]

Thailand and China would also have liked the luxury of non-involvement but their proximity precluded it, although to a certain extent Thailand tried to deal with the Cambodian threat by ignoring it. They maintained the view that a diplomatic solution was the only viable alternative for them, unlike the Vietnamese who could opt for a military invasion. However, to be on the safe side the PRC, US and ASEAN all pledged additional aid to Thailand in order to resist any possible Vietnamese moves, however unlikely they might be. Throughout the second and third Indochinese wars Thailand attempted to maintain its distance from the fray by accommodating virtually everybody, with the possible exception of the Vietnamese.

By contrast China had very definite goals. Blocking Soviet expansionism was seen as their primary security concern and everything else flowed from that particular view of the world. Although China had concerns about Vietnamese regional aspirations they only became dominant when they were perceived to be a mask for Soviet intentions. In spite of Beijing's professed distaste for the internal atrocities occurring within Cambodia the Chinese maintained support for Pol Pot as their only bulwark against a Soviet-backed southern enemy. They were bolstered in this position by Brzezinski's comments about 'regional hegemonism' when he visited China in May 1978.

However, by that time the diplomatic option was beginning to be less attractive to the Vietnamese. In April they had offered yet another 'permanent peace' which the DK government had again ignored. In May the DK initiated a counter-proposal for a ceasefire which Vietnam had in their turn rejected. It is possible that the DK realised they had overstepped the mark and sensing that the SRV were preparing to retaliate decided to pull back from the brink.

Vietnam, however, had almost certainly already made the decision to take action. In fact, Nayan Chanda believed that Vietnam had made the decision to invade Cambodia as early as March 1978.[115] Visits to ASEAN he argued, in addition to the military build-up along the border, plus deliveries of Soviet arms preceded the signing of a Friendship Treaty with the Soviet Union (3 November 1978) all represented an elaborate timetable for a take-over. The final piece in the jigsaw was the formation on 3 December of the Khmer United Front for National Salvation (KUFNS) led by a former military commander of Pol Pot's eastern region, Heng Samrin. This move paved the way for the forthcoming invasion, an analysis shared by Dutter and Kania when they wrote that 'the conflict with Cambodia [could] best be explained as the independent Vietnamese pursuit of their own long-term goal of converting Cambodia into an obedient, if not totally subservient satellite'.[116] In other words, to put Cambodia on the same footing as Laos. It had little to do with Soviet needs, at least in the Vietnamese minds. For them the 3 November Treaty merely enabled them to utilise military and economic resources, beyond their normal scope, as a means to resist any Chinese threat.

Just as the Vietnamese were running out of patience with the DK regime the ASEAN nations were coming to terms with it. They possibly began to realise that Pol Pot's xenophobia and consequent isolationism could actually be quite useful in that a potential adversary was removed by being effectively neutralised. Vietnam, however, as the target of that xenophobia were in no position to be so relaxed and on 22 December 1978 they launched a major offensive. Ironically on 26 December 1978 Elizabeth Becker is reported in the *Washington Post* as saying that while she was 'travelling about the country [she] saw little evidence to support the widespread belief of Western and Asian diplomats that Vietnamese troops are taking over large chunks of the country'. The first invasion reports began appearing in newspapers on 3 January 1979 and Khieu Samphan was quoted in the *Washington Post* as referring to Vietnam as 'the Cuba of Asia' (p. A1) and stressing that the invasion was primarily designed to 'fulfil expansionist ambitions of the Soviet Union in Southeast Asia' (p. A1). On 7 January Phnom Penh fell to the Vietnamese and Heng Samrin assumed leadership of the newly formed People's Revolutionary Council of the People's Republic of Kampuchea (PRK). The invasion simply reinforced a definition of the world that the US had already developed.

1979 was an important year in the analysis of US foreign policy because it contained three specific events which confirmed in the administration's mind its own version of reality; these were the Vietnamese invasion of Cambodia, the Chinese invasion of Vietnam, and the UN debate on the credentials of Democratic Kampuchea. The response to the first event was immediate. The United States called for a complete withdrawal of Vietnamese troops from Cambodia and the non-involvement of China and the USSR. Pol Pot announced the resumption of the guerrilla war and Ieng Sary rushed to China where he was promised an initial $5m aid. The reaction of the US indicated the shift in favour of the Brzezinski world-view and is reinforced by their responses to the punitive Chinese invasion of Vietnam in mid-February. In late 1978 and early 1979 China carried out what amounted to a marketing exercise. A Chinese official was quoted in the *Washington Post* (11 Nov. 78, p. A4) as saying that '[China] must watch and see how much aggression [the Vietnamese] make against Cambodia, then we will decide about measures we will take'. The implicit warning obviously went unheeded and Deng Xiaoping subsequently conducted a tour of Japan and the United States hawking the idea of limited, punitive action. As Brzezinski recalls, Deng 'had concluded that it [any action] must disrupt Soviet strategic calculations and that "we must consider it necessary to put a restraint on the wild ambitions of the Vietnamese and to give them an appropriate limited lesson" ... all [Deng] asked for was moral support in the international field from the United States'.[117]

The US agreed to support the Chinese by *not* supporting the Soviets. The US would demand the withdrawal of Chinese forces from Vietnam but it would be linked to a parallel demand for Vietnamese withdrawal from Cambodia. When this policy was pursued the Soviets reacted by asking for a greater level of condemnation from the US of Chinese actions. The President told Brzezinski 'to stay on the course we [had] previously determined. In effect a slight tilt in favour of the Chinese.'[118] In effect a *major* tilt in favour of Brzezinski. Vance believed that acquiescence with the Chinese action would drive Vietnam irretrievably down the Soviet track, and so it proved. According to a presidential statement ten days after the Chinese invasion captures the hands-off approach:

> we have expressed our very firm disapproval to the Chinese about their crossing the Vietnamese border, and we have expressed our strong disapproval to the Soviets and to the Vietnamese for the Vietnamese crossing of the Cambodian border.[119]

Previously, on 20 February, the President had stated that '[we] have opposed both military actions'.[120] Both statements suggested an equitable public stance but within the administration the shift towards the Chinese had become irrevocable; and it had irrevocable consequences.

An immediate consequence was even closer linkage with ASEAN. At the expanded ASEAN foreign ministers meeting (2 July) Vance 'reaffirmed that the United States would support ASEAN and observe the Manila Pact and furthermore agreed to expedite US military assistance to Thailand' which had been agreed during the visit to Washington of the Thai Prime Minister Kriansak Chomanand in February.[121] This was a confirmation, by Vance, of Brzezinski's return to Cold War mentality, assuming of course that he had ever genuinely departed from it. ASEAN, which really meant Thailand since it was they who had the most urgent problem, continued to support Pol Pot, even voting for his continued representation at the Havana meeting (3–9 September) of Non-Aligned Nations. ASEAN members other than Thailand were 'located along a continuum whose extremes were marked by the positions of Thailand and Indonesia', between immediacy and disinterest.[122] The Cambodian seat at the Non-Aligned conference was eventually left vacant after huge disagreement. For Thailand, however, the urgency was more immediate. They saw a KR presence on the border as a double-edged sword since it simultaneously invited Vietnamese interest and provided a deterrent.

Most analyses continued to view the situation from a balance of power perspective which saw Vietnam as a Soviet puppet and Cambodia as a Vietnamese puppet. In May Vance was still trying to resist that interpretation by proposing that the US should enter into negotiations with Vietnam over the Cambodian issue, believing that continued isolation would drive a potentially independent Vietnam, Cuba-style, into the Soviet orbit. Brzezinski effectively killed this initiative by arguing that the US should acquire Chinese agreement before proceeding, knowing full well that it would not be forthcoming. By aligning itself with the Sino/Thai axis the US had effectively become an ally, twice removed, of the KR.[123]

It was at this point, mid to late 1979, that the US was thrown back onto the prongs of the moral dilemma generated by the administration's early utterances. It was becoming obvious that the US was backing the KR, albeit 'twice removed', and it was also becoming apparent that humanitarian issues were re-surfacing as a result of increased media attention. ASEAN had put down draft resolutions at the United Nations in both January and March. They both 'called for a ceasefire and withdrawal of all foreign forces' and both were vetoed by the Soviet Union.[124] Nevertheless, ASEAN was in a relatively strong position although primarily still being driven by Thailand's security concerns. Given Thai dominance in ASEAN and Chinese support for them it came as no surprise when, on 27 September, Washington warned both the Vietnamese and the Soviets that in the event of any overspill of the conflict into Thailand 'the United States would give full support to Thailand'.[125] Such a move was entirely consistent with the United States' definition of its own security interests.

In the UN, however, the US cloaked their impulses in references to sovereignty and humanity. At the opening of the General Assembly

(GA) the Vietnamese made an attempt to remove the UN seat from the DK but was defeated 6–3 in the Credentials Committee. In the General Assembly China, the ASEAN countries and the US all voted for continuing DK accreditation, a result which haunted the US for the next 13 years. It was described by a senior official as a choice 'between moral principles and international law. The scale weighed in favour of law because that also served our security interests.'[126] Less than a month later, however, the President was referring to a 'human tragedy of horrifying proportions unfolding in Kampuchea ... [which] is beyond politics. It is a matter of simple and urgent humanitarian concern.'[127] In the same hearing Holbrooke spoke of the need for 'the fastest possible public signal to the international community that the Congress of the United States is moving in the right direction'.[128]

Within a month, the US demonstrated their commitment to act 'beyond politics' by increasing the supply of arms to Thailand in an effort to prepare them for cross-border Vietnamese incursions, and also assisted Son Sann in the formation of the anti-communist Khmer People's National Liberation Front (KPNLF) on the Thai border. As Elizabeth Becker said, 'Immediately after the Vietnamese overthrew the Pol Pot regime and installed the Heng Samrin government in Phnom Penh, Washington began a campaign to punish Hanoi.'[129] By this stage the administration was so suspicious they even believed that reports of famine were part of a ploy to extract aid for the Heng Samrin government which would, in some sense, give *de facto* recognition to the government. In late December Stephen Solarz asked Richard Holbrooke whether any thought had been given to linking the normalisation of relations with Vietnam to Vietnamese acquiescence in allowing aid through to the Cambodians and Holbrooke totally rejected the idea.[130] It appeared that weaving the fabric of the US cloak was not a high priority, and as such the cloak remained transparent.

The United States, then, had settled into a matrix of geopolitical alliances at various levels with China, ASEAN and the Khmer Rouge while simultaneously attempting to remain rhetorically neutral and even-handed at the UN. As the year ended the first moves were made by the KR to sanitise its act under pressure from China and the US; Pol Pot stepped aside in favour of Khieu Samphan because, as Brzezinski said, 'the US public would not permit an open alliance with Pol Pot, and neither would the rest of the world'.[131]

In 1980 US foreign policy towards Cambodia was effectively frozen. 1980 was, in Carter's own words, 'pure hell – the Kennedy challenge,

Afghanistan, having to put the SALT treaty on the shelf, the recession, Ronald Reagan and the hostages ... always the hostages! It was one crisis after another.'[132] Notice, no mention of Cambodia. The quote above was taken from Hamilton Jordan's book on the last year of the presidency. The entire book does not contain one reference to Cambodia. Nevertheless, there were still sufficient statements from other sources which were aimed at consolidating US foreign policy towards Cambodia. For example, it was explained that one of the reasons that any thoughts of normalisation with Vietnam had vanished was because the Soviet Union had 'significantly enhanced their military capabilities in ... Southeast Asia' by utilising Khmer ports.[133] The Chinese supported this view in a particularly hostile statement in the UNGA on 24 September 1980. The Chinese delegate Huang Hua stated that:

> By means of supporting the Vietnamese invasion of Kampuchea the USSR had strengthened its control over Vietnam and moved into Cam Ranh Bay ... support for the Vietnamese aggression in Kampuchea were certainly not 'accidental' events, but premeditated acts; not 'defensive' measures, but offensive and aggressive moves; not 'local' problems, but major issues affecting the overall situation of the world.[134]

Vietnam automatically responded with allegations of American imperialism but the Vietnamese were becoming more and more isolated and their annual attempt to unseat the DK at the UN was again defeated in October. They were also repelled by the Thais in June when they crossed the Thai border in order to put a stop to the 'voluntary' repatriation of Cambodian refugees. They managed to stem the flow of refugees but only at the cost of confirming US suspicions, which were duly exhibited by Ed Muskie at an ASEAN meeting in Kuala Lumpur on 25 June where he restated US commitment to the association.

Ed Muskie had relieved Cyrus Vance after his resignation on 21 April 1980 following the failure of the hostage rescue mission. Muskie managed to accommodate both the Brzezinski and the Vance positions towards the Soviet Union by locating them sequentially, which is to say that only when the USSR had realised that co-operation was in their best interests would it be possible for the US to adopt a less confrontational approach. By the end of October and effectively the end of the presidency, Brzezinski was promoting the same view, arguing that there was a 'balance of power from which we must build stability'.[135] For him 'active cooperation between the major powers of the world [was only possible within a] stable framework of deterrence'.[136] Brzezinski's brand of idealism was, therefore, only achievable within parameters set by realistic concerns.

CONCLUSION

United States foreign policy during the Carter administration began on a wave of optimism that morality could provide the foundation for international affairs; but gradually it came to be defined and implemented in predominantly realist terms. It may have been that any attempt to base 'foreign policy on the cornerstone of human rights...[would] always come to grief on the rocks of national interest and power', but this need not have been the case.[137] The tragedy for Carter was that he came to believe that it *was* the case and he adjusted his values accordingly. Had he not done so Cambodia may well have had a higher priority than it ever achieved. The problem was that 'Washington was accustomed to creating reality, not adjusting to it',[138] and the reality it created attached limited significance to a region from which it wished to be politically dissociated. An added difficulty was that Washington's reality was not, until later in the term, very coherent; it was the product of competing realities *within* the administration, predominantly those of Carter, Brzezinski and Vance. Initially there was a direction, albeit one with which Brzezinski was uncomfortable, but increasingly the balance shifted. As it did so, Brzezinski's balance of power, state-centric world-view came to be more appealing, particularly to Carter, who found himself pressured by the *realpolitik* perception of a Soviet Union interpreting his human rights preoccupations as signs of weakness.

Oddly, those human rights preoccupations did not appear to include Cambodia unless it forced itself onto the agenda. This only ever occurred with the assistance of outside agencies, be they NGOs, the media, or established allies. A reliable indicator of the importance attached to an issue can be the number of mentions it warrants in subsequent accounts. As has already been noted above there were *no* references to Cambodia in Hamilton Jordan's book and in Carter's own *Keeping Faith* there are only four, three of which referred to the Vietnamese invasion and the other being a passing reference to the Nixon bombing campaign. In *Power and Principle*, Brzezinski made it more of an issue but usually as the result of comments on foreign policy towards China. Only when a geopolitical issue arose in which it was useful to take a stance on Cambodia was it deemed to be worthy of comment. Considering that human rights was a central plank of Carter's campaign philosophy, the lack of attention paid to a country governed by the 'worst violator of human rights' is an indictment of the Carter presidency.

The fact that it was Brzezinski's vision that finally prevailed was a key factor in the continuing marginalisation of Cambodia. The prevalence of his view was closely linked to the fact that his attitude was the most acceptable at the time. As Hamilton Jordan put it when referring to the difference between Vance and Brzezinski, 'Cy's calm approach sounded good, but Zbig's tough approach felt good'[139] – and at the end of the Carter presidency, feeling good was a luxury. It was not that the Vance view was without support but that he personally seemed unable to galvanise that support when he was challenged. For example, when India proposed seating the Heng Samrin government at the UN there was heated debate at the US mission between those who believed, as Vance probably did, that the US had to vote with the USSR and Cuba on human rights grounds and those that favoured the *realpolitik* option of non-confrontation with the Chinese. It was said that 'Secretary Vance figuratively held his nose and instructed the mission to vote for the Pol Pot regime.'[140] Vance disliked confrontation but he *could* take principled stands, as he did with his resignation. It is interesting to note that Vance said he 'had disagreed with policy decisions in the past' but had remained loyal to the Cabinet position.[141] He chose to make his stand not on an issue of human rights or moral indignation but on an issue of operational tactics and what he himself described as his anger 'that such a momentous decision had been made in my absence'.[142] Sadly personal indignation forced Vance to action while the suffering of others merely encouraged him to 'hold his nose'. In November 1979 Vance said that 'Some issues transcend politics. [Cambodia] is one of them.'[143] Perhaps for Vance 'transcending' can be interpreted as opting out.

The Carter administration suffered in what Stanley Hoffman described as the 'the hell of good intentions'.[144] In this particular hell '[t]he quest for human rights and the quest for world order are not identical.... The issue of human rights ... by definition, breeds confrontation.'[145] There can be little argument with Hoffman's analysis but his conclusion, that such a 'quest' was doomed, need not necessarily have been true. Surely it is a question of which issues are chosen to be confronted and on what grounds. To imagine a non-confrontational world is too idealistic but to imagine one in which issues are confronted for moral reasons rather than those of *realpolitik* seemed possible during 1976. The problem was that Carter himself did not remain true to his beliefs. When they were tested, and it is unlikely that his presidency was any more traumatic or unlucky than any others, he failed his beliefs, they did not fail him. When Brown switched to the Brzezinski camp, acquiescence was Carter's easy way out. Raymond Moore sees successes only when Carter returned to centrist politics[146] but in reality they were defeats for his original vision.

Carter chose Brzezinski and Vance to actually present the moral dilemma. They, in turn, chose staff who mirrored themselves. The conflict between the two camps grew as the term progressed. Eventually Carter opted for the Brzezinski policy variant and Vance was marginalised. From that moment US foreign policy in general, and towards Cambodia in particular, was predictable. This conclusion refers not only to the US but also to the other groups. China believed that the Cambodian/Vietnamese conflict was driven by the Soviet Union's hegemonistic ambitions with Vietnam acting as its proxy. They interpreted this as a lack of respect, and the idea that any Asian nation could choose alliance with the Soviets rather than the Chinese was intolerable. The Soviet Union, of course, argued precisely the opposite. Brezhnev stated that the Kampuchean people were grateful that the Vietnamese had overthrown Pol Pot 'and that it was only natural for the Soviets to assist such an effort'.[147] The Vietnamese and Cambodians were merely playing out their centuries-old antipathies with the help of powerful backers who enabled the conflict to be sustained beyond its natural life-span. ASEAN was concerned only to protect its 'zone of peace' so that its economic expansion could continue without undue interference.

ASEAN's potential was also a prime factor in the more pragmatic stance of the later years of the Carter administration and the following statement from the President in May 1980 needs only to be compared with the tone of the inaugural address to illustrate the point:

> Our friendships with the ASEAN nations [are] growing week by week, month by month, because we see that accurately as the fastest growing economic region of the world.[148]

No mention of the human rights abuses of members such as Indonesia and Thailand which presumably should have been an important issue for a President whose 'commitment to human rights [was] absolute'.

Ultimately the foreign policy of the United States towards Cambodia during the Carter presidency was predictably, if reluctantly, realist. The personalities within the presidential court produced competing world-views which eventually coalesced around Brzezinski's pragmatic, *realpolitik* approach. It could be argued that the change was not actually in Carter but in his audience, that expectations about the world changed and Carter could not. To a certain extent this might be true, Carter's views did not really alter, he seemed merely to lack the resolve to defend them when they came under attack. The American public were entitled to pose Jimmy Carter's own question – 'why *not* the best?' Henry Kamm put the case most clearly in the *New York Times* magazine:

> Washington ... adopted the attitude it believed best served the United States world interests. But ... [d]id not the extraordinary evil of the Pol Pot regime admit of a less one-sided and preachy – and more moral – American policy?[149]

President Carter came into office vowing to radically shift US foreign policy away from the realpolitik of the Kissinger era, and essentially failed to do so. In his own terms, perhaps, his foreign policy was a failure. However, since Cambodia might be considered as relatively unimportant, that particular failure was also relative. US foreign policy towards Cambodia proceeded without generating a great deal of controversy in the face of other more pressing issues, particularly the hostage crisis. During the Carter presidency US foreign policy towards Cambodia may be best described as a major failure for the President as an individual while being only a minor embarrassment for the administration.

2 The First Reagan Administration, 1981–85

> *To those neighbours and allies who share our freedom, we will strengthen our historic ties and assure them of our support and commitment. We will match loyalty with loyalty. We will strive for mutually beneficial relations. We will not use our friendship to impose on their sovereignty, for our own sovereignty is not for sale.*
>
> Inaugural Address of President Ronald Reagan, 20 January 1981

Reagan's inaugural address was a fairly accurate indicator of the policy themes of the next four years. The primary concern of the inaugural was economic: 'These United States are confronted with an economic affliction of great proportions.' The second concern was the intrusiveness of government: 'In this present crisis, government is not the solution to our problem; government is the problem.' Both concerns highlighted the predominant Reaganite view that America was a country in moral, economic and strategic decline. It was a country made great by the pioneer spirit but devalued during the Carter period by the erosion of that spirit. Reagan concluded his inaugural by affirming that he 'did not take the oath [he'd] just taken with the intention of presiding over the dissolution of the world's strongest economy'.

Thus from the outset *foreign* affairs was subordinated to the economy. This is not to say that it was unimportant because Ronald Reagan was also a visionary. When he spoke of evil empires it was not mere rhetoric. From his days as President of the Screen Actors Guild through his 1964 support of Goldwater's candidacy to his presidency, Reagan retained a right-wing, quasi-Christian view of the world. It is not simplistic to characterise his world-view as that of the pioneer, the frontiersman. This view of the world still saw frontiers which needed to be tamed. Beyond the boundaries which the United States controlled were uncivilised people with threatening ideologies, cultures and religions. They were easily categorised, to paraphrase the Bible, 'they that are not with me are against me'.[1] Foreign policy, therefore, had an active, missionary tone, although it has been said that it was not always easy to discern whether that tone was present in

Reagan's 'operational' as well as his 'declaratory' statements.[2] Coral Bell, for example, argued that there was often a mismatch between Reagan's words and deeds. As a result it may well be true that the 'experts' who described Reagan's foreign policy as mediocre failed to distinguish between style and substance.[3]

Cambodia did not figure prominently on either the main economic or the peripheral foreign agenda and as such remained very much on the margins of US foreign policy. Nevertheless, Indochina still held a unique place in the American psyche and as such provides a useful case study for the analysis of US foreign policy. Although Cambodia had a relatively minor place in the hierarchy of issues, when it did demand attention it invariably threw the spotlight on crucial concerns of the Reagan administration as well as reviving traditional concerns of US policy abroad.

During his presidential campaign Reagan made much of what he called the 'gross-hypocrisy' of the Carter administration's record on human rights. He specifically cited the fact that they 'supported the United Nations seating of the Pol Pot [regime] which had slaughtered millions of its own people'.[4] A reasonable comment and an issue the Reagan administration would later confront themselves. The realities constructed by both individuals and organisations in that confrontation, as well as the matrix of interactions between them, directs the ensuing analysis.

THE ADMINISTRATION

The three levels of the Reagan court appear to be very similar to those of Jimmy Carter. The crucial difference, however, was the amount of influence wielded by the various courtiers. As with Carter, the President stood very clearly atop the pyramid. What differentiated the Reagan administration was the relative importance of the contributions made by the level two and level three players as well as his allegedly hands-off management style. On level two were the Secretary of State (SoS), initially Alexander Haig, and the Secretary of Defense (SoD), Caspar Weinberger. The SoD had, therefore, supplanted the NSA at level two in the Reagan hierarchy.

During the 1980 election campaign Reagan had continually vowed to downgrade the position of NSA. He did not want another Brzezinski. The reduction in power was accomplished by the *structural* diminution of the NSA role. Reagan's appointment of weak characters, particularly in the first term, further diminished the position of NSA. His lack of close control over NSAs who were perceived as low status effectively emasculated the post:

> Reagan never took charge ... of his national security establishment, allowing feuding between the State Department and the Department of Defence to have a debilitating effect on United States' policy.[5]

The NSA was deliberately located at a level below the SoS and the SoD.

The NSA was not the only post-holder to suffer. The role of 'crisis manager', a position traditionally the preserve of the SoS was handed to the Vice-President (VP) George Bush. SoS Haig was unhappy with this change but was reassured that he would retain the leadership on foreign policy issues. As Haig recalls, the President said that on such matters, 'I'll look to you Al'.[6] Haig was not destined to last very long but did attempt to stabilise the role of SoS in the way the President wanted. Defence, under Weinberger, became more and more intrusive and the personality clash between himself and Haig's successor, George Shultz, did not make matters any easier. The position of the Defense Department was strengthened by the massive rearmament schedule in the first term. From that position of strength it was relatively easy for Weinberger to undermine Haig's position. However, rather than diminish the role of SoS, Haig's removal strengthened it, due to the arrival of the steadying hand of George Shultz. While Shultz was stabilising the position of the SoS on level two the high turnover of NSAs confirmed the positioning of the NSA on level three. The decline of the NSA was only really halted in Reagan's second term with NSA number six, a certain Lieutenant-General Colin Powell.

Richard Allen, the first Reagan NSA, was recruited from the Hoover Institution at Stanford. Like the later NSAs chosen, Allen appeared to be happier administrating the facilitators rather than resurrecting the assertiveness of a Kissinger or Brzezinski. Structurally he was also constrained by having to report to Edwin Meese, the presidential counsellor, rather than directly to the President, as did his predecessor. Allen was soon replaced by William Clark who tried to enlarge his role, successfully at first. Extremely loyal, he was reported to be well-liked and trusted by Reagan and by the summer of 1983 'was widely regarded as having become the most influential figure in the White House'.[7] Such assessments now appear exaggerated because he was removed in October 1983, reportedly because of his continual disagreements with James Baker, the White House Chief of Staff (CoS). By replacing Clark the White House (WH) staffers became predominant once more.

Glen Hastedt argues that Reagan over-reacted to the power wielded by previous NSAs; so much so that the 'national security adviser became a non-person with little foreign policy influence or stature'.[8] In Hastedt's view this led to the demise of the NSC as a co-ordinating force and severely damaged Reagan's foreign policy potential. The combination of structural reassignment and less forceful personalities probably relegated the NSA to the third level, a relevant but not central level. Level three's primary significance lies in its interaction with the media and the consequent burden of reinforcing presidential image.

At level three, regarding foreign policy issues, those most responsible for progressing the Reagan vision were Jeane Kirkpatrick (US Ambassador to the United Nations) and, particularly with respect to Cambodia, John Holdridge (Assistant Secretary of State for Asian and Pacific Affairs). This is not to dismiss the influence of others. Stockman and Anderson in their roles as presidential advisers obviously contributed but perhaps not quite as fulsomely as Stockman, for example, indicated in his book *Triumph of Politics*. As has been previously mentioned the NSA was marginalised. The so-called 'troika' of WH staff – James Baker (CoS), Michael Deaver (D/CoS) and Edwin Meese (Presidential Counsellor) – was extremely influential within the administration but rarely troubled itself with foreign concerns; and conspicuously absent in any meaningful sense was Vice-President George Bush.

Jeane Kirkpatrick was probably most significant, in a symbolic role, through her powerful rhetoric. An example was her statement to the Third Committee of the United Nations on 24 November 1981. She quite openly attacked the perceived duplicity of the UN in its handling of human rights abuses. She isolated the central problem as being one of 'double standards'. She stated that 'it is neither fair nor reasonable to judge the human rights violations of some nations harshly, while ignoring entirely the gross abuses of other peoples'.[9] She continued in the same 'hard-ball' Reaganite style, berating the UN, and by implication the non-aligned movement, for their reluctance to live up to US expectations. Ironically the rhetoric could as easily have been applied *to* the US and as such Kirkpatrick's statement had a slightly surreal tone.

However, it only appears surreal if you ignore the genesis of such style. Kirkpatrick, in company with Reagan, Shultz, Allen and Casey (head of the CIA), was a member of the *Committee for the Present Danger*. This committee was formed as a Republican counterbalance to the Carter administration in order to bring to the attention of the American public and establishment the dangers inherent in what came to be referred to as the 'years of neglect'. The committee argued that the US was in decline because of a lack of will on the part of President Carter; the decline could, therefore, be halted and reversed only by positive will, an act of faith – and, of course, Reagan could provide that faith. Kirkpatrick's myopic tirade against the UN was indicative of the certainty with which the new right viewed its mission, Kirkpatrick was a rhetorical archetype of the Reagan years.

John Holdridge did a similar job for Reagan in Congress. As the Assistant SoS for East Asia and Pacific Affairs it fell to Holdridge to explain and defend the administration's position on Indochinese matters. He did so with clarity and resolve. In one fascinating exchange with Sub-Committee Chairman Stephen Solarz (D, NY), Holdridge subtly demonstrated the confidence of a competent team player in a winning team. By 1982 Solarz had become a very effective Chairman and interlocutor but he was rarely able to intimidate Holdridge. The following lengthy exchange demonstrates this very well:

SOLARZ: You know we have restrictions in the foreign aid bill against aid to SWAPO and other such organizations. The Khmer Rouge certainly makes these groups look like boy scouts by comparison. I think you ought to take a very close look at this.

HOLDRIDGE: As I say, it is not our policy to provide any aid to the Khmer Rouge, but we are doing what we can to meet the humanitarian needs of all of the women, children, and refugees all along the border.

SOLARZ: There is more than one way to meet legitimate humanitarian needs. If you are disinclined to take an administrative initiative, there may be a legislative one. But we can go into that later.

HOLDRIDGE: I think that is a pitfall you ought to be very careful about, Mr Chairman, recalling some of the things which happened during the Kampuchean war.

SOLARZ: Such as?

HOLDRIDGE: Legislative restrictions; I think in retrospect one might want to question whether this was an advisable policy.

SOLARZ: I don't think the American people and their Representatives in Congress would look with much enthusiasm at our providing aid, whether it is humanitarian or any other kind to people who are, in effect, under the jurisdiction of the Khmer Rouge.

HOLDRIDGE: Let me say this, Mr Chairman. We have been providing aid under some certain circumstances directly into Kampuchea which was distributed by the Vietnamese or by the Heng Samrin forces. Now are you going to stop that, too?

SOLARZ: I have no brief for Heng Samrin or the Vietnamese, but when the whole nation was on the verge of starvation and the question was whether a civilization would survive, it was right to provide aid. I think that was a somewhat different problem than the one we have here. In any case, unless it can be established that our aid literally spells the difference between life and death for the people who are there, which I suspect in this instance it does not, then I think the argument for aid to the Khmer Rouge camps is not a powerful one.

HOLDRIDGE: On the other hand, I would be hesitant to try to describe the situation in any of the camps. This is like the committees in some of our hospitals which have to decide whether or not a person gets dialysis, a scarce dialysis machine. Do we want to take the occasion to exercise the power of life and death, say, over infants or ...

SOLARZ: I suspect that there is a need for greater aid in all of the other camps. Anything you give to the camp controlled by the Khmer Rouge is material that is not available to the camps controlled by the others.[10]

Holdridge impressively dealt with hostile questioning, concerning a complex moral situation, in a subtle and controlled manner. The content was almost immaterial, it was the manner of the performance and the certainty of tone which is crucial – substance and image were fused.

Having the right staff about him, people like Holdridge, was one of the reasons for Reagan's effectiveness as a leader. His personal appeal fostered a strength of character and a fierce loyalty. Melanson argued that Reagan gave others his strength.[11] Reagan said as much himself in an oft-quoted remark:

I believe that you surround yourself with the best people you can find, delegate authority and don't interfere as long as the overall policy that you've decided on is being carried out ... when I've heard all that I need to make a decision, I don't take a vote, I make the decision.[12]

Reagan also utilised the 'monarchical potential' of the presidency to realise his vision.[13] For Reagan the vision itself was the unifying force and it was essential for him to have 'a vision and state it forcefully.... People who intrude with the facts are "doomsayers" and "hand-wringers" who must be ignored.'[14] As a consequence it became unlikely that anybody in the Reagan team would significantly alter the central thrust of foreign policy although the tactics of implementation was left almost entirely within their scope. Within the Reagan team it was possible to become an important member but there was only going to be one leader.

LEVEL ONE

Ronald Reagan has been described as lazy, laid-back and uninterested in detail. It is said that he had a loose administrative style within which he delegated too much and 'was inattentive to the prime ministerial aspects of the job'.[15] All of this may have been true but he also had a clear belief in certain basic ideas which, despite their alleged lack of intellectual rigour were nevertheless powerful instruments for focusing the administration's energies. The basic ideas were easy to understand and appealed to deep-rooted American emotions with which both the public and his subordinates could readily identify. Reagan's long-term anti-communism, nurtured during his days with the Screen Actors Guild and consolidated during his time with the Committee for the Present Danger, was the central pillar of his views on foreign affairs. He also seemed genuinely to believe that Nixon and Carter had all but thrown away *his* America and his duty was to resurrect it.

Strangely his cowboy image, which might have been such a liability, proved to be an asset. Not only did it complement his simple message but to the 'rhetorical president' his previous acting skills were conveniently the tools of his new trade.[16] His presentational abilities enabled him to promote the image of a 'can-do' presidency which he managed to protect throughout both terms of office. Being the 'great communicator' was the crucial element in making the message palatable; he seemed to understand what America wanted and provided it.

He was able to do so either because he genuinely believed it or because he had been saying it for so long that it became second nature. As early as 1962, for example, Reagan had spoken of the 'war' with communism saying that '[t]here can only be one end to the war we are in...Wars end in victory or defeat.'[17] Twenty years later little had changed with Reagan declaring that the Soviet Union was 'the focus of evil in the modern world'.[18]

Reagan envisaged the solution to America's problems as residing in a minimalist domestic government and an anti-communist foreign policy. He made this vision very clear to his administration. Nevertheless, some analysts identified *two* Reagans, 'Ronald the Radical' and 'Ronald the Reasonable'.[19] The former was the strong ideologue committed to 'new right' philosophies dealing in rhetorical 'red meat', the latter was a pragmatist who realised the constraints of any given situation and was prepared to be flexible, building, or building on, a consensus. It was the 'two Ronnies' that Hill and Williams described as the 'pragmatic ideologue'.[20] Reagan himself might not have agreed with descriptions of himself as someone susceptible to compromise since he liked to project a straight-ahead, no U-turn image. He is said to have likened himself to FDR as a non-appeaser.[21] It may be that *all* the descriptions of Reagan were true and that was why he appealed to the electorate.

Much has been made of Reagan's 'no-hands' approach to management. It was argued, particularly in the second term, that such an approach actually meant that nobody was at the helm. However, in the opinion of those close to Reagan, this was not the case. Martin Anderson, a presidential adviser, explained that while Reagan's approach could appear 'curiously passive',[22] it did not necessarily signify an inability to make decisions; when a decision had to be made the President was more than capable of doing so. Anderson also contends that Reagan certainly had direction and that it was easily discernible if reference was made to his pre-election years.[23]

Another criticism levelled at Reagan was of intellectual shallowness. As David Stockman put it, '[his] body of knowledge is primarily impressionistic: he registers anecdotes rather than concepts'.[24] There may be some validity in Stockman's claim but it is equally plausible that the 'great communicator' sanitised and simplified concepts for public consumption.

None of the above is meant to ignore the oft-cited criticisms of Reagan the man, but this was also the man who won *two* elections and probably would have won a third if the constitution had allowed it.

The 'teflon' factor may not have been an accident, the strength of purpose not a front, and the idealism not a sham. During Reagan's acting days it was the star's name which carried the film not the director's or the producer's, and Reagan probably saw his presidential role in the same way. As Michael Foley argues, Reagan clearly illustrated that 'political leadership can ... be generated almost exclusively by impulsive appeals to the unthinking instincts for past visions, old faiths and traditional prejudices'.[25] Reagan would not have considered Foley's description a criticism. There was a mysticism in his view of the world and America's place in it that touched a positive nerve in the American psyche. In 1982 Reagan said 'I have always believed that this anointed land was set apart in an uncommon way, that a divine plan placed this great continent here between the oceans to be found by people from every corner of the earth who had a special love of faith and freedom.'[26] That one sentence sums up Reagan's reality, the well from which his foreign policy inevitably sprang.

LEVEL TWO

A problem in identifying the important influences upon, and views of, the actors at level two is that the crucial position of Secretary of State was held by two men during the first term. Alexander Haig, the President's first SoS initially seemed to be the ideal choice. A vastly experienced Army general who had been an assistant to Kissinger in the Nixon administration and who had also served competently in the difficult post-Watergate Ford presidency, he appealed to the Europeans because of his previous SACEUR (Supreme Allied Commander in Europe) duties and the formidable array of contacts he had established. However, he very quickly lost status. He probably alienated the White House insiders as early as the inauguration day when he presented the President with a memorandum detailing how he perceived his role; not surprisingly it was an SoS with huge power.[27] Haig's major problem was probably a failure to realise, early enough, where the power lay within the White House system. According to Glenn Hastedt he over-zealously attempted to dominate foreign policy, no doubt emboldened by the President's 'I'll look to you Al' indicator.[28] However, the views he advocated on behalf of the State Department isolated him from the President.

  Haig, the self-styled 'vicar' of foreign policy never quite mastered the intricacies of the bureaucratic 'politicking' which characterises the

White House. He made enemies of Meese and Baker, two members of the powerful 'troika', by attempting to assume control of the administration in the immediate aftermath of the Reagan assassination attempt. In June 1982, after less than eighteen months, Haig was driven from office. He had antagonised the troika and failed to win his turf battles with the DoD. Perhaps being a military man was actually a disadvantage in that Defense knew him too well. Another factor in his downfall was the manner in which Weinberger (SoD) had 'consistently spelled out the guidelines of the new administration's foreign policy', a tactic which effectively undermined Haig's efforts to accrue foreign policy power to himself.[29]

George Shultz replaced Haig in June 1982. Like Haig he was essentially a conservative, a pragmatist, *not* an ideologue. He was enormously respected and had great stature coming into the job which, when added to his vast experience, enabled him to survive both terms. Despite the fact that they had been colleagues in the Nixon administration there was an uncomfortable relationship between Shultz and Weinberger. Shultz did manage to achieve the predominance in his capacity as the President's foreign policy adviser that had eluded Haig. One ploy he used to develop that position was to be the President's man rather than the State Department's. Haig had prevaricated and fallen between those two stools.

Shultz had to be the consummate politician because his views often did not coincide with those expected of the State Department's representative – to paraphrase Allison he did not consistently 'stand where he sat'.[30] As an example, he had particularly hard line views on terrorism and tended to favour military action, such as the Libyan air strikes. Shultz seemed to be a quietly efficient manipulator and the ideal right-hand man for Reagan. He had limited missionary zeal, there was no Shultz doctrine, for example, but he could garner support and implement the President's wishes.

In contrast to Shultz, Caspar Weinberger, the other key player at level two, saw himself very much as the representative of the DoD in the various decision-making arenas. He would willingly defer to professional expertise and was, as a consequence, widely accepted as a successful champion of the military's position. The result of Weinberger's strict interpretation of his role was to distance himself from the foreign policy debate except when it directly impinged on his department. Thus Weinberger would engage in foreign affairs only if it seemed likely to have an effect upon his stance that US defence forces should be able to undertake 'simultaneous reinforcement of

Europe, deployment to SW Asia, the Pacific, and support for other areas'.[31] By the time he had enunciated the Weinberger Doctrine in late 1984 his reluctance to use the military was evident. He never really seemed sure of the benefits of using force and was generally wary about the consequences. For Weinberger, force would be used with great care and only as a last resort, and force in low-intensity conflicts must adhere to a restrictive set of conditions before it would even be contemplated.

At level two, then, it appears that the realities of the players were less crucial because they were flexible. Both Haig and Shultz were pragmatists. Haig had little genuine vision and was comfortable accepting the Reagan world-view. For example, his comment that the 1970s were 'a decade when negotiations often seemed to be a substitute for strength' was pure Reaganite rhetoric.[32] As for Shultz he had been a fellow-traveller on the Committee for the Present Danger and could, therefore, be expected to follow the presidential lead. Weinberger clearly saw himself as the Defense Department's advocate. In an administration which did not welcome the advocacy approach his style tended to marginalise him on foreign policy matters, although the massive defence build-up in the early 1980s gave him some influence when he needed to use it – as he did when marginalising Haig.

LEVEL THREE

At the third level there were many players but few with any genuine input into the policy-making level of foreign affairs. The troika, while powerful in the development of domestic policy implementation and White House politics, did not have a significant influence in external matters other than protecting the President from the intrusions of unwelcome facts. Other than Jeane Kirkpatrick at the UN and John Holdridge of the State Department, very little was seen of the others. The NSC had been neutralised by the demotion of the NSA and the various presidential advisers, including the Vice-President, tended to be Reagan converts. Kirkpatrick's real importance, therefore, lay in her ability to project Reagan's vision more effectively than most. Coral Bell said that Jeane Kirkpatrick's rhetoric 'was a major factor in creating the Reagan image abroad'.[33] Holdridge performed much the same function as Richard Holbrooke had done in the Carter administration. Although Holdridge did not have Holbrooke's depth of knowledge on South East Asia he nevertheless made an important Congressional contribution in his role as the administration's front man.

CONFLICT

The major difference between Reagan's first term and the Carter presidency was the lack of conflict between the courtiers on the scale of Brzezinski and Vance. Obviously there were tensions. Weinberger and Haig, and Weinberger and Shultz did clash, but their battles were generally over procedure and not ideology. There was the disaffection of Stockman, and towards the end of the four years the breakdown of the troika's power and the rise of Donald Regan. However, the first period of Reagan's presidency was mostly characterised by a homogeneity that the Vance/Brzezinski confrontations had denied to the Carter team. Reagan's particular management style may have been 'hands-off', careless on detail, and informed by a type of moral absolutism, but it *was* unifying.

Somehow even Reagan's frailties seemed to benefit him. He was, for example, reportedly impatient for action once a decision had been made and this 'sense of impatience was picked up on by subordinates ... who felt they had a presidential mandate to realize goals regardless of the institutional or legal obstacles in their path'.[34] In later years this was to lead to what the Tower Commission euphemistically termed 'insensitivity',[35] but during the early years it contributed to the 'can-do' appeal of the administration. Reagan's lack of a grasp on detail and concepts also allowed him to focus on his vision. It is impossible to ignore the achievement of Reagan in unifying his administration even if it was greater than the achievements of his presidency as a whole.

FOREIGN POLICY

The direction of Reagan's foreign policy was inevitable given his belief that *all* the evils of the world emanated from communism in general, and the Soviet Union in particular. Such a simple world-view completely reoriented the globalist attitude prevalent during the Carter years. Previously globalism had meant interaction or, in extreme cases, intervention *within* the international system but

Reagan believed that he had to operate *despite* the system. An indicator of this was the way in which the US became highly critical of the UN, withdrawing from the UNESCO, withholding 40 per cent of its regular budget payments and threatening to withdraw from other agencies. They continued to withhold $10m in protest at certain aspects of the Law of the Sea Convention and the Division for Palestinian rights until very recently. According to Kegley and Wittkopf, multilateralism was replaced by a 'global unilateralism'.[36] A Reagan comment during his 1980 electoral campaign echoed that assessment; he said the US 'did not seek leadership of the free world, but there is no-one else who can provide it'.[37] The implication was that it was a burden the US would reluctantly have to accept.

The attitude towards the UN was also consistent with the no-nonsense image that the administration wished to project. The image was promoted more by force of rhetoric rather than force of arms. Melanson contended that Reagan realised that while the American public could be made to feel good by the rhetoric, they were also reluctant to risk any Vietnam-type involvement or, even worse, a superpower confrontation; the result, Melanson believed, was 'an essentially cautious foreign policy that largely replaced deeds with words'.[38] This view aligns with Bell's contention that 'the technique of making words stand in for deeds ... [is] classifiable as a foreign policy technique'.[39] The technique was demonstrated by Jeane Kirkpatrick, for example, who was brutally frank with the UN when she stated that 'the central goal of our foreign policy should not be the moral elevation of other nations, but the preservation of a civilized conception of our own national self-interest'.[40] Again the sentiment accords with the unilateralist, tough-guy stance Reagan wished to promote.

Casting the Soviet Union as the lightning rod for all the world's ills suited the Reagan philosophy perfectly. He needed an overall thesis upon which to base his foreign policy, and the domino theory was easy to pronounce and easy to understand. Thus when Reagan told the American people that it was 'time they realized that it was they who were the last domino', they appreciated the danger.[41] So much so that he was able to keep US Marines in Beirut because it was 'central to our credibility on a global scale'.[42]

The Soviets were not only the enemy in the sense of maximising their power; they had to be further demonised by casting doubts on their ability to operate within the world community. At the opening of the 1983 General Assembly, Reagan explained 'how different the Soviet's conception of truth and international cooperation is from

that of the rest of the world'.[43] Once the Soviet Union had been identified as the source of all evil it became comparatively easy to classify
all those who sided with it as evil and those who lined up against it as
fighters against evil, thus the Contras were freedom fighters while the
Sandinistas were totalitarian communists.

It was not sufficient, however, for Reagan alone to portray the
image; others had to play their part. Part of the new image included
revising the Vietnam story. In one of the earliest public revisionist
statements, Jeane Kirkpatrick said 'I don't think that we were driven
out of Vietnam – I think we left. I think that's an important distinction and one we should not lose sight of.'[44] Two years further into the
administration, however, George Shultz put a more realistic hue on
policy rhetoric when he said, 'We cannot pay any price or bear any
burden. We must discriminate. We must be prudent and careful.'[45] If
the general tone of the rhetoric did have its desired effect at home, it
had an equal but negative effect abroad as the following excerpt from
the Vietnamese News Agency (VNA) shows:

> The threat made by a US diplomat shows that the Reagan admin-
> istration is still addressing the world in the rough language of the
> imperialist ringleader.[46]

One of the practical consequences of a foreign policy which aimed to
confront a single enemy was the need to redress a perceived shortfall
in military parity with that adversary. This was achieved by a substantial defence build-up in the first five years to the tune of $1.5 trillion.
It could be argued that the build-up permitted the US to bargain with
the Soviet Union from a position of strength in the second term.
Whether such an analysis is true or whether it was just a consequence
of the dynamics of internal Soviet affairs is actually irrelevant; a
reality had been constructed, primarily by Reagan, and it to be continually reinforced by the rhetoric.

Interestingly, much of the rhetoric was delivered by aides and
asides. Reagan did not deliver a major foreign policy address himself
until January 1982 and he never met with the Soviet leaders throughout his first term. He created the image of resolve through a series of
sound-bites. An entire foreign policy was 'implemented through
rhetoric and a refusal to deal with outsiders'.[47] Perhaps it was necessary to carry out foreign policy in that way since Shultz has argued
that the administration's ability to conduct foreign policy was
constantly undercut by Congress.[48] Whatever mechanisms were used
and whatever leadership style was employed, there can be little doubt

that the thrust of US foreign policy was distinctly Reagan's. While there might have been a split between the 'pragmatists' (Haig, Shultz, Carlucci, Powell) and the 'ideologues', such as Kirkpatrick, both groups nevertheless accepted 'the outlines of Reagan's original agenda'.[49]

The problem for Reagan in Indochina was that the requirements of the Reagan Doctrine (support for anti-communist 'freedom fighters') were tempered by fear of the Vietnam syndrome.[50] During the Carter administration Reagan made the following comment:

> Remember when anti-war protesters and some well known public figures ridiculed the 'domino theory'.... Well South Vietnam fell in 1975 and Laos shortly thereafter. Now Cambodia ... is faced with attack by the North Vietnamese communists ... it seems the dominoes are really falling.[51]

Note that he is still referring to *North* Vietnamese communists, three years after the fall of Saigon. Reagan, at least rhetorically, constantly attempted to reinterpret Vietnam but in reality Indochina was of little concern to him and merely represented another arena in which he could demonstrate his anti-Soviet philosophy. Achieving any tangible results in the region was incidental to the maintenance of the image.

Reagan's foreign policy in that first term was built around three clear objectives – first, increase military strength and thus threaten the Soviet reliance on a favourable correlation of forces; second, be prepared to use the US military without seriously damaging either it, or public opinion; third, restore national pride and morale and avoid any humiliations. Rhetoric was the tool most consistently chosen in the pursuance of all three goals. Reagan merely 'internationalized his McCarthyism'.[52] He completely reversed Carter's notions of interdependence, preferring to believe that 'Washington's policies should not have to adjust to the world – a strong assertive America could make the world adjust to Washington'.[53] He had also skilfully selected level two staff who could rhetorically promote his vision, as evidenced by the following quotations from Shultz and Weinberger:

> America has a moral responsibility. The lesson of the post-war era is that America must be the *leader* of the free world; there is *no one else* to take our place.[54] (*George Shultz 1985*, emphasis added)

> The United States is, and always should be, a *global* power, with global concerns and responsibilities that are an integral part of our national security.[55] (*Caspar Weinberger 1981*, emphasis added)

Reagan translated his reality into general foreign policy axioms and those to whom he had delegated authority were expected to adhere to, and promote, those axioms. Reagan left them alone to do so – and they did so effectively.

THE ADMINISTRATION'S REALITY

Three important pillars supported the administration's Indochinese reality. First, was a residual emotional attachment to the region. Martin Herz, a former US ambassador in Saigon explained to a Congressional hearing that as the United States' 'exit from Cambodia in 1975 was under less than honourable conditions ... the United States does, indeed, have some responsibility for what is happening in Cambodia'.[56] Admittedly Ambassador Herz was not at that time a member of the administration but the sentiments he expressed did seem to have a constituency throughout the American political establishment. The second pillar was, to a certain extent, a similar plea for continued involvement but generated from a completely different perspective. Alexander Haig explained it as follows:

> In Southeast Asia, we had abandoned our influence almost totally, and if it had not been for the Chinese, who were doing America's work for it in that region, the rest of the dominoes might have fallen after South Vietnam and Cambodia and Laos.[57]

Here too was an admission of responsibility, but for what Haig perceived to be *national* security interests not moral interests. Haig wanted the US to 'do its work' in the region. The third pillar was the most important for the Reagan administration since it affected the core of the Reagan presidency – economics. George Shultz mentioned it almost in passing in a *Foreign Affairs* article in 1985. He pointed out that 'for the past five years, our trade with East Asia and the Pacific has been greater than our trade with any other region and its relative importance continues to grow'.[58] There were many other references to the trading importance of ASEAN (Association of South East Asian Nations) in particular, and one comment early in the administration clearly shows the significance accorded ASEAN. John Holdridge stated, to a sub-committee hearing in July 1981, that ASEAN 'economies, all spurred by the forces of the free market, are among the fastest growing in the world. Taken as a whole, ASEAN constitutes the fifth largest trading partner of the United States.'[59] It could be argued, therefore, that the three pillars of US foreign policy towards Cambodia during Reagan's first term were the well-being of the US economy, national interests and moral concern, probably in that order.

Shortly after Holdridge's statement in July 1981 he was again appearing before the Sub-Committee on Asian and Pacific Affairs (October 1981) and his statements there, as well as one by former State Department South East Asia specialist Douglas Pike, are also highly significant. Pike's contains interesting comments on the situation seen from the perspective of an ex-government employee perhaps speaking a little more freely from the safety of academia. Holdridge's statement is probably one of the clearest enunciations of the Reagan administration's policy goals with respect to Cambodia. It is worthwhile examining both statements closely.[60]

Pike made a relatively short statement in which he emphasised what he considered to be the two key factors in US policy towards Indochina – the Vietnam syndrome and the 'bear' syndrome. He argued on the first point that America should learn to confront the memory of Vietnam. He said that '[t]his Nation is never going to recover its full psychic health until it takes Vietnam out of its collective consciousness and examines it.'[61] The 'bear analogy' is recounted by Pike to illustrate how the Vietnamese politburo should be characterised when assessments are attempted. He referred to a sign he saw in his childhood which said 'Please do not feed the bears because the bears will bite you, *because they are bears*.' He went on to explain that the '17 men ... [who] have run [Vietnam] for 40 years'[62] are like those bears. Therefore, when seeking an explanation of Vietnamese actions he explained that:

> the thing you must always keep in mind, is that they did what they did because it is the essence of their nature to so act. This is not meant to be pejorative it is merely characterizing them – if they bite, they will bite because they are bears. It is their nature.[63]

Pike argued that the ancient antipathy between the Vietnamese and the Khmers was an example of the Vietnamese 'nature' and concluded that the invasion of Kampuchea was not hegemony but an error of judgement. 'It was not an invasion for hegemonistic purposes. It was an effort to solve the Pol Pot problem. They did not solve it. They simply went deeper into the swamp.'[64]

Holdridge opened *his* statement by claiming the endorsement of world opinion for the US objectives in the area. Those objectives were:

- the preservation of the security of the ASEAN states, and particularly that of Thailand, which confronted Vietnam's army of occupation in Kampuchea;
- withdrawal of all Vietnamese forces from Kampuchea;
- Khmer survival and national self-determination;
- reduction of Soviet military influence and elimination of Soviet military access to Indochina.[65]

He continued by adding:

> This administration, like the previous one, has given its wholehearted endorsement to the ASEAN-sponsored UNGA resolutions on Kampuchea as the best basis for a settlement of the Kampuchea problem.[66]

He was careful to include the human-rights conscious Carter administration in his statement. By so doing he could deflect criticism of continued support for Pol Pot. He also firmly tied US policy to ASEAN initiatives, possibly deflecting any future blame. These October comments simply reiterated Holdridge's July statement which was made while the International Conference on Kampuchea (ICK) was in session in New York. In this he said that the US:

> firmly supported the progress and stability of our friends and allies in the Association of South East Asian Nations as the heart of our policy toward the entire region. In cooperation with ASEAN we seek to restrain the aggressive ambitions of Vietnam. We seek to curb growing Soviet military influence in the region.[67]

The Pike and the Holdridge statements were public manifestations of the administration's policy of containment and support for friendly regional allies. There were, of course, disagreements over tactics. Shultz, for example, having defined Cambodia as a low-intensity conflict,[68] disagreed with Weinberger's criteria for becoming involved in such events. Shultz contended that 'the need to avoid no-win situations cannot mean that we turn automatically from hard-to-win situations that call for prudent involvement.... [T]hose who shrink from engagement can always find an alibi for inaction.'[69] The 'Vietnam' fear, however, meant that even if the Shultz view were to be implemented elsewhere it was unlikely in Indochina. Whatever other options were open, or realities created, American military personnel on the ground in Indochina was not one of them.

The issue which most obviously identified the administration's foreign policy towards Cambodia was the acceptance, or otherwise, of the credentials of the government of Democratic Kampuchea (DK) at the United Nations. The policy of the US operated on two inter-related levels. On one level it was a stand against tyranny, on another a defence of the state-centric international system. In the early 1980s the concept of sovereignty was not as contentious an issue as it is in the post-Cold War era, being still generally accepted as the defining factor in international relations. At the previously mentioned Congressional hearing, Assistant SoS John Holdridge stated that:

> in September [1981] the UN General Assembly voted overwhelm-ingly for a third year in a row to seat the UN delegation of Democratic Kampuchea ... not because of any affection for the brutal Khmer Rouge regime, but rather because they wished to block any move to confer legitimacy on the regime installed in Phnom Penh by the Vietnamese army, and which is, of course a complete creature of Vietnam.[70]

Almost a year later the UN was again preparing to debate the DK seat. Prior to that vote the Conressional Sub-Committees on Asian and Pacific Affairs, and Human Rights and International Organizations convened jointly to discuss the question of 'The Democratic Kampuchea Seat at the United Nations and American Interests' (see n. 10). Of particular interest during that hearing was the clarity with which the Reagan administration's position was stated and in contrast the genuine soul-searching in which others engaged. The unusual contradiction was probably the result of a *joint* hearing.

Earlier in this chapter Reagan was quoted as referring to the 'gross hypocrisy' of Carter's position on seating Pol Pot at the UN. In his prepared statement Don Bonker (Chairman of the Sub-Committee on Human Rights and International Organizations) referred to Reagan's comment and set the tone of the hearing:

> On October 17, 1980, candidate Reagan characterized the Carter Administration's human rights policy as a 'gross hypocrisy' because that Administration supported the United Nations seating of 'the Pol Pot Communist Cambodia regime which had slaughtered millions of its own people.' Today, the Reagan Administration will try to explain in Congress why it, too, supports Pol Pot's seating at the UN.[71]

His statement went on to advocate leaving the seat vacant rather than allocating it to the Heng Samrin People's Republic of Kampuchea (PRK) government. Bonker pointed out that 'the issue of Pol Pot's credentials at the United Nations is a rare instance of continuity between the Carter and Reagan administrations. And both Administrations are wrong.'[72] He also described the Coalition Government of Democratic Kampuchea (CGDK) as 'a paper coalition [which] does not justify international recognition, nor does it obscure the heinous crimes of the Pol Pot regime'.[73]

Stephen Solarz, by now the Chairman of the Asian and Pacific Affairs Sub-Committee realised the inflammatory nature of the remarks and in an attempt to defuse them said, 'but of course, circumstances have changed somewhat and we are here today to examine the significance of those changes'.[74] The problem for Solarz was that Bonker had already undercut the only real 'change', i.e. the formation of the CGDK. How the administration's representative, John Holdridge, dealt with this and other difficulties is instructive. Basically he contended that Bonker's point was bankrupt. He argued for support of the CGDK application on the *technical* grounds that there was no superior claimant, which he inferred from his own interpretation of UN rules, 'We do not regard the Heng Samrin regime as a superior claimant.'[75] He also argued that the US position was directly supportive of ASEAN. The coalition was valuable, not because it provided a fig leaf of respectability for the Khmer Rouge (KR) but because it gave 'an additional democratic component to the DK'.[76] He deflected criticism that the US position supported the KR by stating that '[t]here should be no doubt in anybody's mind about US policy toward the Khmer Rouge regime. The administration opposes the return to power of the Khmer Rouge.'[77]

What then was the American objection to leaving the seat vacant as France, for example, had advocated? Holdridge countered with a 'thin-end-of-the wedge' argument. If a vacant seat were declared, very shortly the vacuum would be filled as it was with Hungary. In this view he was supported by Son Sann (KPNLF) who by that stage had become the preferred option of the US government. Son Sann had said earlier that in his 'opinion, to leave the seat vacant [was] very dangerous ... [it] might go to the Vietnamese side'.[78] The problem with that position is that it simply avoids the moral dilemma, which is probably wise but nevertheless leaves the administration open to severe criticism on ethical grounds. As Solarz put it during the 1982 debate, the dilemma was also 'how to balance America's strategic interests with its concern for human rights'.[79] In a later hearing, former Ambassador James Leonard argued that the 'vacant seat' strategy could, in fact, be sustained over a long period thus invalidating the slippery slope contention. Leonard believed that the US had to vote for the vacant seat because '[w]e would not be in the extraordinarily ambiguous situation of appearing, in spite of our assertions to the contrary, to be supporters of Pol Pot'.[80] Despite misgivings of that kind the Reagan administration maintained its stance. It was not without reservations but, as Alexander Haig was later to write, those reservations were overridden:

> In the United Nations, we took the difficult decision to support the Khmer resistance movement as a means of opposing the Vietnamese military presence in Kampuchea. Son Sann and Prince Sihanouk were two leaders of this movement; the third was Pol Pot, and it was with considerable anguish that we agreed to support, even for overriding political and strategic reasons, this charnel figure.[81]

Although the decision was difficult there was really no alternative given the government's foreign policy goals. In the hierarchy of US foreign policy interests anti-Sovietism stood high on the list and since Cambodia had become a Soviet client, albeit once removed, it was, therefore, necessary to oppose Cambodia. It was also necessary to back the resistance movement against Cambodia, despite the fact that one of its members was the Khmer Rouge, a client of China which was now an ally against the Soviet Union. Finally, ASEAN, the United States' major economic partner in the region, had actually sponsored the DK recognition resolution – the political and strategic reasons for continuing recognition were overwhelming.

Support for ASEAN as a regional organisation with credibility and legitimacy assumed an ever more central role in US policy. In 1983 John C. Monjo (Deputy Assistant SoS) said that 'support for ASEAN and its approach to the Kampuchean problem is the cornerstone of US policy in South East Asia'.[82] A year earlier Holdridge had similarly asserted that 'ASEAN is the keystone of US policy toward Kampuchea and Indochina. We fully support ASEAN's strategy and respect ASEAN's leadership role in the region.'[83] And a year prior to that Holdridge had commented that 'our policy rests upon the maintenance of solid bilateral relations with each of the five [ASEAN] countries'.[84] There was, therefore, a continuity of policy in this regard which also served another useful purpose in shifting responsibility for backing the

DK at the UN away from the US. Joel Pritchard, a member of the Asian sub-committee reminded his colleagues in October 1981 that 'in the last UN ... we voted for Pol Pot [and] it was ASEAN pleading with us that was the deciding factor',[85] Pritchard's implicit message being that the US was merely supporting its regional ally.

A final function of supporting ASEAN was simply that of assisting allies (Thailand and Philippines already had security treaties with the US) who were members of the Association, in Thailand's case, a senior member. As a result, backing ASEAN satisfied three criteria – economic, ideological, strategic. Economically, ASEAN was the US's fifth largest trading partner; ideologically, 'all of the ASEAN nations share[d] a basic pro-Western political and philosophical orientation';[86] and strategically, 'positive, active support for ASEAN [was] the most effective means of curbing the ambitions of Vietnam and the Soviet Union'.[87]

Constructing a reality which included support for Pol Pot should have required a subtle use of language. However, what actually happened was a series of blunt statements of intent rather than any attempt at explication. John Monjo, for example, made the following comments in 1983:

> The US continues to give diplomatic and political support to the non-communist elements in the coalition ... we do not provide aid of any kind or have any contact with the Khmer Rouge and our welcoming of the coalition does not imply any support for the Khmer Rouge.[88]

He went on to say that the 'coalition has greatly enhanced international support for ASEAN's strategy on Kampuchea'.[89] Again responsibility was shifted to ASEAN. It became an article of faith that the coalition was good, but only the non-communist element. This distinction was referred to so regularly that eventually the initials alone, NCR (non-communist resistance), sufficed. Government members continually affirmed the NCR:

- The United States has given moral and political support to the non-communist Khmer and will continue to do so ... Under no circumstances would we provide any direct support to the Khmer Rouge, and we do not intend to deal directly with them.[90] (*John Holdridge 1982*)

- Without a viable non-Communist alternative, the Kampuchean conflict would have but two possible victors: Pol Pot or

Vietnam's Heng Samrin ... We will never support a strategy which restores the former to power, nor can we accept Vietnam's aggression.[91] (*John Holdridge 1981*)

- We will continue our political and humanitarian support for the [non-communist factions of the] coalition.[92] (*John Monjo 1983*)

Officials also encouraged belief in the efficacy of the NCR military component. For example, when Solarz asked Monjo whether the NCR was gaining in strength he replied 'Yes, we have indications that it is gaining strength this year.'[93] This, in spite of the fact that independent witnesses such as Carlisle Thayer and James Leonard (at the same hearing) insisted that the 'forces of Prince Sihanouk and Mr Son Sann [were] not very substantial; they're certainly no match for the Vietnamese'.[94] It was in the administration's interests to promote the notion of a non-communist force as the flagship of a *democratic* resistance to the Vietnamese occupiers.

Simultaneously it was also necessary to maintain the demonisation of the Vietnamese themselves. The American reality, in which the Soviet Union was the source of all evil, viewed Vietnam as the source of all regional evil. The US spokesman at the General Assembly debate on Cambodia in October 1983 argued that 'Hanoi had sought for three decades to dominate all of Indo-China.'[95] He accused them of 'a double hypocrisy in that [they] had supported the Khmer Rouge both before 1975, when that genocidal régime was installed in power, and after'.[96] John Holdridge supported the hegemonic view when he said that Hanoi still had ambitions to 'inherit the mantle of hegemony of France in Indochina'.[97] These views and the Vietnamese occupation of Kampuchea were the basis for most US rhetoric of that period.

A further complication was the often controversial MIA (US servicemen Missing In Action) issue. However, in reality, the MIA problem alone would not have obstructed a settlement should other developments have permitted one, even though Richard Armitage (Deputy Assistant Secretary for East Asian and Pacific Region (DoD)) did publicly commit both the State Department and the Defense Department to a full accounting of MIAs.[98] Although MIAs were sometimes mentioned in connection with possible normalisation of relations with Vietnam the real problem remained the fact that Vietnam were still 'bears'. John Holdridge explained as follows, 'It is the policy of this administration that normalization of relations with Vietnam is out of the question as long as Hanoi continues to occupy Kampuchea and generally remains a menace to other countries in the region.'[99] The US saw a nation which had humiliated them chastising a despot they had denounced but had been unwilling or unable to remove. With their impotence again exposed the spiteful policy initiatives should not have been a surprise.

Conversely, a nation that the United States had previously demonised, China, had by this time become a virtual ally. The 'China card', which had been played by other administrations, was also part of Reagan's pack. As early as June 1981, SoS Haig and Assistant SoS Holdridge visited Beijing and made some revealing statements during their short stay. At a banquet at the end of the visit Haig remarked that 'American and Chinese policies are both rooted in an objective appraisal of strategic realities', he added that their 'talks had shown that Americans and Chinese can work together to oppose efforts by other nations to achieve global or regional hegemony'.[100] Obviously by global he meant the Soviet Union and by regional Vietnam. At an earlier press conference he had admitted that a good deal of their discussions had focused on the challenges posed by the Soviet Union and announced that 'the USA intends to introduce legislation amending US laws which lumped the PRC with the Soviet Union'.[101] For both the US and China, Vietnam had become a convenient target.

The problem was that if Vietnam was targeted too successfully, and normalisation did occur, the result might be a strengthening of the Vietnamese economy to the point where the Soviet Union could stop providing such massive aid; this, in turn, would relieve pressure on the Soviets. The Chinese are said to have believed that Soviet expansionism (Vietnam, Afghanistan, Poland, etc.) represented 'an enormous financial drain that eventually [would] cause policy changes'.[102] The received wisdom in the State Department at the time was that while finances were a factor, strategic interests would continue to dominate. Time appears to have vindicated the Chinese analysis.

While Al Haig accepted that accommodating the Chinese was a central plank of US policy, '[in] terms of the strategic interests of the United States and the West ... China may be the most important country in the world',[103] his successor seemed less inclined to do so. It is argued that Shultz believed *any* level of support for the KR was untenable and that opposition to the Vietnamese should be firmly linked to ASEAN.[104] Throughout Shultz's time, ASEAN's interests, particularly Thailand's, were paramount. The fact that they generally paralleled China's was irrelevant. Shultz's tactic of playing down China's importance may have paid dividends because John Holdridge opined that 'despite the original Chinese position of saying they had to bleed Vietnam, they would be amenable to political solutions'.[105] To a certain extent though, the Chinese were *always* 'amenable to political solutions' as were most of the other regional actors.

Such pragmatism presented the Americans with certain dilemmas; they were forced to weave the perceptions of relevant others into their own construction of reality. This necessitated running adjustments to attitudes. For example, in July 1981, Alexander Haig told the International Conference on Kampuchea (ICK) that 'Vietnam's seizure of Kampuchea pose[d] a direct threat to the security of Thailand and undermine[d] the stability of the whole region',[106] whereas less than three months later Holdridge was saying that 'the Vietnamese would find it very difficult to move in strength against Thailand'.[107] Another inconsistency lay in the maintenance, by the US, of an embassy in Vientiane despite the presence of 50 000 Vietnamese troops in Laos. When questioned on this Holdridge explained that Laos 'seems to us not in the same category as Kampuchea ... which is an occupied country'.[108] When questioned further his rationalisation of the difference seemed to be merely temporal. There had, he argued, been 50 000 Vietnamese troops in Laos for almost 'two decades. It's a problem that has existed over a long period of time.'[109] Such an explanation implies that time grants legitimacy, the very point Vietnam also wished to press. Since US policy was so closely linked to Thailand the most obvious explanation would derive from the economic interrelationship between Laos and Thailand. Such rhetorical inconsistencies illustrate the manner in which diverse factors are accommodated in constructed realities.

Questions regarding types of aid exposed the same problems. Given that Vietnam had to be resisted and Cambodia liberated it was obvious that aid would be provided. How, and what type was the contentious issue. At a hearing in 1982 Stephen Solarz asked why the US was 'not providing military support to the KPNLF or Moulinaka'.[110] Holdridge replied that it was 'because military support is something which I believe elements of this committee and other elements of Congress and the American public opinion would not support ... we are not disposed to give military support'.[111] In 1981 the same two men sparred again:

SOLARZ: Are we considering providing military assistance, directly or indirectly, to any of the resistance movements in Indochina?
HOLDRIDGE: No.
SOLARZ: Not in Cambodia?

HOLDRIDGE: Not in Cambodia.

SOLARZ: In Laos?

HOLDRIDGE: No.

SOLARZ: Vietnam?

HOLDRIDGE: No.

SOLARZ: Then what did you mean in your statement on the trip with Secretary Haig that we had to put diplomatic, economic and I think yes, even military pressure on the Vietnamese?

HOLDRIDGE: That was a collective 'we' ... I wasn't talking about the United States.[112]

Holdridge prevaricated because he recognised the difficulties in providing any type of military aid to resistance groups and the NCR's liaison with the KR only made them worse. In 1983 deputy assistant SoS for East Asian and Pacific Affairs, John C. Monjo, stated, in a reply about military aid, that he was able 'to provide, in writing, a sort of an outline of what assistance we believe may be being offered to the three forces'.[113] Although he distanced the US by using the term 'being offered' he also inadvertently said *three* forces. How much the US contributed to the KR, either directly or indirectly, is not relevant here since it is the effects of perception on decisions that is under scrutiny; but it is still interesting to note that the information to which Monjo referred remains classified.

Essentially the Reagan administration rested its policy on the decisions which were generated by the International Conference on Kampuchea. The ICK took place early in Reagan's first year and provided a convenient benchmark for all future policy statements. Despite Chinese opposition to a clause in the draft resolution which called for disarmament of *all* resistance groups following Vietnamese withdrawal, the 'United States believed that the ... [ICK] provided the framework for negotiation of a comprehensive political settlement in Kampuchea.'[114] The ICK framework provided a convenient fit with the administration's view of the world – support for ASEAN and Sihanouk in a long-term, low-risk plan designed to isolate Vietnam and the PRK. As a result statements needed to perform three functions: demonise Vietnam and PRK, marginalise other players such as China and the KR and eulogise the notion of absolute sovereignty. The administration's policy towards Cambodia perfectly mirrored its overall world-view.

ALTERNATIVE REALITIES

As illustrated in the previous chapter some of the clearest examples of states defining their own realities with regard to Indochina are revealed in international and national gatherings such as the UN, the ICK, and with reference to Cambodia, the Indochinese Foreign Ministers Conference (IFMC). Additionally, there were concerns expressed in Congress which also provided alternatives to the administration's viewpoint. There were essentially five separate realities, those of the opposition in Congress, the Chinese, ASEAN, the CGDK, and the Vietnamese/PRK axis with the close support of the Soviet Union.

Vietnam/PRK/Soviet Union

The IFMC was the result of a strategy, on the part of the Vietnamese in association with Laos and the PRK, in which a *de facto* acceptance of the status quo was the primary goal. To this end it was important that the three Indochinese countries were linked with ASEAN and involved in the political process *prior* to any international conference. Since the ICK was scheduled for July 1981 the IFMC convened on 27 January 1981 in Ho Chi Minh City. In his opening address Nguyen Co Thach (Minister of Foreign Affairs, SRV) stated that 'no questions relating to South East Asia can be settled without discussion and agreement between the countries in the region, especially between the Indochinese countries and the ASEAN countries'.[115] The conference's closing statement called for a

> regional conference with ASEAN countries in March 1981 alternately in Vientiane and an ASEAN capital.... After the two groups of countries had signed an agreement on South East Asian peace and stability, an enlarged international conference would be held to endorse and secure it.[116]

Such an agreement would have effectively undercut the ICK and established a small degree of legitimacy for the PRK to build upon.

The conference statement not only called for a regional conference; it also reiterated very precisely the Vietnamese version of reality which consisted of a reactionary and imperialist alliance aimed at subverting PRK sovereignty:

> The main cause of [tension] is the expansionist and big-power hegemonist policy of the reactionary clique in the Peking ruling circles in

collusion with imperialism ... the purpose of the presence of Vietnamese troops in Kampuchea is to deal with the Chinese threat ... it is only temporary. The UN General Assembly's recent adoption of a resolution to continue to seat the genocidal Pol Pot clique at the UN and a resolution demanding that an international conference be convened ... constitutes a violation of [Kampuchean] sovereignty.[117]

The above statements were reiterated, with slight variations, for the remainder of the first Reagan term in attempts at legitimisation. One communiqué claimed that what was particularly serious [was] the fact that the Reagan administration continue[d] to play the China card'.[118] The China card was cited again in 1984 – 'successive US administrations have over the past five years increasingly played the China card to oppose the Soviet Union and the three Indochinese countries'.[119]

The IFMC also tried to isolate Thailand. It linked withdrawal of Vietnamese troops with 'a commitment by Thailand to cease making Thai territory available for the use of the Pol Pot gang'.[120] The IFMC argued that without the provision of Thai bases KR opposition would be unsustainable. This was an assessment with which all parties probably agreed but each reacted according to national interest and the stalemate continued. At the fifth IFMC (Vientiane, February 1982) a proposal was made for 'a demilitarised zone under some form of international supervision so as to ensure security in the Kampuchea-Thai border line region'.[121] Acceptance of such a plan again would have added to PRK legitimacy and assisted the establishment of a customary legal position on the issue.

In April 1983 at an extraordinary IFMC, further attempts were made to set up a dialogue with ASEAN which were described by China as yet another 'diplomatic offensive'.[122] These diplomatic offensives had become even more important since the UN adopted the ICK declarations. The IFMC had to add denunciation of the ICK to their rhetoric – 'the Indochinese countries reiterated their categorical rejection of the erroneous resolutions of the United Nations and the *so-called* UN International Conference on Kampuchea'[123] (emphasis added). The only slight movement came in a July 1982 IFMC when the idea of a vacant seat was tentatively agreed as a short-term solution to the continued seating of the DK.[124]

Naturally there were statements which emanated from sources other than the IFMC which were equally important in defining the Vietnamese reality. As early as 22 January 1981, Nhan Dan (the

People's Daily) responded to Reagan's 'two-China' inauguration reference as 'fully reflecting the two-faced US foreign policy toward China based on an alliance full of contradictions between US imperialism and the treacherous Peking clique'.[125] Linking the Reagan administration to the various resistance groups Hanoi radio was even more acerbic:

> The Reagan administration has begun to involve itself more deeply in directly manipulating these lackey groups in order to use them to oppose and sabotage the Kampuchean revolution as well as to oppose Vietnam. Sihanouk, Son Sann, Pol Pot, Ieng Sary and Khieu Samphan are all dangerous country-selling elements who have offered themselves as henchmen for certain foreign countries after having been thrown onto the garbage heap of history by the Kampuchean people.[126]

Nguyen Co Thach also sought to undermine any alliance by minimising the significance of the NCR – 'Son Sann and Sihanouk are used as make-up on the disgusting face of the Pol Pot criminals to help him retain the [UN] seat'.[127] The cosmetic nature of the coalition was fully exploited by both Vietnam and the PRK. A statement made by the PRK foreign ministry, immediately after a UN vote demanding Vietnamese troop withdrawals, attempted to take the moral high ground and also to test any weaknesses in the US position. It was argued, in the statement, that:

> the acceptance of criminals inside the United Nations to represent their own victims put men of conscience to a severe test ... to vote for a coalition government in which the Pol Pot gang dominates entirely is to go against the call to defend human rights and justice in the United Nations; it is to encourage expansionism and genocide.[128]

It was a persuasive argument since Pol Pot was continually criticised by the US government. The US backing for the coalition later allowed the PRK foreign minister, Hun Sen, to reject talks with Sihanouk claiming that they wanted 'dialogue with China, the USA and ASEAN ... not with their valets'.[129]

However, for the moral argument to be effective it required consistency, which was not always evident. Additionally some of the crude demonisation of the KR may have worked against the Vietnamese by allowing the KR to disprove some of the more absurd claims. The problem was that the repulsiveness of the KR was a central platform of Vietnamese policy. Not only did Vietnam portray itself as the only protection from Pol Pot; it also repeatedly cited a Chinese threat to its security utilising the KR as its weapon within Cambodia. Only 'with the halting of the threat from China [and] its use of the Pol Pot clique to attempt to impede the recovery of the Kampuchean people', could Vietnamese troops withdraw from Cambodia.[130]

Unfortunately for Vietnam it had very little leverage for any of its negotiating stances. In September 1983, for example, Hanoi tried to offer a deal to ASEAN which involved Vietnam withdrawing objections to CGDK credentials at the UN in return for ASEAN dropping its troop withdrawal condition. Given that ASEAN had consistently defeated the Vietnamese over credentials it was not surprising that it rejected the Vietnamese overtures. A month later, Foreign Minister Thach tried again in Kuala Lumpur. He attempted to set up bi-lateral meetings with the Malaysian, Singaporean and Thai foreign ministers – all were rejected. 1983 was a bad year for Vietnamese diplomacy. In March, at the 7th Non-Aligned Conference in New Delhi, Thach had approached the ASEAN ministers present (i.e. excluding Thailand and Philippines) suggesting an 'ASEAN + 2' formula, which would have been the ASEAN members plus Vietnam and Laos. The PRK and CGDK were to be excluded as too provocative at that stage. Originally the non-aligned ASEAN states were receptive, despite the inconsistency with stated ASEAN policy, but China, and Thailand in particular, killed the initiative.

Vietnamese support for the PRK was vital for its survival but Vietnam in its turn also needed support from the Soviet Union. It was provided and accepted because it suited both parties. Vietnam had nowhere else to turn; it needed protection against China, support for a ravaged economy and support in the international community over Kampuchea. The Soviet Union wanted naval projection, which Cam Ranh Bay and later Sihanoukville provided, a strong military presence on another of China's flanks, and finally a greater degree of parity with the US in the region. Thus the relationship between the two became more formalised. The Soviet Union inserted more and more 'advisers' into Vietnam and supervised a certain amount of restructuring, it also provided vetoes in the Security Council as appropriate and could be relied upon to provide them in the future should the occasion arise.[131]

ASEAN

Despite support from the Soviet Union the real problem for the Vietnamese was the presence of a world-view and policy which had both regional credibility and superpower backing – ASEAN's. ASEAN managed to present a homogeneous view in the face of what could have been major obstacles. Although Thailand, as the 'front-line' state, was permitted predominance, the dissenting views of Malaysia and Indonesia were never far from the surface. As early as March 1980 the two had met in Kuantan (Malaysia) and developed the 'Kuantan Principle'. This was an agreement whereby ASEAN would *not* insist on Vietnamese withdrawal from Cambodia providing that Thai integrity was assured and also that Vietnam would disentangle from both Soviet *and* Chinese involvement. The Kuantan meeting, however, occurred only a month after the fall of Kriangsak Chamanand's Thai government and the new premier Tinsulanond did not see how Thai security would be assured until the Vietnamese withdrew. For Malaysia and Indonesia the real problem was Chinese hegemony and there was some concern that Thailand was becoming too close to China. As Phnom Penh radio pointed out, 'at present, the Thai's are feeding the "Chinese tiger" and the "US tiger" and one day Thailand will be swallowed by these two "tigers"'.[132]

What enabled ASEAN to develop a coherent and acceptable policy was adherence to its central principle of ZOPFAN – a zone of peace, freedom and neutrality. Its goal was to create stability in the region through non-interference. Stability would enable the prodigious economic growth to continue. ASEAN's strategy was simple – conflict containment and hopefully eradication. In order to achieve this there were two specific objectives: first, no legitimacy for the PRK; second, Thai security. To achieve the first, the DK seat at the UN had to be retained, there would be no recognition of PRK in any form, there must be support for the resistance. Achieving the second required Chinese assistance in keeping border clashes simmering, it also required US and Chinese financing of the resistance groups either directly or through ASEAN. This strategy was not aimed primarily at a military victory, which was thought unlikely, but at limiting the conflict to manageable proportions and resisting any spill-over. It was long-term attrition. ASEAN believed that such tactics might eventually topple a nation in such dire economic straits as Vietnam. The policy was also flexible enough to permit ASEAN to apply intense pressure (especially through China and the US) on the resistance groups to form a coalition when support for the DK appeared to be waning.

Nevertheless, concerns about the wisdom of this policy occasionally surfaced. In the *New York Times* (16 February 1982) Robert Turnbull revealed that a high-level informal meeting had occurred between ASEAN and US officials in Honolulu in which the US had been urged to normalise with Vietnam in order to undercut its reliance on the Soviet Union. ASEAN's worries were generally related to the super-powers, for ASEAN 'any solution to the Kampuchean crisis ... cannot be permitted to occur at the cost of giving Beijing strategic advantages in the region'.[133] ASEAN resisted any incursions by *any* of the superpowers. Effectively this meant the USSR and China since the US was restrained by its own experiences. Thus the conflict within ASEAN was between Malaysia and Indonesia on the one hand and Thailand on the other. For the former, Chinese expansionism appeared to be the primary threat; for the latter, it was Vietnamese expansionism. Their policy of attrition managed to assuage both parties.

As for a solution, ASEAN favoured a government probably led by Sihanouk, or possibly Son Sann, which contained a suitably sanitised KR component and was neutral and independent. Such an alternative would placate China and allow Hanoi to disengage without loss of face and consequently dilute their economic dependence on the USSR. ASEAN at no stage completely ostracised Vietnam and it was even admitted that bilateral dialogue between ASEAN nations and Vietnam had been ongoing since the New Delhi non-aligned conference in the hope of bringing Vietnam into the ICK orbit.[134] It was emphasised, however, that in no way would this lead to a vacant seat solution at the UN. ASEAN kept the lines of communication open without ever really compromising on their position. They rarely mentioned human rights abuses and stuck rigidly to the line expressed most clearly in a communiqué from the ASEAN foreign ministers meeting in June 1982:

> [The foreign ministers] emphasized that the grounds for their support for the credentials of Democratic Kampuchea were based on the fundamental principles of respect for the sovereignty, independence and territorial integrity of states ...[135]

ASEAN spearheaded the campaign at the UN to keep the DK seat. Its sponsorship of the ICK was a major achievement in that campaign. It had been a difficult task to mobilise world opinion on Cambodia but the ICK in New York, July 1981, attracted 93 participants (79 full members and 14 observers). Despite its role as sponsor, everything did not run smoothly for ASEAN. Vietnam refused to attend the ICK and the PRK was prohibited from doing so; the DK was a full participant; FUNCINPEC and KPNLF were observers. The biggest confrontation, however, came with China who vehemently opposed certain elements of the draft proposal. Nayan Chanda argues that the reason the ASEAN draft offended China was because it was based on the view that China's 'bleed Vietnam white' policy was seriously flawed since it would have meant that should Vietnam *want* to escape the Soviet orbit it would not be in a position to do so.[136]

China refused to accept the disarmament of *all* factions, refused to accept the 'legitimate concerns of neighbouring states', and refused to accept a temporary administration until elections. Eventually a vague French compromise was adopted by consensus which basically focused on 'the violation of the principles of respect for the sovereignty, independence and territorial integrity of States'.[137] The final declaration mentioned the terms 'neutral' and 'sovereignty' several times and concluded by 'deem[ing] it essential for the five permanent members of the Security Council ... to declare ... that ... [T]hey will respect ... the independence, sovereignty etc....'[138] Ironically Vietnam's letter of explanation for their absence cited the same principles for their opposite actions.[139] They interpreted any international involvement as 'a distortion of the situation in the country and a flagrant interference in the internal affairs of a sovereign State' – the People's Republic of Kampuchea. They also pointed out that Democratic Kampuchea 'existed only on Thai territory'.[140] For some considerable time the General Assembly endorsed the principal components of the ICK declaration – ceasefire agreements by all parties; withdrawal of all foreign forces under the supervision of UN peace-keeping/observer groups; no armed factions able to prevent or disrupt the holding of free elections; holding of elections under UN supervision; appropriate measures for the maintenance of law and order – ASEAN had not achieved everything it wanted but the congruence around its basic view of the world was close enough to justify some satisfaction that *its* reality might prevail.

China

China's reality differed from ASEAN's only marginally and not crucially. The Chinese prioritised threats as they perceived them, and the Soviet Union was at the top of their list. As a consequence most statements relating to Cambodia would contain a reference to that threat. In response to an IFMC, for example, the National Chinese News Agency (NCNA) stated that '[t]he Hanoi-staged ... conference ... [was] apparently part of the Soviet-Vietnamese diplomatic offensive. The objective is to keep pushing their hegemonism in the name of opposing the alleged threat from China'.[141] The Chinese primarily viewed Vietnam as a tool of Soviet imperialism and the PRK as a Vietnamese puppet. Its allies then would be anybody who opposed those enemies. It was possible, therefore, for China to see ASEAN *and* the KR *and* the United States as allies.

The Chinese position at the ICK perfectly illustrated this point. It used the US to pressure ASEAN to modify the draft resolution which contained anti-KR and pro-Vietnamese proposals. On the total disarmament question China argued that it would 'demoralize other peoples fighting their aggressors';[142] it was not the province of the conference, which was to demand Vietnamese withdrawals; it puts 'on a par the resistance forces against Vietnamese aggression and the forces of the puppet Heng Samrin regime, the spawn of that aggression'.[143] On the subject of an interim administration China also referred to sovereignty, arguing that 'removing the legitimate government of a UN member in the name of the world body itself is unacceptable ... because it will create a precedent of depriving weaker states of their sovereign rights under the same excuse'.[144] That particular view was also embraced by all other nations who had promoted the sovereignty theme.

For internal consumption, however, China retained some chastising rhetoric for the US. In February 1982, for example, Peking Radio derided the view put by SoS Haig that US foreign policy was 'more reasonable' arguing that in reality it 'frequently pitted itself against the vast Third World countries on some major issues'.[145] Deng was also under pressure immediately after Haig's visit to Peking in June 1981. An arms deal was concluded which attracted some criticism. First of August Radio commented that the Chinese people '[would] never tolerate a certain person [Deng] ... making unprincipled concessions to the USA in the name of so-called Sino-American friendship'. Having the United States as an ally and simultaneously criticizing it could be seen as the rhetorical expression of 'dual-track diplomacy'.

Notwithstanding China's concerns over the US, the Soviet Union remained their central threat and their reaction to that threat was the basis of the political reality. In an article in the *Red Flag* of 1 February 1982 entitled 'Soviet expansion in South-East Asia', the case was made that the withdrawal of the United States had provided the USSR with an opportunity of 'filling the "vacancy" and supplanting the USA. Its strategy has been to use Vietnam as its Cuba in Asia.'[146] Later that month the *People's Daily* explained all Soviet actions from a hegemonistic perspective. It stated that detente was 'a component part of their offensive strategy' because it concealed the offensive; it argued that 'anti-imperialism [was] a sugar coating on the strategy of expansion' and concluded that the Soviets only supported Third World countries 'reckoning to bring them within the Soviet monolithic system'.[147]

CGDK

The formation of the Coalition Government of Democratic Kampuchea (CGDK) allowed China to continue opposing the Vietnamese. China was content to back the DK government so long as it suited their purposes, and appeared successful. As soon as the KR alone began to be an impediment China had no hesitation in backing the idea of a coalition. In late February 1982, for example, ASEAN began applying pressure in order to get some sort of coalition formed. Malaysia had begun to make noises about the difficulties entailed in continuing to support the DK's UN seat and China fell in with that view. They did, however, favour a 'tight coalition' over the 'loose coalition' advocated by ASEAN.

Both Sihanouk and Son Sann offered to head the coalition. The DK wished to subsume the other groups and not form a *new* organisation, whereas Son Sann wanted KPNLF dominance of any alliance. In December 1981 Son Sann visited Washington and requested US military aid *only* for the KPNLF, in order to confirm his position. Sihanouk, having changed tack a number of times, eventually agreed with Khieu Samphan (21 February 1982, Beijing) to form a 'tight' coalition between themselves, possibly hoping to attract Chinese military aid. Khieu Samphan was reported as saying that 'in order to fight diplomatically we agreed that we should do so on the basis of the legal status of Democratic Kampuchea. This is because [DK] is an independent sovereign country ... and is a member of the UN.'[148] Within four months, however, another Sihanouk *volte face* led to the 22 June 1982 Kuala Lumpur declaration of the formation of the CGDK with Sihanouk as president, Khieu Samphan, vice-president in charge of foreign affairs and Son Sann as prime minister. The coalition served two main purposes: first, it sanitised the KR; second, it took *from* the KR its legitimacy as a member of the UN. Additionally it provided the prestige of Sihanouk's presence. Sihanouk, with typical modesty, stated as much in May 1981 at a press conference in Peking when he said 'I remain more popular than all the other Cambodian leaders with my people.'[149]

However, despite Sihanouk's 'special' position, the KR retained what amounted to a veto because the CGDK declaration stated that

> in the event of an impasse ... which renders the coalition government of Democratic Kampuchea inoperative [then] the current state of Democratic Kampuchea led by Khieu Samphan will have the right to resume its activities as the sole legal and legitimate state of Kampuchea and as a member state of the UnitedNations ...[150]

The declaration also explicitly mentioned that the implementation of the ICK recommendations was the main reason for its existence.

The debate regarding the CGDK at the 1982 General Assembly was predictably divided into the anti-Vietnamese faction, which argued for the withdrawal of foreign troops, and the pro-Vietnamese faction, which spoke of 'the need for foreign troops to safeguard the integrity and sovereignty of the people of Kampuchea'.[151] The only voice which was at variance with the bi-partisan approach was that of the Indian minister for external affairs P. V. Navasimha Rao who argued that the point was to remove *both* the KR and the occupying troops. He articulated a point of view which concerned many neutrals when he added that 'the advent of an alliance of convenience whose real content is too thinly veiled to need any unmasking should not distract our attention'.[152] In similar vein the Philippine Foreign Minister exposed what many claim was the sole reason for the CGDK; he said that the coalition had provided the *mantle of legality* for the struggle of the anti-Vietnamese forces'[153] (emphasis added). Whether the coalition was a genuine alliance or a cosmetic device to enable continued support for anti-Vietnamese factions is basically irrelevant; the CGDK provided confirmation for a variety of realities.

Congress

Nowhere was this more obvious than in the conflicting realities which existed within the US Congress. Because Congressional hearings accept testimony from a variety of sources there exists within the transcripts a diversity of opinion encompassing the full spectrum of views about the Cambodian problem. It is interesting to compare them with the administration's reality.

During Reagan's first term Stephen Solarz (D, NY) had established himself in Congress as 'Mr Cambodia'. He was Chairman of the Sub-Committee on Asian and Pacific Affairs and had often expressed a particular interest in Cambodia. Solarz, who is Jewish, felt particularly strongly about the parallels between the Khmer Rouge and the Nazis.[154] His statements are replete with references to the holocaust and genocide and he made strenuous efforts to distance the US from any association with Pol Pot. Hearings on Cambodia in 1981, 1982 and 1983 illustrate Solarz's dilemma in trying to operate within a reality constructed by others.

In a hearing shortly after the ICK, Solarz professed himself disappointed with the performance of the United States' delegation at the conference because they had not made enough of the Pol Pot horrors. He also refused to accept Chinese assurances that the KR had learned from its mistakes saying that he did 'not consider the murder of 2 million people a mistake'. He went on to state that 'any arrangements ... which do not provide for the disarmament of the Khmer Rouge faction constitute a recipe for the return to power of Pol Pot'.[155] At the same hearing Son Sann gave testimony. He accused the Vietnamese of indulging in 'a veritable genocide of Cambodian people'.[156] He goes on to use the word 'genocide' twice more in the next two sentences. He was appealing to the moral conscience of the Americans after Solarz had admitted 'a very real US responsibility' in Cambodia. However, Son Sann also had the political wherewithal to reject Solarz's efforts to get him to agree that the disarmament clause in the ICK declaration was not sufficiently strong. Son Sann's sole aim was to extract military aid from the Americans for his KPNLF and he was not unduly concerned with the wording of resolutions because 'if the Khmer Rouge do not want to disarm, if they want to return to power, they will do so'.[157]

Son Sann was also fairly sanguine about the practicalities of joining forces with the KR in a coalition. While he would have preferred to continue alone he recognised the impossibility of such a course without massive US aid. Conversely Solarz still believed that any association with the KR would taint the process. In October 1981, at the height of the negotiations about a coalition Solarz made this statement:

I know we have made it clear we don't endorse Pol Pot or approve of what he did, but our words will sound very hollow if a new coalition is formed in which it appears that the DK is the dominant force, even if whatever diplomatic or political help we give is directed only to certain elements within the coalition. I can't stress this strongly enough, that I think this coalition policy is moving in the direction of disaster.[158]

A year later events had overtaken Solarz. At a hearing in September 1982 on the merits of voting on the acceptance of the CGDK's credentials at the UN he asked:

Is it possible for the US government to have any moral claim to a concern for human rights if it associates itself in any way, shape, manner or form with the Pol Pot assassins who killed their own people in an act of autogenocide never before seen in modern history? We will, in this regard, want to examine closely the extent to which the establishment of a Cambodian coalition expunges the moral stain which would otherwise blot the conscience of our own country were we, perhaps for reasons of strategic necessity, to once again cast our vote in favour of seating the DK at the UN.[159]

He probably knew the unpalatable answer. It took a further year for the CGDK figleaf to be finally set in place. During the September 1983 sub-committee hearing the vacant seat issue was raised again. This time the witness was ex-Deputy US Permanent Representative at the UN, Ambassador James Leonard. He stated quite clearly that the notion that the CGDK had enabled support to continue was flawed. His own judgement 'was that an empty seat would be defensible for a considerable period'.[160] An interesting exchange followed in which Solarz came full circle in sanitising the KR role in the CGDK:

SOLARZ: What would be the benefits of supporting an empty seat?
LEONARD: I think, obviously, the moral basis, which is also the political basis for our position, would be enhanced by [not supporting the DK].
SOLARZ: ... we're not voting to seat Pol Pot; we're voting to seat Sihanouk and Son Sann as the heads of a coalition government in which Pol Pot serves.[161]

Solarz's comment was clearly a defensive reaction but Leonard's point, that *any* association with Pol Pot was based on the faulty premise that it was the only way of maintaining pressure on the

Vietnamese, was irrefutable. He argued that this was wrong on two counts – first, it failed to account for the hatred of Pol Pot, and second, it allowed the Vietnamese to continue to portray themselves as saviours. It was a strong argument against the US position. Another dissenting voice at the hearing was that of Professor Carlisle Thayer (Visiting Fellow at Yale). He argued, in some quite heated exchanges with Solarz, that there was little hope of a resistance battle-field victory. He also contended that 'the PRK had ... emerged as an effective government in its own right. This is often overlooked.'[162] He thought that given greater aid the PRK could develop independently from Vietnam. He believed that the level of aid provided to the resistance was inadequate and gave false hope which consequently prevented recovery. In Thayer's opinion it was better to accept the reality that 'Vietnam [was] a dominant power in Indochina; it [was] likely to remain so, and the cost of overturning th[at] position [was] too great and one that [he] believe[d] the nation would not bear'.[163]

In debate, then, Congress appeared uncomfortable with certain elements of US policy but gradually it fell into line after airing its conscience. Late in 1983 a resolution (H. Con. Res. 176) was passed which contained the following points:

- support the ASEAN position;
- urge other nations to do the same;
- urge other nations to cooperate with ASEAN in 'maintaining economic and diplomatic pressure on Vietnam';
- support the UN Border Relief Operation (UNBRO);
- give humanitarian and political support to the non-Communist Khmer nationalist forces.

Nearly three years into the Reagan presidency, Congress and the policy elite seemed, more or less, at one.

The alternative realities constructed by the participating players such as ASEAN, China, Vietnam, PRK, CGDK and the USSR, as well as those developed by observers such as Congressional partici-pants, highlight the difficulties continually encountered by those responsible for the formulation of US foreign policy. They must simultaneously resist and accommodate the alternatives in order to survive. Each reality was remarkably consistent with the type of prediction which might have been expected given the world-views of the various actors and taken separately each reality has an internal consistency.

AMALGAM OF REALITIES

During the first Reagan presidency the ASEAN nations were suspicious of China's long-term intentions in the region. They were particularly concerned with the possible ramifications of China's dual-track diplomacy in which China was content to deal simultaneously with governments *and* insurgent groups. States like Malaysia and Indonesia, with their own insurgency problems, were thus able to be more relaxed about Vietnamese expansionism because they viewed the SRV as a buffer against China.

In addition to pressure from China, ASEAN also had to accommodate US pressure. Despite ASEAN protestations that disarmament of all factions was non-negotiable, prior to the ICK, the US eventually forced them to accept it. The US was no doubt 'eager to cement [their] new relationship with Peking'.[164] As compensation ASEAN was accorded the leadership role by the US in a variety of statements. During three days of discussions with ASEAN foreign ministers in July 1984, George Shultz 'reiterated strong support for ASEAN'.[165] In 1983 he had told another ASEAN conference that the US would resist taking a more active role in Indochina preferring to allow regional actors to occupy the leading role; 'we will follow your lead', he is quoted as saying.[166] However, ASEAN was still concerned about US rapprochement with China. They believed that China's insistence on 'bleeding Vietnam white' would only serve to reinforce a Soviet presence in the region which was in contrast to ASEAN's policy of limiting superpower involvement not increasing it. For ASEAN, especially Malaysia and Indonesia, it might even have been preferable to have a strong Indochinese group which could be minimally dependent on the USSR.

Despite statements to the contrary it is unlikely that ASEAN could have retained support for their position without the formation of the CGDK. In late 1981, for example, several European states were threatening to withdraw recognition of DK credentials. In conjunction with US and Chinese pressure on the KR and the KPNLF respectively such actions prompted the three resistance factions to submerge their differences and form the CGDK. Proof of its legitimacy came with the increased vote at the UN. In 1981 the vote for retention of DK credentials was 77–37–31; in 1982 it had risen to 90–29–26. The negotiations between the three groups started in earnest when Sihanouk, Son Sann and Khieu Samphan signed a declaration of intent on 4 September 1981. Originally their stances had seemed irreconcilable but pressure from external backers gradually brought them together.

Throughout this period Sihanouk had attempted to either dominate the alliance or to stay aloof, playing the role of mediator, an elder statesman. Although Sihanouk viewed himself in that way, it is alleged that he was merely tolerated by the KR, KPNLF and also by ASEAN because of his cosmetic value.[167] Throughout 1981 Beijing applied almost continuous pressure on Sihanouk to take on a leadership role in any type of anti-Vietnamese coalition which could encompass the KR. Despite these reservations it was acknowledged that Sihanouk had the trust of the majority of the Khmers and as such he was, and remains, invaluable. As president of the CGDK he was able to continue in the monarchical role that he coveted and which suited him so well.

A major difficulty for the CGDK was the lack of total US acceptance of the complete entity. Reagan himself was keen to point this out in May 1984. He said, 'the United States does not recognize the Khmer coalition as a government. We welcomed it as a vehicle to press for a settlement based on the ICK ... principles.'[168] Throughout this period the US, at least publicly, pledged all its support for the NCR. Despite the official US position they remained reluctant to provide the military aid necessary for the success of the NCR factions. ASEAN asked the US to become the major arms supplier to the NCR in an attempt to redress the imbalance held by the Chinese supplied KR. The problem for the US seemed to be that China, with arms, and Thailand, with sanctuary, would have continually restored the imbalance and the NCR could have become a financial sink-hole.

The US allowed ASEAN and the CGDK to take the lead because it was convenient, although it did agree to make so-called 'fungible funds' available. In an article by Nayan Chanda in August 1984, several unattributed sources are quoted who vouch for the existence of this system of providing aid.[169] The US was, therefore, able to provide non-lethal aid to ASEAN which in turn released capital which could then provide lethal aid:

> money earmarked for humanitarian assistance ... [was] handed over to ASEAN countries, who use[d] an equivalent sum from their own budgets to buy weapons and ammunition for the resistance.[170]

The US maintained a distance despite pressure from ASEAN, evidenced by visits in early 1984 by the Malaysian and Thai prime ministers to President Reagan. Eventually ASEAN did extract an increase in aid to $15m, although not any fundamental change in policy, at a meeting with George Shultz early in July. The US remained interested, at a distance, concerned but not entangled. This was precisely the position they wanted. Although the Thais may have reasoned that receiving lethal aid would have tied the US government into a more tangible commitment to Thailand, in the event of Vietnamese invasion, the US clearly rejected any such notion.

In order to promote their policies the US used various fora, but the message remained the same. The Cambodian problem was the result of Vietnamese regional hegemonism backed by Soviet expansionism and could only be remedied by the withdrawal of foreign troops under the auspices of the ASEAN inspired ICK declaration and with the regional actors leading. Jeane Kirkpatrick's statement to the General Assembly in 1984 was informative on this point:

> Vietnam aided and abetted by the Soviet Union continued its illegal occupation of Cambodia and its oppression of Cambodians ... Prince Sihanouk and Premier Son Sann, and the organizations they led, were the true embodiment of Khmer nationalism.[171]

Sihanouk also addressed the General Assembly, as the president of the CGDK, and echoed the US statements.

Dissenting voices, such as those nations who supported the Vietnamese line, were gradually drowned as the mood in the UN inexorably moved against them. Even the Soviets, whose rhetoric remained firm, began to decrease their aid to the Vietnamese. It fell from $134m in 1980 to approximately $65m by 1984.[172] Although many subscribed to a view offered by Ben Kiernan, that the CGDK was 'neither a coalition, nor a government, nor democratic',[173] it was, nevertheless, convenient.

The Vietnamese, for their part, continued with the only tactics available to them. These entailed trying to establish customary legitimacy while simultaneously attempting to isolate individual components of the alliance against them. They were failing because their opponents would not acquiesce in the former nor succumb to the latter. Again there were some who agreed when Nguyen Co Thach made the following statements to the 1984 General Assembly:

> The forces of imperialism ... want to destroy Vietnam economically so that they can teach the Asian, African and Latin American countries the lesson that the peoples of the world may win a war of national liberation but will be beaten on the economic front.[174]

However, those who agreed lacked power. They consisted mostly of members of the non-aligned movement who had been rejected as serious players since they banned the CGDK from their 1983 conference. In the final declaration of that conference a mere two lines were reserved for Cambodia.

The story of the interface of realities during the 1981–85 period was one of US predominance, primarily by dissociation. They prodded and pressured regional actors into an agreement. It appeared that even the Vietnamese were grudgingly acquiescing by not challenging the CGDK seat at the UN after its failure in 1983. Although no end was in sight, damage limitation and stability *were* achieved.

CONCLUSION

During his testimony to the sub-committee in 1983, Carlisle Thayer defined US foreign policy towards Cambodia in the process of criticising it. He said that '[t]railing behind ASEAN and seeking not to offend the People's Republic of China is an abrogation of a positive role the United States *could* play'.[175] However, that was precisely the point, the US did not want a 'positive role'. It wanted to influence the situation without commitment. It wanted the restoration of the Western statist imperative. Alexander Haig had already stated that the 'purpose of the [ICK] was to restore Kampuchea's sovereignty and independence',[176] and Holdridge explained how it would be done:

> the course of action most likely to result in the removal of Vietnamese troops from Kampuchea is to make the occupation as costly as possible ... [by] a process of diplomatic and economic deprivation ... supplemented by the presence on Vietnam's northern border of hundreds of thousands of Chinese troops and the continuing guerrilla activity of several resistance groups inside Kampuchea.[177]

That was US policy at the beginning of the Reagan presidency and so it remained until the end of his first term. The problem throughout was to square these views with the abhorrence of the Khmer Rouge. At a hearing in 1983 Son Sann provided the perfect justification. When asked by Stephen Solarz how he could live with Pol Pot he said '[we must] choose, who is the number one enemy. We have chosen the number one enemy of our people, it is the Vietnamese invader.'[178]

Given this justification it only remained for the US to produce a policy that would not lead to greater entanglement in the region. Reagan himself provided the rationale when he explained that:

> if our involvement appears to be less than in other areas of the world, it is only because of the success the ASEAN countries have had in managing the economic and political issues they face, independent of a heavy US presence.[179]

Above all, however, Cambodia remained a peripheral issue, as it was during Carter's presidency. In his address to the UN General Assembly in September 1984 only two sentences were reserved for South East Asia out of an eight page speech and both simply praised and supported ASEAN. Despite the neglect of Cambodia, the US purportedly still placed a 'concern for human rights [at] the moral centre of its foreign policy'.[180] Another indication of the marginal importance of the region was the paucity of references in the Congressional records; between 1981 and 1984 there were only six logged references. Cambodia only seemed to matter when it was directly related to Reagan's *bête noire*, the Soviet Union. Therefore, it was only when Vietnam erred and was clearly supported by the USSR that Cambodia became significant. Douglas Pike, however, did not agree that the Vietnamese occupation had anything to do with Soviet regional ambitions, arguing that:

> the Vietnamese are [not] in Kampuchea because of China, or because of the Soviet Union, or because of the United States. They are there because they made a series of bad mistakes in handling Pol Pot and now they are stuck.[181]

He may well have been right, and in fact the US policy actually made it more difficult for the Vietnamese to extricate themselves, but Pike's explanation did not match the Reagan administration's reality and as such was an irritant.

Cambodia was essentially a side issue and as such did not demand attention other than when an external factor raised its profile. The policy elite *accorded* status to an issue and Cambodia rarely warranted any attention. While Reaganite rhetoric on Cambodia occasionally dealt with human rights issues, in substance almost all US foreign policy initiatives were tied firmly to the *realpolitik* requirements of defeating the evil empire, and even there the relationship between words and deeds was rarely as close as was claimed at the time. It appears that the reality constructed by the Reagan administration regarding Cambodia was largely rhetorical but for what was essentially a peripheral issue that was probably sufficient. In his first term Reagan was expected to radically alter the direction of foreign policy. Actually he only altered its *rhetorical* direction. Whether this represented an alteration in substance is, of course, debatable.

3 The Second Reagan Administration, 1985–89

There is only one way safely and legitimately to reduce the cost of national security, and that is to reduce the need for it ... America must remain freedom's staunchest friend, for freedom is our best ally and it is the world's only hope to conquer poverty and preserve peace.

Inaugural Address of President Ronald Reagan, 21 January 1985

The analysis in this chapter will focus on whether the dissociation of image and substance, which allegedly existed in his first term, continued during Reagan's second term and whether the new policy elite significantly altered the balance of foreign policy. In his second term Reagan was confronted with the unravelling of the reality in which the Soviet Union was the source of the world's ills. Did it become necessary for the new principate to completely reconstruct reality or did it merely need fine tuning?

Ronald Reagan's second inaugural speech was remarkably similar to the first, concentrating as it did primarily on the economic. It began in self-congratulatory tone explaining how, when Reagan had taken the 'oath 4 years ago, [he] did so in a time of economic stress' but that he had believed there were 'no limits to growth and human progress' and he had been 'right to believe that'. His second pledge of 1981 had also been delivered with the economy 'finally freed from government's grip'. The moral, economic and strategic decline of the Carter years had been halted and reversed during the first term. True to the promise of his first inaugural, he had not presided 'over the dissolution of the world's strongest economy'. A 'time of reckoning' had finally arrived and the second administration would not be found wanting.

It was more than two-thirds of the way through the address before the President mentioned foreign issues. In this area he concentrated on arms reduction: 'We seek the total elimination one day of nuclear weapons.' What would become known as the Strategic Defence Initiative (SDI) was unveiled as 'a security shield that will destroy nuclear missiles before they reach their target'. Finally, employing the

95

rhetoric of freedom, Reagan once again invoked the images of the old west, of Valley Forge and even the Alamo, in an elegiac final section.

As with the first inaugural, there was little evidence of specific foreign policy directives, only general exhortations to 'go forward today, a nation still mighty in its youth and powerful in its purpose'. Reagan, the self-proclaimed missionary for American values, was still running a primarily rhetorical foreign policy. Appropriately for an ex-film star, American popular culture, and the cinema in particular, was happy to catch Reagan's mood and reflect, enlarge and transmit it onto the mass consciousness. Films such as *Rambo, First Blood Part Two, Heartbreak Ridge* and *Top Gun* embraced revisionist views of the Vietnam experience which clearly mirrored what was to be a strong theme throughout the first half of the second term (Reagan II).

Ironically another film, the British-made *The Killing Fields*, which was released in the first week of Reagan's second term, put Cambodia back onto the domestic agenda more forcefully than for many years. Although the antithesis of the *Rambo*-esque philosophy, it also caught the public imagination. At least superficially the two films exposed the contradictions in US foreign policy. The contradiction, which the Reaganite foreign policy machine never seemed inclined to resolve, was between a clear moral tragedy (*Killing Fields*) and a reluctance to fully engage militarily (*Rambo*). Any reality needed to accommodate both.

THE ADMINISTRATION

The differences between the court of the first Reagan administration and that of Jimmy Carter were to be expected, the changes from Reagan I to Reagan II perhaps less so. The head of the Reagan II court naturally remained Ronald Reagan himself, although after the Iran–Contra scandal he was significantly diminished compared with his first-term self. However, the most controversial and arguably destructive change occurred at level two with the job swap between James Baker and Donald Regan. In contrast to this upheaval, George Shultz, who had arrived in June 1982, stayed until the end of the Reagan presidency. In that time he managed to become 'the vicar' of foreign policy that Haig had hoped to be. He provided a continuity that gave the foreign policy community at least a semblance of stability and efficiency.

When Regan and Baker exchanged the Treasury and CoS jobs the important change for foreign policy was that Regan moved onto level two and accreted to himself so much power that he directly affected US foreign policy in general and consequently policy towards Cambodia. The 'troika', of which Baker was a member, had never really involved itself in the foreign policy process and was, therefore, not included at any level of the analysis of Reagan I. Regan, however, involved himself in everything, damagingly so according to the Tower Commission on the Iran–Contra affair.[1] Caspar Weinberger remained at level two by virtue of his position as Secretary of Defense. He made few pronouncements on foreign policy issues other than to reiterate what he considered to be the limited role that US military forces had 'in the larger framework of national power'.[2] Only when it was clear that foreign issues affected Defense did Weinberger become engaged.

At level three the number of actors increased in the second term. Whereas in the first term only Kirkpatrick and Holdridge had any real say in US foreign policy towards Cambodia, the position changed during Reagan II. David Lambertson (Deputy Assistant SoS, East Asian and Pacific Affairs), Karl Jackson (Deputy Assistant SoD, East Asian and Pacific Affairs), Kirkpatrick's successor Vernon Walters (an ex-CIA deputy director), and the National Security Council's John Poindexter all made significant contributions to the administration's construction of Cambodian reality.

LEVEL ONE

It has been argued that Ronald Reagan's ability as a communicator was more relevant to his continuing popularity than any policy content. It has to be acknowledged, for example, that although his ratings plummeted in the immediate aftermath of Irangate, by the end of his presidency they had recovered to 60 per cent approval.[3] It is ironic, therefore, that during his second term, when he actually became far more accommodating towards the Soviet Union, he retained a belligerent image. One reason might be that one of the most powerful influences upon public opinion, the 'movies', can have at least a two-year gestation period. *Rambo*, for example, although released in 1985 was, in fact, started in 1983, only two years into the first Reagan term.

Some commentators thought *Rambo* was 'the quintessential reflection of [the] reactionary current in American popular culture'[4] and it is surely no coincidence that the *Spitting Image* version of Reagan often saw his head atop a Rambo torso. In his first term Reagan had clearly promoted such a view although Coral Bell argued that even then it was false. She concluded there was a gap between 'declaratory' signals and 'operational' signals and she cites, as an example, the downing of the Korean airliner in September 1983. After the civil airliner was shot down by Soviet fighters over Soviet airspace Bell states that there were 'symbolic gestures of rage', such as a denial of landing rights for Gromyko's visit to the UN, which did not fit with the reality of failing to rescind a major grain deal.[5] Her view was confirmed when George Shultz said that 'President Reagan made sure the world knew the full unvarnished truth about the atrocity: nevertheless, he also sent our arms control negotiators back to Geneva because he believed that a reduction in nuclear weapons was a critical priority.'[6] Thus the image of an ideological zealot unwilling to compromise is a little strained.

Nevertheless, Reagan's image was a powerful factor in his popularity with the electorate. In an article in the *New York Review of Books* (28 June 1984) Robert Kaiser explained this phenomenon as follows:

> Many Americans don't want to hold Reagan responsible for the actions of his government, because in all other respects they find him such a satisfactory President. For them the President's position as head of state and government is secondary to his performance as master of ceremonies.

Within his court Reagan was initially protected by the 'troika'; when they were removed Donald Regan stepped in and reinforced the 'teflon effect', albeit by marginalising the President.

Reagan's *style* has also been criticised quite savagely, not least by the Tower Commission, for its 'hands-off' nature. In an interesting analogy Philip Geyelin likens President Reagan to Arthur Miller's Willy Loman and asks whether the American public should be entitled to ask 'more of a president than that he be "out there in the blue, riding on a smile and a shoeshine"'.[7] They probably are but for some reason they seem not to bother. Reagan *did* build up an almost mystical air of invincibility in public opinion which was only punctured by the Iran–Contra affair – although even that was not irretrievable; he was not, for example, threatened with impeachment and he did survive his full term.

However, his laissez-faire approach did not mean that *his* vision of foreign policy did not predominate. I. M. Destler said that Reagan 'may not have grasped, or cared about, the details; he may not have faced the contradictions; but *his* priorities, *his* values were pursued'.[8] The Reagan vision, albeit based on a simplistic zero-sum Soviet–American competition, did persist despite obvious obstacles. One theme in the second term was a revisionist view of the Vietnam war. Reagan believed the received anti-war wisdom was a significant obstacle to American progress.

He began his revisionism during the 1980 election campaign, referring to Vietnam as a 'noble cause',[9] and very early in his second term he said that 'the great disgrace, to me, of Vietnam [was] that they were fed into this meatgrinder and yet no one ever had any intention of allowing victory'.[10] In this interpretation, defeat was not inevitable, victory had not been 'allowed'. Such an explanation was entirely predictable given a reality which could not accommodate the idea of the fallibility of the American way. The failure had to lay with those who ignored American values and *not* with the values themselves.

Reagan's world-view did not appear to have altered in his second term even though circumstances had. The certainties of the Cold War had begun to crumble with Gorbachev's accession and the pragmatic element of the Reagan style became more evident. He did not need to be 'a kind of bellicose cowboy figure'[11] any longer because the bellicosity had done its job. The contradictions identified by Bell through her declaratory/operational dichotomy can be explained within the framework of the 'pragmatic ideologue' persona. They were not contradictions but rhetorical ploys – executed successfully according to some analysts.[12] Reagan still held firmly to his 'anointed land' view of America and its role in the world and essentially that view continued to drive US foreign policy in the second Reagan term.

LEVEL TWO

At the second level Shultz had become the 'real "Vicar" of foreign policy'[13] but there were still reservations concerning his influence on the foreign policy process. He was described 'as an experienced, moderate and responsible leader ... a sensible and pragmatic voice',[14] which may well be true, but he also presided over the foreign policy fiascos of Reykjavik and 'Irangate'. Michael Smith argues that Shultz never really established his grip on the foreign policy community and that Irangate merely proved this point in 'spectacular fashion'.[15] Shultz allowed the bureaucracy a freer hand and thus a stronger role than was, perhaps, wise. Shultz himself conceded that he had great difficulties, especially with the NSC. He explained to his own staff, '[t]here is a management crisis in foreign affairs here', and, therefore, his task was to make the NSC irrelevant.[16]

Despite Shultz's urbanity and generally acceptable diplomatic demeanour, his public statements epitomised the Reagan administration's belief that they had 'reasserted America's leadership as an engaged, global force for prosperity, security and democratic change'.[17] The tone, and even the content to a certain extent, could have been drawn from a Reagan inaugural. Above all Shultz was a team player. His articles for *Foreign Affairs* are reworkings of *Current Policy* papers. He seemed content to play the role the team most needed and the one the team's manager so designated. Given the role that foreign policy played in the Reagan administration Shultz was probably perfectly cast – he did not make waves and in a stoical fashion promoted the policy directives as he interpreted them.

By contrast Caspar Weinberger appeared to remain a team player only in pursuit of the Defense agenda. Weinberger concentrated on resurrecting the status of the military in the policy-making process and concentrated on building up the defence budget. Ideologically he was close to the Reagan position, minus the elegiac component. His pragmatism was, perhaps, the greatest point of departure from the purely Reaganite stance.[18] He remained resolute in advocating the maintenance of force levels and structure, even in the face of the 1985 Balanced Budget and Emergency Deficit Control Act, better known as the Gramm, Rudman, and Hollings Act. Thus the majority of his time during the second Reagan term was taken up defending Defense. His influence on foreign policy was consequently limited.

It is argued that Weinberger and Shultz clashed,[19] although it can also be seen with the Iran–Contra issue that they were prepared to pragmatically combine on specific issues. Unfortunately, when they did agree on the inadvisability of arms sales to Iran, they did not prevail. Weinberger and Shultz were not likely to have been friends, but they both appear to have been able to accommodate each other when it was mutually beneficial; neither was an ideological zealot.

In the short time that Frank Carlucci served as SoD he seemed more amenable; he was, for example, 'more flexible on budget, choice of weapons and arms negotiations'.[20] His relationship with Shultz was easier not least because Shultz had supported Carlucci's candidature for the job. This was despite their clashes over the enhanced role for the NSA pushed by Carlucci when he was in the job.[21] However, as with his time as NSA, Carlucci's was a short-term appointment to ease tensions and restore order. He did not, therefore, unduly concern himself with foreign policy issues and does not figure significantly in this analysis of the foreign policy elite.

Donald Regan, however, *was* significant. His influence was all-pervasive. The exact details of the job exchange which transferred Regan to CoS and Baker to the Treasury are still somewhat sketchy. Regan claims that Baker was simply tired of the strain involved in his White House duties.[22] Whatever the reasons, the swap happened and its ramifications have been characterised as dire. The main criticism concerned the manner in which Regan gathered power and in the process isolated and marginalised the President. As Tip O'Neill put it, '[w]hen you have a president who likes to delegate, assisted by a White House Chief of Staff who likes to amass power, it's a formula for disaster'.[23]

Regan replaced the loyalty, political wisdom, Washington credibility and selflessness of the troika with himself and the troika slid imperceptibly into the backgound. Where the troika had displayed responsibility when Reagan delegated to them, Regan 'crudely exploited the vacuum created' by such delegation.[24] The reason he exploited it is debatable. Norman Ornstein in the *Washington Post* assumed simple self-aggrandisement; Regan 'glorified in national television opportunities, insisted on being photographed standing by the president's side, looking over his shoulder or whispering in his ear, and boasted frequently about his power'.[25] Regan himself disputes such an analysis arguing that at 67 years old he had no personal ambition, only the desire 'to get Ronald Reagan's agenda translated in law'.[26] He was 'not power mad [only] trying to put the President's policies into effect'.[27] This may actually have been true, but power can be seductive and Regan's rhetoric and actions do not suggest passivity. For example, in his own book he describes his duties as follows:

> All duties formerly exercised by Baker, Meese and Deaver devolved on me – personnel, the coordination of information, the choice of issues, the flow of paper, and the schedule that controlled the President's travel and other movements and determined who would see him and who would not.[28]

Those are not the words of a self-effacing civil servant. Regan also engineered cabinet rank for himself, unlike his predecessor. Additionally, by controlling access to the President, whether by accident or design, he effectively maximised his own power. He thus emerged 'as chief of staff for both domestic and foreign policy'[29] and consequently needs to be situated at level two.

Had Regan been more capable then the administration may have survived such a concentration of power. However, it has been argued that Regan generated a 'growing disorder'[30] which eventually culminated in the Irangate affair and part of the disorder was the result of hiring weak staff. Regan employed the classic tactics of those who covet power – they isolate a superior in order to emasculate them and employ weak subordinates in order not to be threatened by them; it is also the classic error. Regan insinuated himself into every corner of the administration and had a disproportionate and inappropriate influence over the NSC. The Tower Commission concluded that 'more than almost any Chief of Staff of recent memory, he asserted personal control over the White House staff and sought to extend his control to the national security advisor'.[31] The President had already marginalised the NSA by depriving him of Cabinet status. Regan simply compounded the situation, insisting that the NSA could only access the President through the CoS.

The interesting point here is that while the NSA had been formally relegated to level three, the lack of control which came with such relegation allowed the NSC to generate their own agenda and indulge in renegade actions which reverberated up through level two and even into level one. The Iran–Contra affair merely confirmed the impression that a hands-off managerial style was vulnerable when subordinates did not exhibit self-restraint. After the Tower Commission report there was no alternative but to remove Regan. In February 1987 he was replaced by Howard Baker, who was in turn replaced by Kenneth Duberstein, two inconsequential James Baker devotees who saw out the presidency without rocking the boat – a period of calm being essential.

At the second level then it was not so much the world-views of the actors which effected the foreign policy process but the 'bureaucratic infighting' that resulted from a marginalised and rogue NSC not performing its policy coordination function.[32] No foreign policy initiatives could gain attention over the demands of Irangate. A group (the NSC) who had been deliberately relegated by the President had effectively usurped the foreign policy agenda by indulging in operations of dubious legality.

LEVEL THREE

Given that the NSA, as least formally, could be said to have been relegated to level three he was nevertheless pre-eminent at that level. The other important actors, for the purposes of the Cambodian issue, were the State and Defense Department assistant secretaries with responsibilities for East Asian and Pacific Affairs – Paul Wolfowitz (State), Karl Jackson (Defense), David Lambertson (State) and Gaston Sigur (State).[33] Their importance to the presentation of the administration's constructed reality is demonstrated in the absolute consistency of their public statements. They were aided and abetted by deputies such as John Monjo and by other third-level actors like Vernon Walters who succeeded the ebullient Jeane Kirkpatrick as the US Permanent Representative to the United Nations. Walters, as an ex-CIA deputy director and senior military officer, did not have the high public profile or charisma of Kirkpatrick, and although he served for the majority of the second term he consequently had limited influence.

As previously stated, the role of the NSA and the NSC was pre-eminent at this level and had considerable repercussions at other levels. The NSC was designed to provide comprehensive analysis, alternatives and follow-up in order to facilitate the decision-making process. By sidelining the Council, Reagan deprived himself of those assets. The Tower Commission said that at 'no time did [the President] insist upon accountability and performance review. Had the president chosen to drive the NSC system, the outcome could well have been different.'[34] Strangely, in parallel with its decline in status, the NSC increased in size. Under Carter and Nixon the NSC consisted of 40–50 staff, whereas under Reagan it rose to 70. The number of NSC sub-committees increased to 25 with an additional 55 mid-level committees.[35] All of this led to a 'loss of control and increasing absorption in bureaucratic minutiae, at the cost of providing strategic direction and imposing policy coordination'.[36]

Lack of control, increase in numbers, more military personnel and absorption in bureaucratic minutiae provided fertile ground in which the devil made work for idle hands. Reagan had succeeded in diminishing the role of the NSA and had simultaneously marginalised the NSC. The NSC did not, however, disappear but generated work for its idle hands and one of its projects eventually turned into the Iran–Contra affair. The Tower Commission found that 'NSC staffers assumed direct control of an operation that was well within the jurisdictions of the State Department, Defense Department and the

CIA'.[37] The Commission further concluded that this was a deliberate policy. Poindexter (NSA, 12/85–1/87), for example, explicitly stated that he 'did not want a meeting with RR, Shultz and Weinberger' on this matter.[38] Oliver North has also said that Robert McFarlane (NSA, 10/83–12/85) 'directed that no copy be sent to the secretary of state and that he, McFarlane, would keep Secretary Shultz advised on the NSC project'.[39]

Similarly John Poindexter argued that it was his duty to protect the President by *not* informing him of the illegal activities of the North operation. He told the Congressional investigation, 'I made a very deliberate decision not to ask the president, [about the diversion of funds] so that I could insulate him from the decision ... on this whole issue the buck stops with me'.[40] Unfortunately it was not Poindexter's decision as to where the buck stopped, although in terms of indictments he was right. The President is shown, either by duplicity or incompetence, to be responsible – either he knew, in which case he was duplicitous or he did not, in which case he was incompetent.

As a result of Irangate, Frank Carlucci was appointed as NSA to succeed Poindexter and conduct 'a wholesale house cleaning of the National Security Council staff'.[41] He did so and stabilised the NSC to such an extent that the remaining two years of the administration were relatively trouble-free. Level three is characterised on the one hand by a group of loyal and conservative civil servants and on the other by an out-of-control, rogue NSC. There was little, if any, conflict between the two because the covert nature of the NSC's operations meant that contact was limited.

CONFLICT

The main cause of conflict within the second Reagan court, Donald Regan, has been dealt with in some detail above. Donald Regan's accession undoubtedly caused tensions but the traditional battles between Defense and State were also evident. They were fuelled not only by the personal antipathy between Weinberger and Shultz, but additionally by the divisiveness generated by Regan's manipulation of the policy-making machinery. On a rare occasion that Weinberger and Shultz had agreed – the *non*-viability of the arms to Iran scheme – 'both were overridden and excluded by a renegade NSC';[42] an NSC that Regan virtually controlled due to his close association with the NSAs. Regan was also allegedly contemptuous of both the Congress, 'a damn nuisance',[43] and the media. Neither attitude was particularly helpful to an administration which was increasingly at odds with Congress as the second term progressed, and both were in complete contrast to the urbane cordiality of Regan's predecessor, James Baker.

State and Defense continued to fight each other with varying degrees of intensity. On intervention, interestingly, they exchanged hawk and dove garb, with State often advocating intervention and Defense being reluctant to commit US forces without almost total assurances as to victory and casualty levels. George Shultz described Weinberger as being 'extremely wary and reluctant to use the formid-able capabilities lodged in the Department of Defense'.[44] On arms control, they assumed their more predictable stances. What Phil Williams calls the 'squeezers', that is to say the conservative ideo-logues of Defense, and the 'dealers', the pragmatists of State, disagreed completely on how to approach arms control negotiations.[45] The 'squeezers' wanted to accelerate the competitive strategy of an intensified arms race while the 'dealers' wanted to conclude an agree-ment with Moscow. However, on the foreign policy approach towards Cambodia there was little real conflict. State had developed a stand-off approach, Defense was not concerned because it was unlikely to affect force levels and Regan was disinterested because there was little, if any, status in the issue.

FOREIGN POLICY

What *did* affect foreign policy, however, were perceptions held by the members of the court both individually and collectively. Michael Smith argues 'that the development of Reaganite foreign policies up to 1985 had been relatively cost-free and had not produced the need for agonising choices; in 1986 some of the choices not confronted in previous years came home to roost'.[46] Smith's analysis assumes a 'development' of policy but it is probably more accurate to describe the process as reactive. Policy sprang from a simplistic world-view, held by Reagan and promoted by his court, in conjunction with the loose control exerted by the White House over the foreign policy process. Kegley and Wittkopf, for example, argued that 'the import-ance of the president's cabinet as a collective body proffering foreign policy advice ... declined to almost nothing'.[47] Ironically Reagan had tried to make the Cabinet *more* central to foreign policy decision-making because it would simultaneously undercut the NSC. However, very quickly he began to fall back on the advice of his personal staff.[48] The advice he received reaffirmed the 'American way' ideals espoused by the administration during the first term.

However, as with the first term the ideals were tempered with reality, even in some of the public pronouncements. George Shultz, for example, felt able to say, in 1985:

> The United States of America is not just an onlooker. We are participants, and we are engaged. America is again in a position to have a major influence over the trend of events – and America's traditional goals and values have *not* changed.[49]

This represented an explicit pronouncement of an American *duty* to be involved in world affairs. It was a clear statement of foreign policy. However, Shultz also said '[w]e cannot pay *any* price or bear *any* burden. We must discriminate.'[50] And at resignation Alexander Haig said:

> The idea that the United States, acting alone in an interdependent world, can somehow renew the mythical golden era of the immediate post war years when [the United States] seemed invulnerable to international or economic developments is a dangerous illusion.[51]

Thus the perception of US foreign policy within the elite was one of interventionism balanced with a pragmatic realisation of constraints upon such intervention. Those constraints might be self-imposed as with the Weinberger Doctrine, or externally imposed as with the need to react to other superpower actions. The problem was that the first term had created a belligerent mood across America. *Rambo* was described at the time as an 'absurdly overwrought comic strip action which shamefully caught the mood of America at the time of its release'.[52] However, that time was 1985, the *start* of the second term. It may have been deemed necessary by the administration to temper that mood by admitting the limitations on action that even an American president must accept.

An early manifestation of the new approach to foreign policy was the enunciation of the Reagan Doctrine in the 1985 State of the Union address. This doctrine committed the US to aid counter-revolutionary forces in their wars against the Soviet Union's Marxist clients. A consequence of this policy was the need to repeal the Clark Amendment (1975) which had prohibited funds to assist anti-communist groups, an amendment described by Haig as 'a blatant restriction of executive authority'.[53] The amendment was repeated in mid-1985 with relative ease, an indication of the changing mood of both the public and Congress.

It seems plausible to suggest that the mood had changed primarily because of a concerted effort on the part of the administration to exorcise the 'Vietnam syndrome' by the simple tactic of revising it. In an extraordinary address at the State Department on 25 April 1985 George Shultz explained both the substance of the revisionist view and its consequences for US foreign policy.[54] He began by arguing that the reassessment was 'not merely a historical exercise. Our understanding of the past affects our conduct in the present, and thus, in part, determines our future'. By inference, rewriting the past to inform the policies of the present will produce an 'acceptable' future.

The language of the address is also replete with elegiac reassessments:

> The President has called our effort a noble cause, and he was right. Whatever mistakes in how the war was fought, whatever one's view of the rationale for our intervention, the *morality* of our effort must now be clear. (p. 14)

> A lot of rethinking is going on about the Vietnam war – a lot of healthy rethinking. (p. 15)

Perhaps the most interesting and illuminating section deals with the isolationist impulse generated by the original interpretations of the war. It is worth quoting at length because it encapsulates the central rhetorical thrust of the early months of the second Reagan term:

> For a time, the United States retreated into introspection, self-doubt, and hesitancy. Some Americans tended to think that American power was the source of the world's problems, and that the key to peace was to limit our actions in the world. So we imposed all sorts of restrictions on ourselves. Vietnam – and Watergate – left a legacy of congressional restrictions on presidential flexibility, now embedded in our legislation. Not only the War Powers Resolution but a host of constraints on foreign aid, arms exports, intelligence activities, and other aspects of policy – these weakened the ability of the President to act and to conduct foreign policy, and they weakened our country. Thus we pulled back from global leadership. (p. 14)

The notion of self-imposed constraints actually damaging the country and forcing the abdication of the responsibilities of power was expanded when Shultz ended the address by stating that 'when America lost faith in itself, world stability suffered and freedom lost ground' (p. 16). Thus not only were domestic divisions over Vietnam seen as weakening the US, they also adversely affected the world's chances of freedom. The obvious conclusion was a reassertion of US leadership and by implication intervention. Of course, as has been previously mentioned, this would need to be done without actually inserting US troops in any situation other than where overwhelming superiority, and consequently speedy victory, was assured. Shultz was calling for the reaffirmation of American prestige, what Dean Acheson had called 'the shadow cast by power'.[55] That simple vision *was* Reagan foreign policy.

Unfortunately two specific events, more than any other, precipitated a lack of confidence in presidential control. The first was the Reykjavik summit in September 1986 and the second the Iran–Contra scandal. Of the two, Reykjavik was probably a clearer indicator of the malaise within the administration's foreign policy community, while 'Irangate' might be described as the final manifestation of that malaise. 1986 was the year in which Reagan's foreign policy was found to be without substance and the Reykjavik summit demonstrated that most clearly. It was ill-conceived and poorly prepared. The whole event was proposed with very little forethought or indeed analysis, which incidentally should have been the responsibility of the otherwise occupied NSC. Gorbachev's charisma and continually radical initiatives left Reagan to be merely reactive, thus ceding the political advantage to Moscow. Reagan's laissez-faire approach and uncoordinated action were indicative of the lack of control which eventually led to Irangate.

The policy to sell arms to Iran was also handled with an informality that degenerated into chaos. Linda Miller wrote that the:

> Iran–Contra fiasco ... dramatised the weak grip of the White House on both the substance and the process of American foreign policy. Mr Reagan appears to have issued a series of vague directives to an amateurish, over-zealous National Security Council staff whose unorthodox and probably illegal behaviour threatened the reputation of the administration as a whole.[56]

Ironically, it was Edwin Meese, one of the original troika who by that stage had become Attorney General, who initially uncovered the diversion of profits from arms sales to the Contra rebels. On 13 November 1986 Reagan admitted, in a television address to the nation, that 'small amounts of defensive weapons had been sold to Iran'.[57] He went on to explain the transaction in a quite disarming manner. It was undertaken, he said,

> for the simplest and best of reasons: to renew a relationship with the nation of Iran, to bring an honourable end to the bloody six-year war between Iran and Iraq, to eliminate state-sponsored terrorism and subversion, and to effect the safe return of all hostages.[58]

Such a bland and apparently genuine explication reflects Reagan's 'unerring sense of just how far to go'.[59] Miraculously Reagan survived, even in the face of public opinion polls which found that 'roughly half of the citizenry did not believe that the most trusted president in memory was telling the truth'.[60] Reagan managed to survive when the tide turned; whether by luck or ability is, to a certain extent, not relevant. The *implementation* of his foreign policy vision may have been made more difficult but the vision itself remained intact.

With these chinks in the Reaganite armour Congress became increasingly restless and even hostile. By November 1986 the Democrats had taken control and Reagan's last two years in office were not easy. However, it is arguable that the pressures had little effect on foreign policy other than to keep Caspar Weinberger even more distanced from the process as he tried to defend his empire against the phased budget cuts of Gramm–Rudman–Hollings.

Although it might be true that the Reagan vision remained intact, the foreign policy agenda was undoubtedly altered by the events of 1985/86. The fight against the budget deficit had slowed the defence build-up, added to which Gorbachev's peace initiative in Reykjavik in 1986 and the beginnings of Irangate all dampened the likelihood of stronger foreign policy initiatives. If Reagan's foreign policy was 'based not on facts but on moods',[61] then those moods were most accurately reflected by the rhetoric employed, which in turn can be interpreted as policy.

Towards Cambodia the rhetoric was delivered as expressions of the Reagan Doctrine. For example, Caspar Weinberger said that 'Americans cannot ignore their [the Cambodians'] aspirations without betraying our own. If it is proper and just that we should help those who wish to remain free then we can hardly turn our backs on those who have lost their freedom and want it back';[62] and George Shultz spoke about the 'long and noble tradition of supporting the struggle of other peoples for freedom, democracy and independence', and argued that if the Reagan administration were to turn their backs on such a tradition they 'would be, in effect, enacting the Brezhnev Doctrine into American law'.[63]

At every level the Reagan court complied with a foreign policy based on a simplistic anti-communist, pro-American vision. The problem was that in the second term the court was less effective than in the first. Martin Anderson has argued that Reagan's hands-off approach and reliance on personal advisers worked well in the first term only because the staff were 'very, very good, talented, wise and loyal, and almost selfless.... But when [the] staff [was] ordinary – talented, smart but not wise, and loyal more to themselves than to Reagan policy or to the man himself – then mediocrity rule[d]'.[64] After Irangate Reagan had to purge his foreign policy team and a semblance of stability and order was achieved. By that stage, however, it was virtually irrelevant being so late in the second term.

THE ADMINISTRATION'S REALITY

Whether the presidential court was mediocre or not they still needed to construct a reality which would accommodate each separate issue, and Cambodia was no exception. In the dry season of 1984–85 the Vietnamese launched a massive and initially highly successful offensive against all elements of the resistance forces, the Coalition Government of Democratic Kampuchea (CGDK). Very shortly after the offensive a sub-committee of the committee on Appropriations, House of Representatives, met and as part of their work discussed a request for security assistance to specific states including Thailand.[65] The answers of the Assistant SoS for East Asian and Pacific Affairs, Paul D. Wolfowitz, are enlightening in that they immediately reveal the building blocks in the administration's construction of reality. Further questioning also elicited a strong overall policy statement which again outlines the foundations of the reality.

Early in his testimony Wolfowitz clearly identified the heroes and villains. He explained that the 'Vietnamese are pressing their offense intensely against the Cambodian resistance groups and are at present violating Thailand's borders ... [t]he US intends to honour our long-standing commitments to the front-line states'.[66] Wolfowitz designated the Vietnamese as aggressors violating *two* borders, Cambodia's and Thailand's; the Cambodians were 'resisting' the aggressor, and Thailand was a 'front-line' state in the battle against Communism. He continued by arguing that Thailand desperately needed US help in order to modernise its military in order to 'create a credible deterrent to Vietnamese adventurism'.[67] One piece of the jigsaw of reality was thus in place – Thailand was threatened by Vietnam. A second piece was immediately proffered when it was explained that US 'support of this effort is crucial not only because of the importance of Thailand itself but because of the stake we have in the independence, integrity and prosperity of [ASEAN] ... which has a GNP greater than that of China'.[68] He added that taken together 'the ASEAN countries constitute our fifth largest trading partner'.[69] Thus reality also consisted of a group of nations who inherently possessed integrity, independence and, most importantly, prosperity and economic potential. ASEAN's relative importance was gauged on its GNP and its trading relationship with the US.

Wolfowitz was then asked to outline the administration's view of the $5 million aid, which had been approved by the Senate, to the non-communist resistance (NCR). He entered into evidence a letter from William L. Ball III (State Department) which explained that the administration supported the opportunity 'to provide either economic or military assistance to the non-communist Cambodian assistance'.[70] However, the letter added that it was the administration's 'understanding that the non-communist resistance [was] being provided with all the military equipment it can effectively absorb at this time. We do not believe, therefore, that it is necessary or appropriate for the United States to give weapons to the resistance now.'[71] Wolfowitz reaffirmed US commitment to the NCR and to ousting the Vietnamese *and* the Khmer Rouge (KR) from Cambodia. He had, therefore, in a few short sentences, consolidated the status of the various actors within the administration's reality.

When asked for the administration's views on the long-term prospects of the NCR he answered by once again negatively referring to the Vietnamese. He said that he did not believe Vietnamese assertions that their only goal was the removal of the KR since during the recent offensive 'the people they hit first were Son Sann's forces and Sihanouk's forces'.[72] Finally, then, Wolfowitz had established the reality of a non-communist, or rather non-KR, force as a separate entity as well as a notion that if Vietnam were *only* to seek to remove the KR there was hope for some common ground.

Having established what the reality was, Wolfowitz was very pointedly asked what were the reasons for US involvement, 'for what policy goal, would we be providing tax dollars?'[73] In answering, Wolfowitz clearly enunciated American desires which appeared to centre primarily on the need *not* to be involved very closely at all. He answered as follows:

> The goal is definitely not a military victory and no one is deluded enough to think the Vietnamese are going to be beaten militarily. The goal is a political settlement ... in which Vietnam's legitimate security concerns – and it has them – are met. That is to say, you have got to come out of it with a Cambodia that is generally neutral and non-aligned...[but] the most important thing is that we don't intend to act in a way that this becomes ... a US effort, with the countries whose interests are most directly affected having bailed out of it. We say we are supporting ASEAN. We mean it. That is our policy.[74]

So the question as to US policy goals was answered, 'most importantly', by saying that it was to support, *not* to be drawn in because the Vietnamese are militarily unbeatable. The lessons of the Vietnam War may have been revised for other regions but they remained unchanged with regard to Indochina.

An issue Wolfowitz did not address was Soviet involvement. If, as the administration had suggested, the Soviet Union was at the root of the world's problems, then there must be an involvement and it needed to be exposed. An obvious forum for this activity was the United Nations (UN) and there Vernon Walters presented the administration's view of the Soviet role. When the General Assembly (GA) reviewed the 'situation in Kampuchea', in November 1985, Walters spoke in the debate. He spoke of the 'puppet regime' which had been set up by Vietnam who, 'aided and abetted by the USSR, continued its illegal occupation of Cambodia'.[75] He embellished the demonisation of the Vietnamese by claiming that 'Cambodians faced the prospect of cultural genocide and the extinction of their national identity'.[76] However, there was also recognition that in order to achieve the political settlement the US wanted, there would need to be some accommodation with the Soviet Union. He conceded that the 'United States was prepared ultimately to discuss with the USSR ways to contribute to [the ASEAN proposal's] progress, and was also prepared to contribute to reconstructing Cambodia's economy'.[77] Although muted this statement held out the hope of negotiation and, therefore, constituted a softening of US attitudes.

The softening prefaced an uncertain period for Shultz. On 6 July 1985, for example, Shultz responded to a proposal by the Malaysian Foreign Minister, Ahmed Rithaudden, for 'proximity talks', i.e. an informal gathering in which *any* interested parties would be represented, by saying that he did not 'think anything that ha[d] implicit recognition of the puppet arrangement the Vietnamese have in Cambodia [was] a good thing'.[78] However, six days later Shultz reversed his position and stated that the proposal '[deserve[d] the backing of the international community, and the United States certainly supports it'.[79] It is at least plausible that the change in stance resulted from a need to reflect the softening ASEAN position which itself represented a realisation that the various negotiating positions had effectively stagnated. Only a year earlier Shultz had been berating the Vietnamese by claiming that their occupation of Cambodia was 'Hanoi's version of the Brezhnev doctrine'.[80]

The difficulty for the US was that only negotiations which involved *all* parties had any hope of success, but that would have involved *de facto* recognition of the Phnom Penh government (the PRK), which was anathema to the Reagan administration. In May 1986 John C. Monjo summed up the dilemma in a State Department bulletin. He argued that Vietnam had attempted 'to enhance the almost non-existent stature of its Cambodian clients ... by suggesting we deal with Phnom Penh directly on this issue. We prefer to continue to deal with the reality of the situation which is that Hanoi controls most of Cambodia's territory.'[81] Monjo was merely restating American reality as a defence against Hanoi's version which was establishing some credibility.

To reinforce the condemnation of the Vietnam/PRK alliance it was necessary to praise the opposing factions and Sihanouk once more became the favoured option. Phyllis Oakley, of the State Department delivered the following statement to the press:

> Prince Norodom Sihanouk has been the leading symbol of Cambodian nationalism during the past 40 years. His leadership has been indispensable in the struggle of the Cambodian people to regain their independence. We believe that his role is central to a satisfactory settlement in Cambodia, and we welcome the opportunity of his visit to express our strong support for him.[82]

Two things are worthy of note here. First, this is the same Norodom Sihanouk whom the CIA had once worked so hard to oust. Second, the comment was made in October 1988 when the United States rhetoric was softening in the hope that a settlement was at last possible. In 1985 the State Department were more distant and spoke of the resistance forces as being able to cope without specific US assistance.[83] By 1988, then, the administration's 'reality' was that Vietnamese ogres had invaded an innocent Cambodia and installed a 'puppet' regime which could only be resisted by the *non*-communist resistance forces led by an 'indispensable symbol of Cambodian nationalism' supported in the first instance by ASEAN who would themselves be steadfastly backed by the United States.

The only variable as yet unmentioned is the Khmer Rouge. While it was obvious to serious observers that any US assistance to the NCR must also have included the KR, at least secondarily, the KR still had to be rhetorically ostracised.[84] A typical condemnation would be of the type given by George Shultz in Bangkok (July 1988) at an ASEAN foreign ministers meeting where he stated that the US was 'unalterably opposed to the Khmer Rouge ever again taking control of Cambodia, and we believe it is essential that any settlement have adequate safeguards to prevent this'.[85]

US foreign policy towards Cambodia had, in the final six months of the Reagan presidency, coalesced around very specific definitions of the situation. So much so that State Department officials were delivering speeches and statements with virtually identical sound bites. The following phrase, for example, was used by both Charles Twining (29 September 1988) and Vernon Walters (18 October 1988) less than three weeks apart:

> Vietnam's illegal occupation remains the root cause of the conflict in Cambodia today and the expeditious withdrawal of all the estimated 120 000* Vietnamese troops we believe are still in the country is the key to resolving this tragic situation. We cannot imagine that the Cambodian people would willingly vote for the return of the Khmer Rouge.[86]

It is not surprising there should be such congruence between two employees of the same department. In fact it might even be commendable. Nevertheless, it is indicative of a very tight definition of what constituted reality for the administration.

These statements were made by level three officials who were tasked to be concerned with South East Asia. At the other levels

---

* For some reason the only difference in the two statements was that Twining used the figure of 100 000 troops whereas Walters used 120 000.

Cambodia was not such an important issue. Analysis of the Presidential Papers for Reagan's second term reveals only one mention in 1985; and this occurred during a welcoming speech for Lee Kuan Yew and consisted of one short paragraph – 'most heartening has been the stand Singapore and its [ASEAN] colleagues have taken against the Vietnamese occupation of Cambodia'.[87] In 1986 there were four mentions which all dealt very briefly with support for the ASEAN position. A typical comment was that 'ASEAN's efforts are consistent with American desires to bring peaceful resolution to the tragic cycle of events that has plagued the Cambodia people'.[88] In 1987 there were even fewer comments than previously. 1988 saw an upturn in quantity even if the quality remained much the same.

There is, then, a degree of evidence which suggests the existence of a very definite administration reality. At the highest level there were only passing, infrequent, and bland comments about that reality. The detail was left to staff at the other levels who demonstrated a similarly neutral tone. In the reality constructed by the administration's declarations there were certain 'facts' – the Cambodian people were caught in a tragedy; the tragedy was generated by the Vietnamese and the KR in that order; ASEAN was an important trading partner; Thai security was at risk; the risk was the result of Vietnamese hegemonism; China was a superpower; superpowers are best dealt with by accommodation from strength; China backed the KR; the USSR was a superpower; the USSR backed Vietnam; Indochina was of only peripheral importance in foreign policy terms. The 'facts' were both established and reinforced by the rhetoric.

ALTERNATIVE REALITIES

During Reagan's second term there were five significant alternative realities. They were constructed by dissenters in Congress, by a coalition of Vietnam/PRK/USSR, by China, by ASEAN, and by the CGDK. In the international arena it was natural that the Reagan reality should be contested and, in obvious quarters, rejected. However, the pressure to which it was subjected by Congress was also considerable if, perhaps, less expected. Examining four particular hearings illustrates not only the construction of alternative realities within the US but also demonstrates the resilience of the elite's version.

Congress

In May 1985, early in the second term, there was a special hearing before an appropriation sub-committee called to debate, among other things, the so-called 'Solarz amendment'. In these hearings Solarz defended his proposal to provide the non-communist resistance with a $5 million aid package while Jim Leach (D, Iowa) as one example, opposed the aid. Solarz's opening statement pointed up an ironic reinterpretation of general American policy:

> In the 1960s the big question for the makers of American foreign policy was whether the United States should oppose wars of national liberation, and, if so, which ones. Now the wheel has turned, and the issue is whether the United States should support wars of national liberation, and, if so, which ones.[89]

The statement provides a fairly basic example of reconstructed reality.

While most witnesses, including those from State, Defense and the Khmer People's National Liberation Front (KPNLF), advocated granting the aid, or even increasing it, Jim Leach was vociferous in his opposition. Leach argued that it was 'not enough to conclude a cause is just. An assessment must also be made that the US involvement advances just goals.'[90] Leach's definition of American national interests involved the advancement of just goals as a predominant criterion. Such a definition would, however, seriously undermine the relatively fixed and ideological reality of the Reagan administration. Leach's moral absolutism was clearly at odds with the President's 'pragmatic idealism'.

In addition to the moral issues raised by Leach there were also practical concerns that the aid would inevitably lead to an Americanisation of the situation. Solarz's answer to such worries actually reinforced the administration's reality. He argued that the $5 million figure was not picked out of thin air but represented only 20–30 per cent of what was actually needed because it was 'important to preserve the principle that the primary responsibility for supporting the [NCR] lay with the other countries of Southeast Asia'.[91] Solarz countered any concerns that there could be a reintroduction of US combat forces by asserting that the '[NCR] have not asked for it; the ASEAN countries do not want it; and the Congress and the American people would never permit it'.[92] His response addressed the single most important factor in any US explanation of the situation – the absolute unacceptability of *direct* US involvement in the region.

In his rationalisation of the case for aid, Solarz again reinforced the basic principles of the US position in Indochina. He spoke of the PRK as an 'international pariah', of the support for aid by our 'friends in SE Asia', and finally of the greatly increased cost that an effective NCR would impose on Vietnam if it continued its occupation. Despite serious attempts to oppose the proposals the aid was approved.

Leach's opposition was relatively muted. Perhaps it was early in a new administration, or perhaps Leach was not naturally aggressive. *His* alternative was not sufficiently powerful to offer a significant threat to the Reaganite definition of the situation. In later hearings, however, questioners were less respectful, perhaps because the issue of the Khmer Rouge had begun to resurface, together with the realisation that the Vietnamese might be genuinely contemplating a withdrawal. If the Vietnamese were to withdraw then attention would be refocused on the Khmer Rouge and the moral time-bomb they represented. In 1987, therefore, Chester Atkins began to question the administration's reality concerning the KR. He said that 'while the United States says it opposes the return to power of the Khmer Rouge, the US supports the use of a revived and rearmed Khmer Rouge as an instrument of policy against Vietnam'.[93] This was a powerful statement and one that reappeared in an important hearing in July 1988. The hearing considered H. Con. Res. 271 'Expressing the sense of the Congress that the President should negotiate with the Government of Vietnam to establish interest sections'.[94]

Ostensibly a hearing to discuss the implications of establishing interest sections in Hanoi, it became a direct confrontation between two tactical approaches, ironically towards achieving basically similar foreign policy goals. The debate concerned the wisdom of holding the original course in the face of a change of circumstances. One view advocated continuing to isolate Vietnam given that those tactics had precipitated the change of circumstances, while the other held that a change in circumstances demanded a change in tactics. Naturally, both alternatives were predicated upon the view that US tactics *had* changed the circumstances, the complete Vietnamese withdrawal of late 1989 for example; of course that may not have been the case. Nevertheless, it had become the reality; both groups agreed that the US tactics to date had been successful.

Both views were expressed early in the hearings by the Chairman, Stephen Solarz, and Senator John McCain of Arizona. Solarz argued that the current tactics of trade and diplomatic isolation were 'beginning to bear fruit' and that a change in policy at that stage might have 'significantly demoralized the Cambodian resistance forces'.[95] He also pointed out that ASEAN did not favour the establishment of interest sections. Senator McCain was not convinced by the ASEAN argument and pointed up the inconsistency of the ASEAN position:

> As far as our ASEAN friends are concerned, let me remind the committee that four of the ASEAN countries have embassies in Hanoi, full-fledged embassies. One-third of Vietnam's free-world trade comes from the ASEAN nations. Their number three free-world trading partner is Singapore. So I find it a bit surprising that [they] criticize us for wanting to set up the barest, most elementary dialogue.[96]

The official replies to the McCain point are especially illuminating because they clearly show a reluctance to move away from, or question in any way, the established reality, i.e. support for ASEAN and distrust of the Vietnamese. In the first instance, Gaston Sigur (Assistant SoS, East Asian & Pacific Affairs) essentially ignored McCain's observations and simply restated administration policy:

> HCR 271 argues that an interests section would facilitate the resolution of the Cambodian conflict. In our view this is the wrong approach. Establishing interests sections would undercut our long-standing support for the ASEAN lead in efforts to achieve a settlement.[97]

There is no refutation of McCain's argument about ASEAN's double standards, simply a reaffirmation that US policy is to support ASEAN. Sigur continued by arguing that HCR 271 would represent a fundamental change in policy. He concluded that Hanoi would take sustenance from the decision while the NCR and others would interpret it as a weakening of US resolve. He actually accepted that Vietnamese withdrawal was genuinely happening and that Vietnam was, at the precise time of the hearings, engaged in negotiations at the Jakarta Informal Meeting (JIM). However, given that success was 'far from assured [the administration] opposed the passage of H.R.271'.[98]

Karl Jackson (Deputy Assistant SoD, East Asia and Pacific Affairs) echoed Sigur's sentiments, again arguing that HCR 271 would give succour to 'the hard-liners in Hanoi'.[99] In the light of a less than satisfactory response from Sigur and Jackson the attack was switched to the question of the Khmer Rouge. Under particularly hostile questioning from Chester (Chet) Atkins, Gaston Sigur seemed less assured. Atkins asked the following question:

I am curious as to how we can have a policy, and you can claim ASEAN has a policy, of no return to power of the Khmer Rouge while as we speak, Thailand is continuing to serve as a conduit for Chinese arms going to the Khmer Rouge and into Cambodia. What is our position on that, and what have we done with the Thais?[100]

Sigur prevaricated before Solarz came to the rescue and stated, 'to be very clear about it, our policy is *not* to urge the Chinese and Thais to terminate their support for the Khmer Rouge prior to withdrawal by Vietnam'[101] (emphasis added). Sigur continued to bluster until a specific exchange with Atkins exposed the primacy of the Vietnamese withdrawal in US regional policy. Atkins asked Sigur whether the US 'commitment to pressing the Thais and Chinese to end their assistance to the Khmer Rouge [was] predicated on Vietnamese withdrawal. In the absence of that withdrawal we are not objecting to any aid for the Khmer Rouge'. Sigur answered, 'I don't like to put it quite that way', and Atkins responded, 'But that is the way it is.'[102] This form of question and answer continued for some time until Solarz refocused on the moral dilemma. He reasoned that the administration found it difficult to respond effectively to the questions because they could not 'permit [them]selves to be in a moral posture where [they] were sort of winking at strengthening these genocidal fanatics'.[103] Jackson immediately retorted, 'We are not winking at strengthening these genocidal fanatics. If I thought such was the case, I would resign my office right now.'[104] They were, and he did not. Ironically the administration was saved on this issue by the Vietnamese. Foreign Minister Nguyen Co Thach took offence at some of Sigur's comments in the hearing and suspended an agreement to search for MIAs, and Congress consequently 'backed away from the interest-sections legislation'.[105]

The other hearing at which the administration's reality was tested also occurred in June–July 1988. The hearing and mark up on House Joint Resolution 602 was entitled 'Hope for Cambodia: Preventing the Return of the Khmer Rouge'.[106] This was a strange hearing during which the process by which alternative realities are constructed was almost visible. Witnesses included, for example, not only Dith Pran, the subject of the film *The Killing Fields*, but the actor, Haing Ngor, who had portrayed Dith Pran in the film. These men were called upon to testify to the horrors that existed in Cambodia, primarily, it seemed, as a backdrop to a debate about the best way to sideline the KR. Stephen Solarz's opening statement admitted as much. He argued that Cambodia had reached a point of both promise and danger. The promise resulted from the impending Vietnamese withdrawal, the danger from the vacuum that withdrawal might create, and which the KR might exploit. He also said that any such exploitation 'would be both morally unacceptable and politically unthinkable ... how to prevent it? That is the question which we gather today to consider.'[107]

Unfortunately, at no stage did the administration's representatives actually address that question, choosing only to chant their Cambodian mantra:

> we are totally opposed to a return to power by the Khmer Rouge ... we have joined with ASEAN in putting political and economic pressure on Vietnam ... we have maintained a total trade embargo ... offered political and material support to the [NCR] ... given strong backing to Prince Sihanouk ... but continue to be sceptical about Vietnamese intentions ... we abhor the Khmer Rouge.[108]

Chester Atkins harangued both Lambertson and Jackson on the timidity of the actions taken by the administration. Again it is worth quoting him at length because his monologue clearly identifies an alternative view of reality. His statement is as follows:

> I frankly want to express my anger at the policy which both of you represent.... We have a policy that is obsessed with the Vietnamese withdrawal ... But withdrawal is happening. We all know it ... the real issue, the fundamental issue is the Khmer Rouge and you both politely dance around what I believe is one of the fundamental moral questions of our time.... And I think we ought to look at our history in this region, because frankly, it is a history of not wanting to know what has happened so that we could cover our moral backsides after it happened. It is a history of the strongest rhetoric accompanied by the most timid actions ... the US is just not willing to go the distance on this issue.[109]

Lambertson's only response was to reassert that 'it would be unrealistic to attempt to convince either the Chinese or the Thai to cut off the Khmer Rouge in the manner suggested while fighting is still going on with Vietnam'.[110] What is demonstrated here is a simple conflict between views of the world; in one *realpolitik* rules, in the other moral issues must be accommodated. Interestingly, the passing of H. J. Res.

602 on 8 August 1988 *did* have a qualifying effect upon at least declaratory US foreign policy towards Cambodia. When signing the law pursuant to H. J. Res. 602 (Public Law No 100–502, 18 October 1988) President Reagan said that he disagreed 'with the wording of certain clauses, which as written could complicate our efforts to work with other governments to achieve the objective we all seek: to prevent the Khmer Rouge from ever again being in a position of absolute authority'.[111] On the same day Vernon Walters told the UN General Assembly that his government had recently 'approved [H. J. Res. 602] and it was signed by President Reagan. It reflects the overwhelming bipartisan sentiment in the United States for a total withdrawal of Vietnamese forces and for the prevention of a Khmer Rouge return to power.'[112]

Walters' statement represents a partial and non-controversial view of reality while Reagan's exposed the rigidity of the administration's pragmatism. Presumably when referring to 'certain clauses', Reagan meant points (3) and (4) of the resolution. Point (3) 'implores those nations continuing to arm the Khmer Rouge to cease the flow of war material and the accumulation of caches of arms that might ultimately be used to terrorize the Cambodian people and to threaten a legitimate government of Cambodia'. Point (4) concerns the Genocide Convention and the call that those responsible 'should be held accountable under international law'. The President's only reservation in confirming these points must surely have been the fear of upsetting the Chinese and the Thais. If that *was* the explanation then it confirms Atkins' analysis of the situation.

The alternative reality constructed in Congress did not contest many of the administration's facts but did reject the emphasis placed upon them, and the speed with which a change in that emphasis should have resulted in policy changes. When Atkins talked of a history in the region and 'the strongest rhetoric accompanied by the most timid actions' he was registering a view which, despite all the other considerations, found the continued influence of the KR abhorrent. He shared that 'fact' with the administration but for Atkins, and others, it was that fact which should have been pre-eminent. Solarz once said, 'a continuation of the Vietnamese occupation would be morally preferable to a return of the Khmer Rouge if that were the only possible consequence of a Vietnamese withdrawal'.[113] If it had been the *only* alternative then presumably policy would have changed; accommodation with Vietnam would have been made, interests sections opened, the US would have led and not merely followed

ASEAN, China would have been admonished and perhaps even sanctioned. An alternative reality need not necessarily dispute facts, it might simply be the result of a different perception of the significance of those facts.

However, some other realities do dispute the facts. When states, either directly or indirectly, involved in the conflict begin to define their own realities such disagreements are revealed. For obvious reasons states with empathetic world-views construct similar or complementary realities. The Soviet Union, Vietnam and the PRK provide just such a case.

Soviet Union/Vietnam/PRK

The basic tenets underpinning the Communist realities were, relatively speaking, not subject to change in quite the same way as in the US where administrations changed on a more regular basis. So that, in 1985, for example, the 'facts' were almost identical to those that had pertained since 1979 – the KR were genocidal; the Vietnamese had assisted the PRK in saving the Khmer people and would withdraw once Cambodian security was guaranteed; the Chinese, willingly aided and abetted by the US and Thailand, and less willingly by the remainder of ASEAN, continued to provide arms and succour to the KR; the Soviet Union provided support for Vietnam; there was a *natural* Indochinese alliance which consisted of Vietnam, Laos and Cambodia; the CGDK was dominated by the KR; Vietnamese security was threatened.

Statements derived from the above were predictable in content, tone and language. Whenever the occupation of Cambodia was at issue notions of 'invitations' and the 'volunteer' status of the Vietnamese in Cambodia were invariably mentioned. When withdrawal was mentioned then the elimination of Pol Pot was also always included, it became almost a collocation. The language used was extremely stylised for Western tastes but it would be a mistake to describe them as codifications, they were simple statements of 'fact' as the Vietnamese saw them. Below is a common example in which Vo Dong Giang (a member of the Council of Ministers) explains the Vietnamese views to the UN General Assembly:

> Should a solution guaranteeing the security and sovereignty of all States and peoples in the region, including Kampuchea, be reached, the total withdrawal of Vietnamese volunteer forces

would be completed before the 1990 deadline unilaterally decided upon by the Governments of Viet Nam and Kampuchea. Kampuchea has declared its readiness to discuss national reconciliation based on the elimination of the Pol Pot clique and the organization of general elections after the total withdrawal of Vietnamese volunteer forces from Kampuchea. (4 October 1984, A/40/PV.23)[114]

In that one short statement the concepts of threatened security and sovereignty, volunteer forces (twice), withdrawal, a Pol Pot clique, the integrity of Vietnam and the PRK, and general elections are reinforced. Less than a month later the General Assembly reviewed the situation in Kampuchea. Maligna Saignavongs (Laos) spoke of the PRK as the sole representative of the Kampuchean people, of the CGDK being a façade for representatives of a 'genocidal regime' and welcomed efforts by ASEAN to develop a dialogue 'on an equal footing, without any side imposing its views on the other and without external interference'.[115] Two simple statements in the UN had thus effectively defined the basic facts of one version of reality.

Naturally embellishments were necessary to enhance the status of this particular version. For example, the policies based upon it had to be seen to be successful and as such political legitimacy and military victories were important factors. Consequently the massive dry-season offensive of 1984–85 was unreservedly claimed as a success. Nhan Dan (the *Party's Daily* in Vietnam) reported the 1984–85 dry-season offensive stating that:

> the Kampuchean armed forces and people, assisted by Vietnamese army volunteers ha[d] won the biggest victory since February 1979 … accelerating the disintegration of the genocidal Pol Pot gang … and the collapse of Peking's scheme against the revival of the Kampuchean people.[116]

Later in the same article Thailand and the US were implicated in the anti-Vietnamese alliance. It was argued that the dry-season successes had angered 'the Peking hegemonist-expansionists and the US imperialists [who had] stimulated their Bangkok puppets openly to carry out armed provocations'.[117] It was a nice touch for the supporters of a 'puppet' regime in Cambodia to apply the term 'puppet' to Thailand.

The final requirement of the Vietnamese–PRK–Soviet construct was to develop a growing legitimacy for the PRK regime and a belief in an eventual *de facto* victory. In an interview with Hanoi radio in early 1985, Hun Sen said that 1984 'could be considered a year when the country's international prestige was consolidated and developed to a higher level than ever before'.[118] Opening the tenth Indochinese Foreign Ministers Conference (IFMC) in Ho Chi Minh City, Nguyen Co Thach said that he was 'confident that within five to ten years time the so-called Kampuchean problem will of itself be settled even in the absence of a negotiated settlement'.[119] Both comments attempted to establish a momentum for the idea that the position in Cambodia was irreversible. It was a tactic used continually; in mid-1987, for example, Nhan Dan was proudly stating that the international prestige of the PRK had continued to grow and the 'fact is that nobody can reverse the situation in Kampuchea'.[120]

Statements from the PRK also attempted to consolidate the regime. For example, Hun Sen always rejected the notion of international control of the country because it implicitly repudiated the legitimacy of his government. He argued that 'Cambodia [was] not a losing country like Germany or Japan in World War Two, it [was] not necessary to bring in a peacekeeping force to keep control over the Cambodian government.'[121] Any idea that the PRK would be dismantled in favour of a quadripartite government had to be rejected. The Vietnamese–PRK reality was built upon the notion that the repetition of certain articles of faith would provide an impregnable structure; viewed from the *inside* it probably did.

The Soviet Union mostly went along with the Vietnamese version and statements of mutual affection were common. At the sixth Vietnamese Party Congress, for example, 'solidarity and all-round cooperation with the Soviet Union', was described as 'the cornerstone in the foreign policy of our party and state'.[122] The Soviet view became slightly more restrained over the course of the period under review possibly because their experience in Afghanistan had chastened them and the reverberations of glasnost and perestroika were being felt in the realms of foreign policy. In an interview with the *Lao Party Paper*, Eduard Shevardnadze made the following, slightly cryptic, remark, 'although we have a certain means of settlement we will not allow ourselves to force any democratic state to accept it'.[123] Presumably his 'certain means' was the withdrawal of financial support. The tone of the statement conveys the menace that the word 'yet' might be added at a later stage. The Soviet Union was beginning to *need* to disengage but did not want to create the impression of an unreliable ally. Nevertheless, it was obvious that Cambodia was not high on Moscow's list of priorities. When Gorbachev addressed the UN in late 1988 he did not mention Indochina at all; and neither did Reagan. Their thoughts were for each other and already client states were becoming less significant.

The ties between the Soviet Union and Vietnam truly represented a marriage of convenience. However, in the late 1980s, it was becoming a relationship of dependence rather than interdependence and both parties were beginning to show signs of discomfort. An interesting observation was made on the relationship by a Vietnamese official talking to Mr Lagomarsino, Chairman of the Congressional Task Force on POWs and MIAs. Lagomarsino quotes the Vietnamese official as saying, 'we beat the French, we beat the Americans, we beat the Chinese and we didn't do that just to become a puppet of the Soviet Union'.[124] It seems most unlikely that the Soviets would not be aware of such a mood, and notwithstanding their reluctance to lose Cam Ranh Bay as a warm water port, would have been quietly pressurising the Vietnamese to withdraw from Cambodia no matter how embarrassing that might prove. Ironically the Soviet policy of disengagement was very similar to the Americans' although generated by a separate reality.

China

The Chinese, by contrast to the Soviets and Americans, continued to be fairly vitriolic in their rhetoric and also quite consistent. Throughout the period of the second Reagan term the Chinese rhetoric never altered. The Vietnamese were expansionist, hegemonic and untrustworthy. The following statements from the Chinese government encompass virtually all aspects of its position on Cambodia:

China firmly supports the anti-Vietnamese patriotic forces in their just struggle, strongly condemns the crimes of invasion by the Vietnamese troops and demands that the Vietnamese authorities immediately stop their atrocities of ravaging and slaughtering the Kampuchean people. (Xinhua)[125]

... if Vietnam continued to make provocations along the Sino-Vietnamese border in a frenzied way, China reserved its right to teach Vietnam a second lesson. (Wu Xueqian, Chinese Foreign Ministry)[126]

The so-called complete withdrawal of troops from Kampuchea by 1990 is a sheer hoax, the aim of which is to eliminate the resistance forces and perpetrate Viet Nam's control over Kampuchea. (Wu Xueqian, address to UNGA)[127]

China's world-view consisted of friends, enemies and those with whom you were required to do business. Movement in and between those categories was infinitely flexible. During the second half of the 1980s China's enemies were the Soviet Union (global) and Vietnam (regional); friends, in a loose sense, included Thailand and the Khmer Rouge; business was carried out with virtually anybody else. For China the overriding reality was represented by the perceived Soviet threat and Vietnam carried security significance primarily due to Soviet support. China believed that 'without Soviet assistance, Vietnam [could] not sustain the fighting in Cambodia for a single day'.[128] If the threats China perceived were removed, then China would be content.

ASEAN

One of the groups with which China did business was ASEAN. Although some of ASEAN's members were still wary of China their policies, to a large extent, coincided. The ASEAN reality consisted of a potential market place riven with discord. All that the situation required was a mediator since for ASEAN it was axiomatic that all parties desired stability in order to trade. ASEAN aspired to be the honest broker. The way ahead consisted of a series of bi-lateral or multi-lateral compromises which would be organised by the ASEAN states. Throughout the period 1985–88 ASEAN was also being courted by the Vietnam/PRK camp in an effort to legitimise themselves and also possibly to sever ASEAN ties with the US. At the IFMC in January 1985, for example, the final communiqué noted that several ASEAN states appeared willing to develop their bi-lateral relations with Vietnam and Laos.[129] This ploy, of undermining the unity of the opposition, was continually employed by the Vietnamese. Although on occasions it seemed to have some chance of success the breakthrough never occurred; in fact, the vote in the UN on ASEAN's annual resolution calling for Vietnamese withdrawal reached its height in 1988 with 122 in favour, 19 against and 13 abstentions. Perhaps the margin of victory reflected the slight modifications made to the resolution. Reference to the KR had been altered to read 'the non-return to the universally condemned policies and practices of the recent past'.[130] This allowed the vexed problem of how to accommodate the KR elite to be side-stepped for a time. Their 'practices' had been disavowed but the individuals themselves were not mentioned.

Tactically ASEAN continued to play whatever cards were available. Indonesia, for example, acted unilaterally, reasoning that a settlement of the Cambodian conflict would remove the reason for Thailand's close alliance with China which they viewed as unwelcome. At separate times ASEAN supported both the eight-point plan proposed by the CGDK[131] and the six-point plan proposed by Hun Sen.[132] Although ASEAN also counselled a regional solution, by 1988 the Malaysian Prime Minister, Mahathir Mohamad, was arguing for an international presence, 'United Nations must accept a role in Cambodia if we are going to have a Cambodia that is viable. Otherwise we are going to throw the Cambodians at the mercy of people who are capable of all kinds of atrocious things.'[133] All ASEANs wanted was to get a process, *any* process, under way as soon as possible. ASEAN needed to halt the conflict because war is bad for business.

CGDK

The same could not be said of the CGDK which was riven by dissent. The CGDK reality consisted of an external invader and internal enemies who would be dealt with in turn. The major unifying element within the loose CGDK was Prince Sihanouk. However, while he was a constant presence, his was not a constant voice. He was constantly redefining the situation, sometimes subtly, sometimes outlandishly. In 1986, for example, he was warning the UN of impending onslaughts by the Vietnamese which would not, however, 'subdue our national resistance and our people's will for independence'.[134] In the same speech, he also offered olive branches by promising a non-aggression pact with Vietnam and no-reprisals against collaborators, but only *after* Vietnamese withdrawal.

A year later Sihanouk was repeating the theme and also building up the credibility of the CGDK forces. He argued that their forces were within striking range of Phnom Penh and their recent eight-point proposal proved their sincerity and although 'the Vietnamese leaders are, by their aggression against Kampuchea, war criminals, just as were Hitler and his Nazi disciples, we will not ask for revenge, punishment or war damages'.[135] The rhetoric was pure Sihanouk, even down to the transference of the Nazi imagery from Pol Pot to the Vietnamese. However, the rhetoric maintained the reality in which the removal of the Vietnamese was paramount with other issues subordinated until withdrawal had occurred.

The KR were just such an issue. Sihanouk was one of the first to articulate the view that marginalising the KR was virtually impossible and eliminating them *was* impossible. In September 1988, Sihanouk made the following comment during a visit to Singapore, 'If you exclude [the KR], they will try to destabilize the new government. So, in order for the new government to have a chance of establishing itself through democratic stability and peace, we must include the [KR] in the government.'[136]

As early as 1985 Sihanouk had been preparing the way for at least a partial rehabilitation of the KR. In February he said the 'people of Cambodia support not only Son Sann and Sihanouk, but they also support the Khmer Rouge. Otherwise, you can't explain why they are so strong.'[137] Later he argued that Pol Pot was 'the only man capable of weakening the Vietnamese ... not winning, but bleeding, so everybody needs Pol Pot'.[138] Sihanouk realised that it was not possible to ignore the KR, they had to be accommodated. Naturally such an interpretation was anathema to the US with its total public repudiation of any involvement for the KR. Perhaps that partly accounts for American attempts to build up Son Sann and the KPNLF. The KR reality was, perhaps, most chillingly expressed by Dr Haing Ngor when he explained their philosophy, 'when the water rises, the fish eat the ants; when the water recedes, the ants eat the fish'.[139] He added that there were no Cambodians who did not understand exactly what was meant by such a statement.

The alternative realities constructed in Congress, Hanoi, Phnom Penh and Moscow, China and Battambang, the ASEAN capitals, and wherever Sihanouk resided, represented either challenges to, or confirmations of, that constructed by the Reagan administration. The amalgam of the various realities constructed below provides a datum from which to gauge the degree of deviation for each alternative.

AMALGAM OF REALITIES

Attempts to define an 'objective' reality inevitably congregate around certain events which can be considered as incontrovertible – a specific UN debate, a meeting in Jakarta, the official granting of aid – these are events that can be agreed. One such 'event' was the dry-season offensive of 1984–85. The Vietnamese launched a massive attack against all resistance groups in their established bases along the Thai border areas. It is generally conceded that the offensive was successful;[140] eight Pol Pot bases, seven of Son Sann's and one Sihanoukist base were destroyed, with joint resistance losses (dead, injured, deserted) amounting to 10 000. That, at least, was the assessment given by Hun Sen at a press conference in April.[141] The truth of his statement was irrelevant since he was able to assert that as a result of the victories a further 15 000 Vietnamese troops were being withdrawn. In the following August, Hun Sen issued another statement, from the IFMC in Phnom Penh, which again indicated that withdrawal was being completed earlier than expected because of speedier victories.[142] Thus the 'image' of a successful offensive allowed the Vietnamese to withdraw with honour.

Of course it might be argued that pressure from Moscow, whose own finances were under stress, had really forced the Vietnamese withdrawal. Hun Sen was able to exert rhetorical pressure by adding, at the end of the August statement, that 'the PRK was willing to talk to Sihanouk and Son Sann provided they dissociated themselves from Pol Pot and his clique'. Five days later Nguyen Co Thach confirmed Hun Sen's version of reality when he repeated Hun Sen's comments during a visit to Jakarta.[143] Although by no means the dominant reality these public statements show how reality develops.

Unfortunately, for Hanoi and Phnom Penh, the offensive only really succeeded in solidifying ASEAN's diplomatic resistance. During the offensive, for example, every ASEAN state expressed their concern to their respective Soviet ambassadors. At the ASEAN foreign ministers' meeting in Bangkok (11–12 February 1985) the offensive merely convinced ASEAN to mount a campaign for military assistance, primarily from the US. As Mochtar Kusumaatmadja (Indonesia) said, 'why should one party only get aid? The Soviet Union is supplying the Vietnamese, and they are the aggressor. While the victims (the Khmer resistance forces) don't get any aid.'[144] The conference communiqué called on the international community to increase assistance to the Kampuchean people, including direct military aid. Another ASEAN Foreign Minister went even further and argued that the international community 'must go all out to build [the NCR] up in military terms'.[145] Therefore, it could be argued that in political terms the result of the dry-season offensive was the opposite of that which the Vietnamese would have hoped for and expected.

Later in 1985, in part as a response to ASEAN's request, the US Congress agreed to $5 million aid to the NCR for FY 1986 and FY 1987. The offensive, and the rhetoric it spawned, had provided only temporary success for the PRK. Even the resistance forces admitted that faults in their own strategies had been exposed by the offensive and as a consequence by 1986 they had 'begun to display an ability to regroup and to revise the nature of their military operations'.[146] This was not the environment the Vietnamese would have hoped for as the result of a militarily successful dry-season campaign.

1986 and 1987 witnessed the gradual acceleration of superpower accommodation, Sino-American, Sino-Soviet, and Soviet-American. These new attitudes trickled down to their respective regional clients. Early in 1986 William Bach made an important and prophetic assessment of the position that Cambodia played in Sino-Soviet relations. He said, 'Cambodia's importance derives mainly from the Sino-Soviet global competition, not from its intrinsic interest to either giant, the conflict will diminish if the two communist states make significant strides towards detente'.[147] Less than six months after that assessment, Gorbachev made his major foreign policy speech at Vladivostok (28 July 1986) in which Sino-Soviet rapprochement was given considerable encouragement. Three months later Deputy Foreign Minister Rogachev announced Soviet willingness to include Cambodia on the agenda of the ninth round of Sino-Soviet normalisation talks.

In 1986, then, the attitude and, therefore, the language of the Sino-Soviet relationship had changed. Gorbachev was still reluctant to abandon Vietnam but he also realised that Vietnamese occupation was a serious obstacle to rapprochement. By the end of the year Truong Chinh, who had taken over the position of General Secretary of the Vietnamese Communist Party when Le Duan died in July, had conceded that Vietnamese leaders had been 'guilty of serious shortcomings and errors', especially economically.[148] It is not possible to prove cause and effect between Soviet pressure and Chinh's statement but it is as plausible an explanation as any other.

If Moscow's desire to normalise with China was pressuring Vietnam then the US's desire to retain Chinese goodwill brought pressure to bear on the NCR. March and April 1986 provided evidence of such pressure when the NCR made their eight-point proposal for ending the conflict which included, among other things, a non-aggression pact with Vietnam. The proposal was made in Peking, endorsed by ASEAN, although the Indonesians were again lukewarm, and supported by the United States. By 1987 the progress towards some sort of settlement was beginning to accelerate. There were signs throughout the year that most parties were preparing to compromise. As regional specialist, Muthiah Alagappa, said, '[u]ntil 1987 the principal actors were not ready for compromise',[149] by 1987 they clearly were. The Vietnamese became more active on the diplomatic front and expressed their desire to resolve the dispute, probably because they were 'feeling the weight of [their] Cambodian policy'.[150] ASEAN's Indonesian intermediary, Mochtar Kusumaatmadja, visited Ho Chi Minh City in July 1987 in an attempt to set up the so-called 'cocktail diplomacy'[151] which would allow the Cambodia parties to meet at a later date in Jakarta 'on the basis of an equal footing, without preconditions and with no political labels'.[152]

Sihanouk, who had yet again temporarily resigned from the CGDK in May, decided to meet with Hun Sen later in the year. This naturally caused a split in the CGDK because any talks without Vietnamese presence tacitly legitimised the PRK. Nevertheless, the two met first in France (2–4 December 1987) and external support for the venture was unexpectedly uniform. Massamba Sarré, the Chairman of the ad hoc committee of the ICK reported that Son Sann and Khieu Samphan had also been invited, that Vietnam and the USSR supported the idea and that China backed Sihanouk, as did ASEAN.[153] And lastly, at least tacit support came from the US. In the first week of August General John Vessey, the Chairman of the US Joint Chiefs of Staff, visited Hanoi as a special representative of President Reagan. He was the first high-level US visitor since 1977 and represented a further indication of the willingness of both parties to compromise.

In 1988 progress continued apace. In January Hun Sen and Sihanouk met again and Sihanouk pressed ASEAN to proceed with 'proximity talks', a request which eventually led to the Jakarta Informal Meeting (JIM) taking place in July 1988. The JIM carried over the proposals of the 'Ho Chi Minh City Understanding' (July 1987) of 'equal footing' and 'no pre-conditions'. At the end of 1987 Vietnam had withdrawn the majority of its forces from Laos and throughout 1988 activity increased. The Secretary General's Special Representative Rafeeuddin Ahmed, for example, twice visited the region in June/July and September in order to circulate 'specific ideas for a framework for a comprehensive political settlement'.[154] The ad hoc committee noted that 'there seemed to be a general convergence of views and interests for an early solution to the Kampuchean problem'.[155]

Perhaps the single most important event of the period 1985–89 occurred on 15 May 1988. On that day Soviet troops began to withdraw from Afghanistan. Within a month the *Washington Post* was reporting that the Soviet Union was sounding out the United States to act as 'guarantors' of a Cambodian settlement – much as they had done with the Afghanistan Geneva accords.[156] At the same time, Nguyen Co Thach had his first meeting for over two years with Thai officials and also announced that he *would* attend the 'cocktail party' meeting in Jakarta (JIM). Prior to JIM the Chinese also issued a formal statement on a Cambodian solution and George Shultz announced that discussions with Deng Xiaoping were 'very fruitful and worthwhile' and the two nations had 'rather similar views on the Cambodian situation'.[157] The Chinese even excused their own backing for the KR on the grounds that it was only an anti-Vietnamese tactic and they did not actually support a KR return to power.[158] After the JIM Shultz confirmed that 'Both Beijing and Moscow [were] believed eager to end the Cambodian conflict in order to mend their own bilateral relations';[159] and in late August the US and China held five days of talks in Beijing which were the first in three years of talks between the two which concentrated specifically on Cambodia.

As the views of most of the actors were beginning to converge around a reality which did not include the Khmer Rouge, so Prince Sihanouk, who had once, and would again, argue that they *had* to be accommodated, began to attempt to distance himself from them. On the eve of the JIM talks Sihanouk delivered a series of answers to questions prepared by Elizabeth Becker of the *Washington Post*. The central theme of his answers was his *divorce* from the KR, coupled with a warning of the responsibility that would have to be borne by CGDK supporters 'for a new holocaust ... which [was] becoming inevitable, with the impending Vietnamese withdrawal'.[160] Sihanouk seized the opportunity to create a reality in which only support for him could prevent a return to the killing fields.

By the end of 1988 Sihanouk had resumed talks with Hun Sen and Son Sann but not Khieu Samphan; he had also visited Ronald Reagan and George Shultz in Washington. Immediately after the Reagan meeting, Sihanouk attempted to force the pace by revealing that he had been 'told that covert CIA assistance to the resistance forces would not only be increased but could also be used to buy weapons'.[161] The State Department immediately denied Sihanouk's assertions. Sihanouk's manoeuvrings provided a telling metaphor for the manoeuvrings of all the actors in the Cambodian drama. The amalgam of realities had condensed to what it usually turns out to be – the resultant of contending superpower interests. The rhetoric had changed subtly to reflect the fine adjustments in world-views, the regional clients reacting accordingly. It is, perhaps, appropriate that the intransigent Chinese should have the final words in this section since they had performed a considerable shift since 1985. On 19 December 1988 Li Peng, China's Premier said,

> If Vietnam withdraws its troops, all sides, including China, should suspend military support to all parties in Cambodia. To put the mind of the international community at rest, all sides may even gradually reduce such military support in step with the tempo of the [Vietnamese] troop withdrawal.[162]

The value of this political rhetoric is demonstrated by the fact that for years after the complete withdrawal of the Vietnamese, China were still supporting the Khmer Rouge, albeit less fulsomely.

CONCLUSION

US foreign policy towards Cambodia during the second Reagan period might easily be described as a highly successful manifestation of the Reagan doctrine. Admittedly the doctrine had quite clearly been less successful in Nicaragua but in Cambodia, by the end of the Reagan presidency, most Vietnamese troops had already withdrawn, the major US goal had thus been achieved. Reagan's own assessment of his foreign policy could also be understood. In his farewell address he said, '[t]he fact is, from Grenada to the Washington and Moscow summits, from the recession of '81 and '82, to the expansion that...continues to this day, we've made a difference'.[163]

Other assessments differed from Reagan's. They argued that Reagan's foreign policy was one of imperial pretension coupled with tough rhetoric but actually characterised by small-scale actions.[164] Gary Wills is even more critical; he argues that during the Reagan period the 'very fabric of our politics was shot through with unreality ... "Keep lying to us" was the implicit plea of the electorate'.[165] Similarly Kenneth Sharpe accused the Reagan administration of turning 'inward to a pattern of deception and lies ... to make reality fit its vision' of what foreign policy should be.[166] Both Wills and Sharpe missed the point: individuals and groups do not make reality fit a vision; the vision is generated *by* their reality, and politics cannot be 'shot through with unreality' because that implies the existence of an objective reality. Reagan's foreign policy, especially towards Cambodia, was remarkably consistent over both terms and that is not a normative statement. The Reagan rhetoric remained tough throughout his presidency and his actions remained low-key. Attacks on Libya and Grenada represented the limited uses of force that Reagan undertook. In Cambodia, the US was not inclined to be the leader and was content to follow ASEAN directly and China indirectly, allowing them to assume the main roles. United States' foreign policy towards Cambodia, under Reagan, accurately reflected the Reagan world-view. More clearly, as Coral Bell had supposed, the main interest in the Reagan years probably surrounded 'the importance of declaratory as against operational signals, image against substance, words against deeds'.[167] As Bell herself conceded, in many instances image *was* substance and Reagan's second term may well have fallen into that category. The Indochinese reality constructed by the Reagan administration changed very little from that of the first term, reinforcing the relative insignificance of Cambodia as a foreign policy issue.

4 The Bush Administration, 1989–93

[Vietnam] cleaves us still. But, friends, that war began in earnest a quarter of a century ago, and surely the statute of limitations has been reached. This is a fact: The final lesson of Vietnam is that no great nation can long afford to be sundered by a memory.

Inaugural Address of President George Bush, 20 January 1989

Unlike the previous chapters, this one addresses a reality constructed from a view of the way the world works rather than one constructed from a view of the world. As the 'pragmatic President' the Bush reality was predicated upon the notion that virtually everything was negotiable. His world-view was concerned with a perceived 'objective' reality and he was the arch exponent of the dictum that politics is the art of the possible. The passage quoted above was as close as George Bush came to being specific in what he himself described as a 'thematic speech'.[1] The Bush inaugural was littered with references to 'new beginnings' and 'new breezes blowing' and 'freedom'. In all there were fourteen uses of 'new' and thirteen of 'free'. This was a speech in which Bush was at pains to promote an image of his leadership style and way of doing business, not of a world-view, because he distrusted the 'vision thing'.[2]

His style was 'folksie': '[w]e meet today on democracy's front porch. A good place to talk as neighbours and friends.' He spoke of the victory of democracy and criticised overly materialistic values; he signalled the beginning of an anti-drugs campaign; he 'yearn[ed] for a greater tolerance and easy goingness about each other's attitudes and way of life'; he saw the 'need for a new engagement ... between the Executive and Congress ... For Congress has changed in our time. There has grown a certain divisiveness.'

However, despite Bush's appeals for goodwill he was not unwilling to coerce agreement if that appeared necessary. He hinted as much at the traditional press conference the day after his inauguration. Bush made it clear that he would attempt to get things done in foreign policy with, or without, Congressional support. He explained that the 'President has unique responsibilities under the Constitution for foreign policy and for the national security ... and I intend to carry those out'.[3] For Bush foreign policy was important and his lack of involvement as Vice-President must have been extremely frustrating.

As with previous administrations it was unlikely that Cambodia would figure prominently on Bush's foreign policy agenda as he took office. However, one event and the circumstances surrounding it, was to generate the first significant change in policy towards Indochina in over a decade and illustrate in a very clear manner how, in order to adjust the administration's foreign policy, it was necessary, and relatively simple, to *re*construct reality. That event was the unilateral withdrawal of Vietnamese forces from Cambodia. The announcement of the withdrawal occurred less than three months after the inauguration. It meant that the number one US policy priority in the region had been achieved. This, in turn, meant the underbelly of US policy was exposed – the involvement of the Khmer Rouge.

The moral debate resurfaced and a strange alliance formed within the US to counter the administration's interpretation of the situation. Individuals from Congress, the media, academia and NGOs congregated around a more or less similar world-view. As early as January 1989 an article in the *Washington Post* encapsulated the elements of this counter view. It invoked the Nazi imagery related to Pol Pot and argued that 'unless the US reordered its priorities and revamped its strategy the Khmer Rouge would return to power' and 'now that the Vietnamese are departing', resisting the KR should be the top priority. The article also rejected the deference accorded to China arguing that 'if Beijing rejects suggestions [to desert the KR], so what?'[4] The fear of a Khmer Rouge return, filling the vacuum left by the Vietnamese, remained a strong theme of the opposition throughout the first half of the Bush administration.

The administration itself did not dismiss those fears, rather it tried to accommodate them within what it considered was a pragmatic acceptance of reality. Less than a month before the Vietnamese withdrawal, for instance, Secretary of State (SoS) James A. Baker III had said that 'giving the Khmer Rouge a role in a future Cambodian government was a fact of life ... you're going to have the Khmer Rouge there'.[5] Naturally other actors with other realities were also relevant but were essentially tangential to the two main competing realities. In simple terms the competition could be reduced to a battle between totally rejecting complicity in genocide and accepting some complicity as the only practical option. However, Cambodia retained a unique characteristic. It was 'the place where the Khmer Rouge lurked in the woods'.[6] It fell to the Bush administration to deal with that fact.

THE ADMINISTRATION

In an effort to avoid another Brzezinski, Ronald Reagan had deliberately downgraded the role of the NSA and in so doing created the environment which permitted Iran-gate. The Bush solution was to select an NSA who could wield the power necessary to control the NSC while remaining a team player. Bush has said of his selection, Brent Scowcroft, when referring to Iran-gate:

> it couldn't and wouldn't have happened under Brent Scowcroft. His conduct as NSC chief was a model.... He didn't try to make the NSC into a policy-making agency. He knew that the United States didn't need two Secretaries of State and two Secretaries of Defense.[7]

Bush was very aware of relative responsibilities, often using team analogies and, therefore, while his admiration for Scowcroft was enormous his [Scowcroft's] influence on foreign *policy* was significantly less than that of the formal holder of foreign policy responsibility – the Secretary of State. It was also true that the Secretary of Defense (SoD) was clearly situated below the SoS on foreign policy matters. As a consequence there is some difficulty in defining, particularly on foreign policy, the levels within the Bush court. Obviously Bush himself is located at level one and that is especially true on international issues which Bush considered his forté. Baker is also clearly on level two. However, it is the relative positioning of the other members of the court which causes some difficulty. The most reasonable explanation seems to be that everyone else is situated at level three, although some actors are more equal than others.

The Bush administration was also very much personality driven in foreign affairs. During the Gulf War, for example, the 'excom' consisted of what was referred to as the 'Gang of Eight', Bush, Baker, Cheney (SoD), Scowcroft, Gates (deputy NSA), Sununu (White House CoS), Powell (JCS) and Quayle (VP).[8] When these eight met they effectively by-passed the NSC structure. Even though Scowcroft and Gates were present they were there as individuals and not really representing the NSC. There was no significant consultation with the

NSC on the Gulf and it is said that the same was true of the Panama coup attempt in October 1989, the December 1989 attempted coup in the Philippines and the Christmas 1989 Panama invasion.[9] Reagan's marginalisation of the NSC ended under Bush, primarily because Scowcroft was a close personal confidant of the President.

The Bush administration was built around personal relationships and experience. Initial appointments were invariably Washington insiders and pragmatists who 'knew the value of loyalty to the boss'.[10] Ninety per cent of the Bush cabinet had previously held government posts, mostly in the Ford administration.[11] The President himself was unparalleled in his experience of the foreign policy machinery having been Vice-President, director of the CIA, ambassador at the UN and an emissary in China. The other crucial element in the administration was subordination to the team. Bush said, 'when you're part of an Administration you don't jump out and try to take credit. You are part of a team.'[12] As Vice-President Bush adhered to the team philosophy. He was loyal himself and, as such, demanded loyalty from others. He developed this culture 'gradually building trust among other members of the elite and cutting private deals with them ... the patrician approach'.[13]

The manner in which close personal friends were appointed to key positions severely restricted the influence that all but the most senior officials could wield. Baker, Scowcroft and Cheney were, for example, described as the 'new "troika" of foreign policy'.[14] If this were true, which is debatable, then Baker was certainly the senior member with Scowcroft more influential than Cheney on foreign policy matters. It is for that reason that Cheney is relegated to level three in this analysis.

At that level a plethora of spokesmen emerged with minimal policy-making responsibilities but vital representational roles. Government officials such as Richard Solomon, Robert Kimmitt and David Lambertson were the administration's front men on Cambodia and all were vastly experienced. The only drawback to the experience of the team were charges that they brought with them the shadow of Henry Kissinger. Scowcroft and Lawrence Eagleburger (Assistant SoS), for example, came straight from Kissinger Associated Inc., a consultancy firm, back into government.

The structure of the Bush administration specifically delineated between policy-making and policy implementation. As an example of this attitude Bush argued that neither the US ambassador to the UN nor the director of the CIA, both posts that Bush had held, should have Cabinet status. The reason given was, in the case of the UN ambassador, that it created unnecessary tension with the SoS and that foreign policy was 'risky enough without having two conflicting voices in the cabinet'.[15] The director of the CIA was excluded simply because he was 'not supposed to be a policy maker'.[16] There was, therefore, a very tight-knit elite which consisted of the President himself and the Secretary of State with other trusted colleagues, such as Scowcroft and Cheney coopted when necessary. At the lower levels the implementers were also trusted, experienced personnel and represented policy in the loyal manner that Bush would have expected.

LEVEL ONE

From the outset Bush was determined to play a more direct role in the whole policy-making process. He encouraged alternative views but made the final decision himself. He held Cabinet sessions which were called 'scheduled train wrecks', in which opinions on a variety of scenarios were aired in front of the President. He would then retire to the Oval Office and phone his formidable array of contacts, but ultimately decided himself. Bush controlled the policy. He was able to achieve that by selecting staff who accepted his notion of team responsibility. However, Larry Speakes argued that being a team player meant, for Bush, not having a strong philosophical base, being indecisive and being unwilling to 'take stands on big issues'.[17]

The lack of a 'philosophical base' was an oft repeated criticism usually codified as 'lack of vision'.[18] This was a charge that Bush himself rejected as being 'off-base'. He argued that his vision was clear:

> It was (and is) a view shaped by my political philosophy – a conservative philosophy based on the idea of America as a beacon of hope throughout the world, and of freedom, justice, and opportunity for all its citizens. Overseas that translates into honouring our commitments to our friends and allies, and maintaining America's interests by a policy of peace-through-strength … Here at home it means viewing government as the last, not the first, recourse in solving problems.[19]

This quotation tends to confirm rather than refute the charge. It was vague rhetoric and lacked a strategic overview which was essentially the accusation levelled at the President. If Bush did have a vision it was of a world that needed to be handled and managed. Intuitively Bush adopted a more hands-on approach than Reagan, it was a problem-solving approach which emphasised an 'involved, knowledgeable, pragmatic president'.[20] The most important aspect of policy for Bush was its feasibility. As he said himself, 'I am a practical man. I like what's real. I'm not much for the airy and the abstract. I like what works ... I do not yearn to lead a crusade.'[21]

Others did not find it so easy to categorise Bush. Hastedt, for example, was unsure where Bush fitted into Barber's typology. He argued that although Bush's traits of caution, pragmatism, willingness to compromise and openness to information would mark him as an 'active-positive' President, his secretiveness might point to a President who could 'justifiably be portrayed as active-negative'.[22] Barber himself had no such difficulty and considered Bush's character to be 'active-positive'.[23] It would, perhaps, be more accurate to describe Bush, in Stoessinger's terms, as a 'pragmatist'.

Stoessinger argues that 'pragmatists' consider a variety of alternatives and will, as a result of those considerations, be prepared to adjust to new realities. The pragmatist

> may lack an overall blueprint or design for American foreign policy. But this does not mean that the pragmatic mind is unable to conceive a general philosophy. The crucial difference is this: the pragmatist always tests his design against the facts of his experience. If the design does not hold up against the facts, the design will have to change.[24]

The 'experience' against which Bush tested his 'design' was almost entirely Cold War. He was reluctant to reject the long-held 'design' of the Cold War without overwhelming evidence that it was no longer credible. As a consequence Bush adopted a 'wait-and-see' approach. Senate Majority Leader George Mitchell described his attitude towards Gorbachev as 'show me', an 'almost passive stance'. The Bush administration for Mitchell seemed 'almost nostalgic about the cold war and the rigid superpower relationship'.[25]

Another facet of Bush's character which was a remnant of the Cold War was his obsession with secrecy. He felt comfortable with, and probably enjoyed, secrecy. He approved his first covert campaign (a $10 million propaganda campaign directed at General Noriega of Panama) in only his second month in office.[26] He is also reported to have failed to inform even his CoS when he sent a secret mission to China in July of his first year.[27] In view of his fascination with secrecy perhaps it is not strange that Bush also leaned heavily on a very personal style. He was personally well acquainted with most of the world's leaders and made it his business to be so. His adherence to 'rolodex diplomacy' became legendary.[28] He was said to have spoken to foreign leaders by phone approximately 190 times in his first five months in office and also had 135 face-to-face meetings.[29]

Bush's diplomatic style served him well in the Gulf War throughout which he 'displayed an exquisite sensitivity to diplomatic nuance and the need for subtle compromise ... his performance went beyond competence to sheer mastery'.[30] The problem for Bush was that his style was anachronistic. It was only appropriate in the Gulf War because that too was an anachronism. The Gulf crisis required ad hoc, reactive decision-making, the type a pragmatist would be comfortable with. For critics of Bush, however, his successful handling of the Gulf only confirmed that while he was good at crises he was not able to make choices with reference to careful long-term strategic planning.[31] Paradoxically, although the Gulf was seen by many as a triumph for Bush's strategic vision, it still lacked 'a wider framework of long-term goals'.[32] In other words, the new world order did not generate the management of the Gulf crisis but was generated by it.

Given that Bush was a 'pragmatist' and that his decision-making style might be described as 'do your best and don't look back'[33] it should not have been surprising that he lacked a grand design. However, he did retain some of the Reaganite rhetoric. In May 1989, for example, he referred to 'the eclipse of communism ... and the ascendancy of the democratic idea'.[34] He was fortunate to a certain extent that during the election campaign foreign policy was not a significant issue and Bush was not, therefore, encumbered by any specific commitments. For Bush foreign policy was something to be managed, to be 'realistic' about.

A part of that management was the need to achieve a greater degree of cooperation with Congress. Bush's appointments were people he considered could deal with Congress effectively in the hope that procedural confrontations which had in the past stagnated foreign policy, could be avoided. He wanted to resurrect a bipartisan approach which entailed 'less congressional micromanagement'.[35] Unfortunately, when he was elected, his position in relation to Congress was 'one of the weakest of any new president in the twentieth century'[36] and it was damaged even further by the failure of the House to pass his budget package in October 1990. In October 1990 the *Washington Post* described Congress's relationship with Bush as ambivalent and awkward, co-operative one minute, confrontational the next. All this in a field that Bush openly relished. In an oft-repeated quotation from a White House press conference Bush explained what it was about foreign policy that appealed to him:

> When you get a problem with the complexities that the Middle East has now, and the Gulf has now, I enjoy trying to put the coalition together and keep it together ... I can't say I just rejoice every time I go up and talk to [House Ways and Means chairman Dan] Rostenkowski about what he's going to do on taxes.[37]

What appealed to Bush was the mechanics of foreign policy management, the personal 'wheeler-dealing', the 'Rolodex diplomacy' and basic hands-on activity. It is argued that this failed to provide 'long-range guidance or substantive coherence across many regions and issues'[38] but it is also true that in a world in a state of flux a reactive approach was the most appropriate. Bush may not have had a grand design but he actually enjoyed the minutiae of foreign affairs and was an excellent practitioner. Issues such as Cambodia would be dealt with reactively, Bush would address Cambodia when it *became* an issue.

LEVEL TWO

On foreign policy matters level two was inhabited only by Secretary of State James A. Baker III. He has been described as both 'the most politically expert individual to hold the [SoS] post'[39] and a 'political crony with limited foreign affairs experience'.[40] There is no doubt that Baker had governmental experience, having been Secretary of the Treasury and White House CoS. Equally as important, at least in terms of his appointment, was the fact that most recently he had been Bush's campaign manager and for three decades before that he had been his political adviser, and was, therefore, extremely close to the President.

Baker's greatest asset was his empathy with, and loyalty to, Bush himself. Baker recognised the need to be a team player and to understand the role of his important, but subordinate position. He was effective because he retained Bush's confidence. One way in which he did that was by letting it be known 'that he perceived himself as the president's man in "the building" and not State's representative at the Oval Office'.[41] As a result he was criticised for not involving the State

Department on key foreign policy issues. Bush tended to involve State and the NSC in the initial analytical stages but marginalised them when the actual decision needed to be made, then he relied almost solely on Baker. The career professionals in State were said to be unhappy at the separation between the SoS and themselves. One is quoted as saying that Baker was 'running a mini-NSC, not State.... We learn what our policy is when we read it in the newspapers.'[42] However, as far as foreign policy was concerned, Baker was a pragmatist in the Bush mould. His style mirrored the reactive decision-making process of the President; the two confirmed each other's views. The President genuinely devolved responsibility for foreign policy development onto his SoS simply because there was unlikely to be any real friction.

LEVEL THREE

For the purposes of the Cambodian issue level three consisted of Brent Scowcroft (NSA), Richard Solomon (Assistant Secretary of State for East Asian and Pacific Affairs) and David Lambertson (Deputy Assistant Secretary of State for East Asian and Pacific Affairs). Although figures such as Robert Kimmitt (Under Secretary for Political Affairs), Dick Cheney, Lawrence Eagleburger and Dan Quale contributed what might be described as cameo performances they did not have significant inputs into foreign policy towards Cambodia. They did present it and defend it so in that sense they would be important in depicting the administration's reality but not in any other really meaningful sense.

Scowcroft's importance lay in the experience he brought to the job. He was only the second person to hold the NSA job twice and was well respected and trusted by the President. He was an informal adviser to Bush and like Baker understood his subordinate position and the importance of the team. He was described by Melanson rather disparagingly as a 'defense policy mechanic'.[43] It is more accurate to describe him as a manager, a 'fixer', which is exactly what the pragmatic Bush wanted. As Kegley and Wittkopf said, Scowcroft 'played an active *managerial* role in an administration committed to lead with foreign policy as its strong suit'[44] (emphasis added). Bush was impressed with Scowcroft's adaptability given that the original charter of the NSC never envisaged it having a policy-making role.[45] The only influence Scowcroft might have exerted was in supporting the Cambodian resistance given his predilection for low-intensity warfare. Scowcroft had specialised in Low-Intensity Conflict during his Air Force days.

Richard Solomon and David Lambertson were the most prominent of the administration's front men in Congress, taking the roles previously occupied by Richard Holbrooke (Carter) and John Holdridge (Reagan). Additional pressure came to bear on level three personnel in Congress. As the administration's policy came under pressure and eventually changed it was left to these civil servants to save the government's face. Scowcroft was not involved in this street-fighting. The real significance of level three personnel was not in the construction of reality but in its presentation and defence. The reality was constructed at the upper levels and it was left to the foot-soldiers to defend it.

CONFLICT

If the battle between Vance and Brzezinski represented the extreme end of the conflict spectrum with Weinberger and Haig, and Weinberger and Shultz increasingly the more moderate end, the Bush administration was at the most benign end of the scale. Naturally there were some small-scale conflicts such as Cheney and Scowcroft on the MX missile deployment issue and Quayle and Baker on the nature of the Soviet threat but there was no real friction. Primarily this was because once a decision had been made the losing faction fell in line behind the President. As has been previously stated everyone at significant levels had served in government before and as such agreed on the principles that guided foreign policy-making; they would participate in the process then accept the decision.

However, probably the most important reason that conflict was relatively absent was that the key players worked to make it so. In a *Washington Post* article David Gergen contended that Baker led on foreign policy in the hope of avoiding the damaging turf battles of previous administrations. Scowcroft, it was argued, agreed to be the administration's 'honest broker' and to remain relatively low-profile.[46] Scowcroft needed to be an NSA above reproach given his influential membership of the Tower Commission – there was no way he was going to be accused of the same offences as those committed by the Reagan administration.

FOREIGN POLICY

The foreign policy developed by the Bush decision-making elite mirrored the group themselves. They were experienced hands who worked hard to create harmony. This harmony stemmed at least in part from 'an utter lack of ideology.... Instead the President and his associates embraced pragmatism, defined by Secretary of State Baker at his confirmation hearings as "being realistic about the world and appreciating the importance of getting things done"'.[47] Incidentally, this was the same hearing at which Baker had referred to the Khmer Rouge as a 'fact of life'. Baker was even referred to, by the administration themselves, as the 'ultimate pragmatist'.[48]

Although it can be convincingly argued that the Bush foreign policy was pragmatic, it did have an interpretation of the world as a place which needed the United States. There was never even a hint of isolationism. The Bush administration represented a renaissance of the Atlanticist tradition. In 1989 both Bush and Baker said that the US as 'the most powerful democracy ... can be a force for freedom and peaceful change unlike any other in this world ... if we fail to do so, we will not be able to run or hide from the consequences'.[49] Bush clearly linked US involvement on the wider world stage with deterring threats to national interest. The pragmatic position was to be involved, Bush said he did not 'believe any other country can pick up the mantle'.[50]

The Bush administration's foreign policy was said to be in a 'cultural lag', analysing the problems of the 1990s with the conceptual tools of the 1970s.[51] It is probably more accurate to suggest, however, that it was simply the natural caution of the personalities involved. Their reactions, or lack of them, to continual Gorbachev initiatives were invariably prudent. A statement by Colin Powell perhaps illustrates the Bush caution most clearly; he said, 'I've seen no particular Soviet capability disappear; I've seen no part of the world where we have an interest go off the map.'[52]

It was that reluctance to tamper with policy principles that had served them so well which informed the major foreign policy review of the early months of the Bush presidency. There was considerable criticism of the policy review, claiming that it had restricted the ability of the administration to be able to react, or even to act, in relation to Gorbachev.[53] For the administration, however, it allowed them time to develop their own image while simultaneously placating a Democratic Congress. Doing nothing during the review had much to recommend it to a conservative administration. Bush justified the review by saying it 'would be imprudent if [he] didn't have [his] team take a long hard look at everything'.[54] The review eventually provided what was referred to as the 'status quo plus' analysis of which Scowcroft said, in a piece of diplomatic rhetoric, 'We have the initial results from the study and it's probably not surprising that the future looks a lot like the present in a straight line projection.'[55]

It was natural that pragmatists should adopt an incrementalist rationality but it was less than satisfying at a time in which genuinely historic events were occurring. The completion of the review was followed by five speeches during April and May 1989 including Bush's 'beyond containment' reference on 12 May when he addressed an audience at the Texas A & M.[56] The speeches all dealt with the new US–Soviet relationship and the changes in Eastern Europe. Bush was anxious to encourage the 'democratisation' and promised preferential economic treatment for those nations with liberalising political agendas (17 April 1989).

Explaining a reactive foreign policy is relatively straightforward and some of the momentous events of the Bush term illustrated pragmatism at work, most notably perhaps the events of 4 June 1989 in Tiananmen Square and the subsequent US foreign policy towards China. In a Senate hearing on 6 June 1990,[57] a year after Tiananmen, the accusations and responses demonstrated the pragmatic *realpolitik* mentality at work and it is, therefore, worth quoting at length. In the opening statements to the hearing Senator Jesse Helms (N. Carolina) was highly critical of the continuation of MFN (most favoured nation) status for China. He highlighted the moral ambivalence of the Bush policy and called for a change in that policy. Richard Solomon's opening response is at the heart of this book. He began by citing F. Scott Fitzgerald's definition of a first class intellect as one which has 'the ability to keep two opposing ideas in one's mind and still be able to function', a definition which is not too dissimilar to Orwell's concept of 'doublethink' in *Nineteen Eighty-Four*. Solomon continued by explaining that the 'foreign policy equivalent is what we have done consistently since Tiananmen: balance the competing demands of hardnosed national interests and our national values, aspirations and ideals'. Finally he says:

> Our approach is to try to preserve a key relationship that serves important national interests while at the same time sending a clear message that Beijing's human rights performance has been and

remains unacceptable, precluding a fully normal relationship. Let us be clear, this administration regards the situation in China with regard to the protection of human rights as deeply disturbing.[58]

Solomon's statement effectively advocates 'double-think' and holds US policy as a hostage to charges of double standards. He did the same when he invoked the 'trade' argument. Again it is necessary to quote at length not least because exactly the opposite argument was used to maintain the trade embargoes on Vietnam and Cambodia:

> the President has concluded that on balance and in view of other sanctions that remain in place, MFN status for China remains in the US national interest and he has acted to renew China's MFN waiver under the Jackson-Vanik amendment of the 1974 Trade Act for another year. Our recommendation and the President's decision were difficult in the light of the fundamental lack of progress in China towards healing the wounds of last June. In the end the President concluded that denial of MFN would inflict serious harm on many intellectuals, workers, managers, and officials inside China who struggle to keep alive the flame of reform and openness to the outside world. We cannot break faith with the people who count on us by destroying the basis of commerce with China ... [c]ommerce is a force for change.[59]

Senator Helms dismissed the 'sanctions that remain in place' as akin to 'beating the Chinese with a wet noodle'.[60] And it is clear that the Chinese themselves were fully aware of the US dilemma; the Chinese premier Li Peng argued that taking MFN status away was not an option open to the US. If they *played* that card then they wouldn't 'have the card any more'.[61]

Although Baker insisted that 'rebuilding that consensus was in [the] national interest',[62] he later admitted that Tiananmen had 'shattered the bipartisan consensus ... for engagement with China'.[63] What the Bush administration failed to realise was that it was not so much the actual policy which shattered the consensus but the manner in which the policy was conducted. Less than a month after Tiananmen, and the imposition of a ban on high level visits, Bush secretly dispatched Scowcroft and Eagleburger to Beijing to discuss the situation. This was not uncovered until 2 a.m. on 9 December 1989 when it was announced that the same two were again en route to Beijing.[64] There was outrage in Congress, who at that time still did not know about the previous visit. Stephen Solarz called it yet 'another example of the

President's tendency to kow tow to Beijing'.[65] Representative Nancy Pelosi (D, Calif) concluded that it made 'everything we've said about our disgust and revulsion at the Chinese government's actions only empty words'.[66] In response Bush simply vetoed attempted legislation over the protection of Chinese students and the Senate upheld his veto. For Bush, Congress had unnecessarily complicated negotiations with the Chinese. Marlin Fitzwater, when left to comment on the Congressional furore, commented that 'The President views China as an important country in world affairs. While he deplores the tragedy of Tiananmen Square last June, China nevertheless remains part of the world around us.'[67]

This acquiescence to Chinese needs appeared to many to be in stark contrast to the 'wait and see' approach adopted with regard to the changes in the Soviet Union. It also seemed at odds with the evolving security situation. With the collapse of the Soviet threat the tensions which had held the strategic triangle in place were seriously weakened. As a result there did not appear to be any likely scenario in which it would be necessary to play the China card against the Soviet Union and as such possession of the card would also be redundant. Why, then, did Bush still protect it so fiercely? Possibly due to his attachment to the status quo and realpolitik. Also his own personal reminiscences of his time in China and the influence of his 'Kissinger boys' clearly played a part. The Scowcroft/Eagleburger trips and Bush's dismissive response to the ensuing criticism has revealed much about the Bush foreign policy towards China. James Baker provided both a definition of the problem and the pragmatic solution. The problem was that 'an anachronistic regime [had] alienated [the US] by lashing out, by seeking to repress an irrepressible spirit. A return to hostile confrontation will not help the people of China nor serve our national interests.'[68] The solution was to maintain a 'policy of engagement toward the People's Republic. We can eventually solve our problems with China only if we maintain the ability to make our case with the Chinese.'[69]

Bush's use of the UN was another example of his pragmatism. Under Reagan the UN had gained almost demonic status, but in a time of economic constraint Bush may have perceived UN legitimised coalitions as the only feasible way of financing military excursions on a large scale. Alternatively it might be argued that he had a residual affection for the organisation from his time as US ambassador there. Whatever the reason, the resurrection of the UN was condoned, fostered and welcomed by Bush. The Gulf crisis and Cambodia proved the worth of the United Nations in different but significant ways. By the end of his presidency Bush was extolling the virtues of the organisation and looking forward to building 'a genuine global community of free and sovereign nations' in which the UN would take the lead, *supported* to the full by the US.[70] Thus US direct involvement could be kept to a minimum, or avoided completely; no ground troops in Bosnia, no troops at all in Cambodia and, in the final weeks of the Bush term, a grand gesture in Somalia.

Of course we now know that the Somalian gesture had some tragic consequences but in December 1992 it seemed a no-lose situation. In Bush's *Address to the Nation on the Situation in Somalia*, broadcast on 4 December 1992, he explained how he had acted in concert with the United Nations and how the seriousness of the situation led the US to tell the UN they were willing to provide more help, and the Secretary General had welcomed the US offer to lead a coalition to get the food through. He told his audience 'that America [would] answer the [UN's] call ... and assist in Operation Restore Hope'. The troops the US would send would be 'America's finest. They will perform this mission with courage and compassion, and they will succeed.'

Despite the fact that the Bush administration was alleged to have been stuck in a Cold War culture their obvious bias towards the pragmatic actually meant they were able to adjust to the changing environment, albeit cautiously. They managed their foreign policy as they did the rest of their administration by employing a careful process of risk aversion. And this was true even when it was unsuccessful as in Somalia.

THE ADMINISTRATION'S REALITY

Bush was inextricably tied to minimising any risk to his presidency. Policy towards Indochina would, therefore, be developed by a process of eliminating unacceptable alternatives – or more precisely by eliminating *domestically* unacceptable alternatives. What were these alternatives? First, *do nothing*; this was unacceptable because of the possibility of a KR victory. A KR victory was unacceptable either for genuine moral reasons or simply because the polls might reflect public unease. Second, *send US troops*; this, despite Bush's 'statute of limitations' comment on the Vietnam War, was an option no President would contemplate. US troops in the Gulf or Somalia was difficult enough, Indochina was out of the question. Third, *support and legitimisation of the Hun Sen regime*; unacceptable because this would have represented a radical change of policy which is only ever a last option for the pragmatist. This left only one viable alternative – *assisting the non-communist resistance (NCR)*. This option had several redeeming features. It continued an American influence in the region, it counterbalanced the possibility of a KR victory, it tied the Vietnamese into hugely expensive support for the Phnom Penh regime, theoretically it did not involve any connection with the Khmer Rouge, and most importantly it did not involve any US troops.

The difficulty which pragmatists encounter is the fact that idealists exist and they construct 'impractical' realities. The solution of the pragmatist is to construct a plausible and, more importantly, a robust reality of their own. This reality must be able to accommodate unpalatable facts, such as Khmer Rouge involvement, which can in turn be disowned by the administration as unavoidable concessions to practicality. Thus, in his testimony to a Congressional hearing in October 1989, David Lambertson could explain that the judgement of Sihanouk and ASEAN was that the KR could not be excluded from any settlement and that the US was prepared to 'accede in that judgement, provided that the worst of the Khmer Rouge leaders [were] indeed excluded from the process'.[71] Son Sen was, of course, later involved. Lambertson's statement was made only months after Baker had said that the US would 'continue to work for a new Cambodia free of both Vietnamese occupation and the Khmer Rouge'.[72] Baker had also said that it 'had been consistent administration policy to oppose [the Phnom Penh] government and support the [NCR]'.[73] Each statement is worded in such a way as to provide ambivalence. The key words – 'provided', 'continue' and 'had been' – all allow for later changes in direction.

The first significant event regarding Cambodia which required comment was the first Paris International Peace Conference (PICC) of August 1989. Statements before and, most revealingly, after the conference establish the administration's reality quite clearly. However, two events prior to the conference must be borne in mind when assessing the US policy. The two events were the final withdrawal of Soviet troops from Afghanistan in February 1989 and the announcement on 5 April 1989 of a similar action by the Vietnamese in Cambodia. The first was a major indicator of the Soviet desire to disentangle themselves from expensive regional commitments and the second, probably causally related to the first, brought the whole issue back onto the agenda. A telling statement was made a year after the Vietnamese announcement by Robert M. Kimmitt (Under Secretary for Political Affairs) when he addressed the Asia Society. He said that with 'the emergence of Mr Gorbachev, we and the Soviets began to focus on extricating ourselves from these conflicts [Afghanistan and Cambodia] and resolving them through negotiation'.[74] A prime aim of both superpowers had become the removal of financially draining commitments. For the US, Cambodia did not represent such a commitment but for the Soviets and the Vietnamese it most definitely did. They now perceived a need to speed up the pace of a settlement and this caught the Bush administration by surprise.

When the PICC was adjourned it was widely considered to be a failure. Two actions, therefore, needed to be taken. First, apportion blame; second, re-establish the status quo. The administration accomplished these two requirements in three Congressional hearings shortly after the conference, one in the House (September 1989), one in the Senate (October 1989) and the third in the House (November 1989).[75] Blame was obviously to be located with the Hun Sen faction (PRK) and the Vietnamese government (SRV). In the November hearing David Lambertson explained that the 'reason no agreement was reached [in Paris] was that Vietnam and the PRK were unwilling to consider any arrangement which diluted in any significant way PRK authority';[76] in October he had said that if 'Hanoi wished to have a political settlement in Paris ... we could have had one'.[77] Another reason given was the PRK insistence on retaining a reference to genocide in any documentation. In the September hearing Richard Solomon explained that in the administration's view the Vietnamese continued to return to the genocide issue because 'the way the international lawyers defined genocide would create a rationale, a legal justification for the Vietnamese invasion and occupation of Cambodia'.[78] This was never a part of the Vietnamese rationale which was based on self-defence, but it shows the US preoccupation with Vietnam.[79] A letter from Janet Mullins, an Assistant Secretary for Legislative Affairs, cemented the Solomon interpretation. She said that 'the Hun Sen faction callously exploited the genocide issue to help block a comprehensive settlement'.[80] The administration's reality was simple, the Vietnamese and their allies were the 'bad-guys', therefore it was *their* actions which had subverted the PICC.

The hearings also provided opportunities to reaffirm basic tenets of US foreign policy on this issue. Solomon explained US priorities in the following way:

> our primary interests begin with support for the security of
> Thailand ... and by our concern for the continuing integrity and
> vitality of ASEAN ... a second element of concern ... has been the
> development of a non-communist third force, if you like, under the
> leadership of Prince Sihanouk.[81]

Lambertson added that Sihanouk must have a 'leadership role inasmuch as he remains the single most authentic symbol of Cambodian nationalism'.[82] Interestingly Solomon's statement used the term 'third force' which established the dissociation of the NCR from the KR. This dissociation process had become increasingly important since the announcement by the Vietnamese of their withdrawal. The exclusion of the KR from any future or interim government was highly sensitive and the administration officials resorted to the rhetoric of pragmatism. When questioned at length on the KR exclusion Solomon simply stated, 'Prince Sihanouk is our lead on this as are the ASEAN countries.'[83] When pressed further, he conceded it was clear there was 'a tension, if you like, between our moral position, which is very clearly to see these people excluded, and looking for ways to deal with the realities of the situation'.[84] He went on to say that 'the position that says freeze the Khmer Rouge out of any involvement being a moral one seems to me self-deluding, because there is a reality out there',[85] a statement which surprisingly drew agreement from Congressman Solarz who said that '[s]ometimes morally correct policies require morally ambiguous actions'.[86]

Earlier in the hearing Solomon had suggested what the reality out there might look like. Ironically he almost seemed to blame the Vietnamese for withdrawing, arguing that they had 'in effect presented the international community with a forced choice between their surrogate ... or the Khmer Rouge'.[87] The implication seemed to be that by taking precipitate action the Vietnamese had forced the administration to make difficult decisions before it was ready to do so. As if to provide thinking time Lambertson said, 'I think the policy that we have pursued for 19 years, frankly, remains still valid.'[88]

In July 1990 the Bush administration was faced with presenting a change in policy on Cambodia to the world, the reason for which will be discussed later. This might have required the construction of an entirely new reality but very skilfully, and under considerable pressure, the administration managed a PR operation analogous to building an annex to an existing structure. On 18 July 1990 Baker announced that, having seen the withdrawal of Vietnamese troops accomplished, the US needed to turn its attention to the prevention of a Khmer Rouge return to power. Specifically he said:

> we have determined that we will open a dialogue with Vietnam about Cambodia. We will be prepared to enhance our humanitarian assistance to Cambodia, and we will be prepared to and will in fact change what has been our policy regarding the seat at the United Nations which has been held by a coalition that includes the Khmer Rouge.[89]

In two sentences Baker had shifted US foreign policy towards Cambodia considerably, but fundamentally the reality remained unaltered because he added that the 'change in policy [did] not constitute a decision to normalize relations with Vietnam'.[90] He reproached Congress over its reluctance to continue funding the NCR and its failure to adopt a bipartisan approach. He also managed to reapportion some of the blame for the difficulties in reaching a settlement when he said that the 'Khmer Rouge ha[d] succeeded in turning the political dialogue into a dialogue of the battlefield'.[91] The blame, therefore, no longer belonged solely to the Vietnamese.

It was vital that the administration minimised the opportunity for criticism by subtly adjusting their language. When asked, two days after the announcement, whether it was a 'new policy' Solomon answered that it was 'an adjustment or – let me get the right word. It is [was] a revision in our policy.'[92] Robert Kimmitt later also referred to a 'policy revision'.[93] 'Revision' became the authorised version after Baker had unwisely referred to it as a 'change'. Baker himself had to adjust the wording, explaining to an ASEAN foreign ministers meeting that the announcement was 'merely a shift in tactics'.[94]

In addition to semantic adjustments the ethical emphasis also changed. Where previously the moral argument had been subordinated to pragmatic considerations Kimmitt, for example, was now able to describe the Cambodia situation as one in which 'US interests are primarily moral rather than strategic'.[95] The new policy was now articulated as being concerned 'to do everything we can to prevent a return of the Khmer Rouge to power'.[96] Within two months Baker told the Senate Foreign Relations Committee that the next logical step was 'a dialogue with Hun Sen's representatives'.[97] Ironically the US representative turned out to be their ambassador to Indonesia, John Monjo, the vociferous interlocutor of the Reagan administration.

From the 'policy shift' announcement to the Monjo meeting took less than two months. To illustrate the speed with which opinions were altering it is worth noting that three months *before* the announcement Thomas Pickering, the US Ambassador at the UN, had been saying on national television that the reason the Cambodia UN seat should remain with the former government, i.e. the Khmer Rouge, was in order that the 'Vietnamese … who are not, in our view, have not been a superior claimant' should not be rewarded.[98] Enormous controversy was generated by the 'policy shift' announcement, but most was over the tardiness of the change rather than its content and the administration played down the change and generally defused the situation.

One of the pillars of the administration's previous reality which had been compromised by the 'Baker shift' was that of normalisation with Vietnam. Although specifically rejected by Baker, events seemed to be pointing in the direction of normalisation and it needed to be managed at the administration's pace. The brake was applied by proposing the so-called 'roadmap' towards resuming normal relations. It was first laid out on 9 April 1991 when Richard Solomon met Trinh Xuang Lang (Vietnam's permanent representative to the UN). The 'roadmap' consisted of four distinct phases:

(i)   when a peace agreement had been signed only then would the US enter into normalisation discussions,

(ii)   when UNTAC was established the US would 'partially' lift trade embargoes on Vietnam and Cambodia,

(iii)   after six months of the transitional process the embargoes would be fully lifted, diplomatic offices in Hanoi and Washington would be established, and IMF restrictions would be eased,

(iv)   after elections there would be full normalisation.

Additionally stages (i) (ii) and (iii) all required progress on the MIA issue.[99] Functionally the roadmap served two purposes: it provided discrete steps based on a US view of reality and it threw the ball back into the Vietnamese court.

From the perspective of this book the interesting aspect of another major event, the PICC of October 1991, was the triumphal way in which it was described by the administration. In their description of the present they also created history, they reaffirmed reality. Thus when Richard Solomon said the agreement signed in Paris was 'the culmination of a negotiating effort initiated by Secretary Baker in the fall of 1989', he simultaneously confirmed its success and Baker's role in that success.[100] In addition to 'proving' that the success of the process was a product of US involvement Solomon also 'proved' that previous lack of progress had been the fault of Vietnam and China. He said there was 'no question but that the settlement process was given its final impetus by the decision of China and Vietnam to resolve their bilateral differences',[101] the implication being that they had always been the problem.

The shift in policy, the roadmap, and the Peace Agreement were relatively successfully handled by the administration. The moral issues, however, presented altogether more difficult situations which manifested themselves in a variety of ways. The most perplexing of these was probably the 'genocide' debate. This debate exposed the limitations of a pragmatic approach when attacked in a morally ambivalent climate. Nowhere is this clearer than in a lengthy exchange between questioner Jim Leach (Iowa) and questioned Michael Young, Deputy Legal Adviser to the State Department, during a congressional hearing in November 1989. There was considerable argument as to whether genocide had actually been committed and eventually Leach asked Young very directly, 'Is it the position of the United States Government that Pol Pot committed an act of genocide in Cambodia?'[102] Young's answer, quoted at length below, almost borders on the surreal since he seems to be implying that the term 'genocide' has not been used by the administration because it is not strong enough to embrace the crimes of Pol Pot:

MR YOUNG: If I could address that question for a moment, I think we do believe that they committed genocide. I think we have tried to avoid the use of that term in part because as we have examined the treaties, particularly the genocide convention, as I am sure you know, the term seemed somewhat underinclusive for what they actually did. They define genocide somewhat more narrowly as requiring the intent to destroy a national race or religious group as such. We believe they certainly did that in some cases, but they went beyond that. They attacked groups that spoke foreign languages, groups that were bourgeois, I guess. It is probably too narrow a term to describe what they did.

MR LEACH: Just so that we are on the record here. This is a premise that also relates to the Vietnam issue. Let me just be very careful. It is the position of the United States Government that Pol Pot committed genocide in Cambodia, yes or no?

MR YOUNG: I think the answer to that is yes, but could I qualify it?

MR LEACH: I appreciate your present situation.

MR YOUNG: May I qualify it? I have actually been in this job just a little over two months and I come from the academic world where we can never say yes or no. I am a little reluctant to put the United States Government totally on record based largely on my ignorance in this matter. It is very clear that we think they engaged in acts broader than genocide.

MR LEACH: Mr Lambertson, you have been in the United States Government for more than a few months. Is it the position of the United States of America that Pol Pot committed genocide?

MR LAMBERTSON: Among other things.

MR LEACH: Is the answer yes?

MR LAMBERTSON: The answer is yes.[103]

Mr Young also said it was the position of the US Government (USG) that 'the participation of those individuals who committed genocide in a multipartite government would not be acceptable given those crimes'.[104] Young's problems arose from the fact that while genocide had obviously been committed, those who committed it would have to be accommodated if any formal settlement were to be reached. A pragmatic reality could cope with such contradictions but an idealistic one could not; and it is virtually impossible for the two to communicate logically with each other since the premises of both are often contradictory. In a written answer concerning the legal question the State Department conceded that:

the United Nations special rapporteur on genocide, Benjamin Whitaker, stated in his report of July 2, 1985 ... that Pol Pot's Khmer Rouge government of Democratic Kampuchea was guilty of genocide 'even under the most restricted definition ... since the victims included target groups such as the Chams (an Islamic minority) and the Buddhist monks'. We agree with that assessment.[105]

Despite the fact that the answer had been 'yes', a reasonable damage limitation exercise was completed, mainly because written answers are rarely reported as widely as the open hearing exchanges and so the issue was buried. Later, after the 1991 Paris agreement, Baker further defused the matter by stating that the US would 'support efforts to bring to justice those responsible for the mass murders of the 1970s if the new Cambodian government [chose] to pursue [that] path'.[106] To date this has not happened.

The moral debate was not only confined to questions of genocide but to the Khmer Rouge in general and in particular the degree of involvement between them and the NCR which the US openly backed. It was the issue that required most frequent attention from the Bush administration. Statements had to represent a very simple reality – the name Khmer Rouge had to equal an evil 'fact of life'; NCR had to stand for the only hope for democratic settlement; PRK/Vietnam were the major obstacles to the achievement of any such settlement. Two statements made prior to the 1989 Paris Conference make the point. In June 1989 Robert Kimmitt said that US support for the NCR would 'depend on the extent to which the non-communists [were] seen as distancing themselves from the Khmer Rouge'.[107] In a similar vein a pre-conference policy paper stated that the ability of the US to support any Cambodian government was 'directly and inversely related to the degree of Khmer Rouge participation, if any, in it'.[108] The difficulty with these statements was that in March 1989 Sihanouk had actually announced the formation of a high Council for National Defence to facilitate co-operation between the *three* resistance forces as 'a step toward merging the *three* forces into a single army'[109] (emphasis added). In testimony to the Senate Foreign Relations Committee David Lambertson dismissed the announcement as mere PR and added that it 'had no significance on the ground in Cambodia'.[110] One reality was simply shrugged aside by another.

Tactically the administration dealt with the continuing situation very defensively. There was a series of rhetorical parries in the immediate wake of the Vietnamese announcement to withdraw. On 9 April 1989 Solarz argued that the US 'should do everything it [could] to bolster the NCR immediately against the Khmer Rouge ... by increasing both quantitatively and qualitatively US lethal and non-lethal assistance to the NCR'.[111] On 20 April 1989 Bush was asked whether he was going to offer military aid to the NCR; he said, 'No, no discussion of that yet, no decision taken on that yet.' The questioner persisted and asked whether he had said 'no decision' or 'no discussion'. Bush said, 'No decision and – not with me – can't recall, but I'm not anywhere close to making a decision of that nature.'[112] A few days later, the unlikely duo of Jeremy Stone of the Federation of American Scientists (FAS) and ex-CIA director William Colby argued that the US should be cutting off lethal aid to the factions rather than trying to increase it.[113] Probably as a response to the media debate Dan Quayle stated in Bangkok that the US was 'considering providing weapons to the [NCR] to bolster their position against both the Khmer Rouge and the government in Phnom Penh'.[114]

Although these prevaricatory statements maintained a certain equilibrium, the State Department obviously felt it necessary to bolster their position and on 1 June 1989 spokesman Richard Boucher explained the exact position according to the administration. A decision had been taken to step up aid to the NCR because of the

> accelerating political process in the wake of Vietnam's announce-ment to withdraw all its troops by Sept 30 [which] was expected to provoke a Khmer Rouge bid to overthrow the Vietnamese-backed regime in Phnom Penh, an outcome the United States and its allies are seeking to avert.[115]

A decision had been taken less than six weeks after Bush was 'not anywhere close to making a decision'. Some in Congress reacted angrily. Senator Robert C. Byrd, for example, said if the US were now 'to play a new role in Southeast Asia that role must be based on a solid, bipartisan, fully debated and understood consensus'.[116] Boucher's statement implicitly accepted the notion that the Vietnamese and the PRK *had* been the only effective bulwark against the Khmer Rouge.

The criticism heaped upon the administration's seemingly amoral stance caused at least 'one senior US official' to admit the adminis-tration 'need[ed] some public debate before we can proceed on plans for any regional activity'.[117] The aid issue was difficult and would not easily go away. A year after the above statement Richard Solomon was still explaining the contradictions in the US policy. During a Congressional hearing he was asked about the US support for a coali-tion which included the Khmer Rouge and which also involved the thorny question of actual military co-operation on the ground. His reply was not convincing:

> To an extent there were marginal collaborations with the Khmer Rouge, politically it created [a] measure of ambiguity about our position … Secretary Baker has made it clear that we are not prepared to even sustain that element of ambiguity.[118]

Robert Kimmitt, perhaps inadvertently, also admitted that the NCR had 'never been a significant military force'[119] which among other things meant that US non-lethal aid had to be sustained. Additionally failure to support the NCR would 'undercut … US credibility'.[120]

The administration tried to ignore the issue as much as they could. However, further reports of KR/NCR co-operation in January 1991 resurrected the debate. A report to Congress, which it had requested as a condition of approving aid to the NCR (autumn 1990), said that 'tactical military cooperation' *had* occurred between the KR and NCR. However, the report argued that this did not contravene legal restrictions placed on the aid since the leadership of the NCR was not 'cooperating in strategic planning'.[121] The administration nevertheless suspended the aid unilaterally and in April 1991 Solomon was forced to admit that no aid had been delivered to the NCR from the funds previously approved due to the reports of cooperation since January.[122] Despite the fact that legal restrictions had technically not been contravened, the administration obviously considered it wise to avoid further controversy. During the Cold War the strategic imperative had often been sufficient reason to back a proxy force but by the early 1990s the public and Congress required more convincing.

What is clear from the statements made by members of the administration is that pragmatism was always the preferred option, and that while certain principles remained strong, they were negotiable. The foundations of the administration's reality remained remarkably constant, even allowing for a major policy shift in mid-term. Within two months of taking office President Bush made the following statement:

> What remains clear ... is the absolute requirement that we maintain ASEAN unity and support for a political settlement in Cambodia featuring an interim government led by Prince Sihanouk.... The goals as ever are twofold: full and permanent withdrawal from Cambodia and the permanent prevention of a return to power by the Khmer Rouge.[123]

In January 1992 he said:

> The key point is this: After being strong, determined and patient, we finally can entertain realistic hopes of building lasting ties of interest and affection with Indochina.[124]

Bush's foreign policy towards Cambodia had been a success. He had achieved his goals, the Vietnamese were gone, the Khmer Rouge did not have any real power in the interim government, ASEAN was essentially intact, relations with China had not been completely severed, the MIA issue was under control, elections were due less than six months from the end of his presidency, and normalisation with the potentially lucrative marketplaces of Indochina was progressing satisfactorily. Whether or not other analysts might query the manner in which the goals were achieved would probably be irrelevant to the pragmatic Bush who would, no doubt, allow the results to speak for themselves.

ALTERNATIVE REALITIES

As in previous chapters there were several alternative realities constructed by interested parties and although they each had subtle differences they tended to group around three particular versions – the Vietnamese/PRK/Soviet view; the Chinese/Khmer Rouge/ASEAN/Sihanouk/Thai view; and finally what might best be described as a *conglomerate* view which took as its central thrust an anti-administration stance. This final viewpoint was held by a group of 'strange bedfellows' in what was essentially an alliance of ideas. This disparate and unlikely association consisted of Congressional members (e.g. Cranston, Solarz, Leach and Byrd), the media (e.g. McGrory, Becker, Jennings, Chanda and Pilger), academia (e.g. Haas, Kiernan, Chomsky, Vickery and Etcheson), NGOs (e.g. Stone and Muskie) and business (e.g. Multinational Business Development Corporation). Some dwelt in more than one camp but each subscribed, for a variety of reasons, to a very similar interpretation of the Cambodian reality.

Conglomerate View

Although academia, the NGOs, and American business were important in sustaining pressure on the Bush administration the two groups who initially applied that pressure were from the Congress and the media. In Congress the debate was reignited by the apparent failure of the Paris Conference of 1989. Immediately after the conference Alan Cranston, Chairman of the Senate Sub-Committee on East Asian and Pacific Affairs, accused the administration of being 'on automatic pilot, which leads nowhere but to lethal aid'.[125] Another issue for the anti-administration alliance was the accommodation of Hun Sen. Michael Horowitz, a former Reagan staffer, said that he 'had never seen such a wide gap between government perception and reality' on the issue of recognising the Hun Sen government.[126] Both the lethal aid and the Hun Sen debates were at root moral dilemmas and the first Senate hearing after the PICC collapse highlighted this fact.

Alan Cranstan opened the hearing in typically combative style and condensed all the problems that this group had with the administration's version of reality into a single, short paragraph:

As Secretary Baker stated in Paris on July 30, on the one hand 'the United States strongly believes that the Khmer Rouge should play no role in Cambodia's future', but on the other hand, again quoting Baker, 'we are prepared, however, to support Prince Sihanouk should he deem it necessary to accept the inclusion of all Khmer factions in an interim coalition, or an interim authority'. I say that that policy wobbles like jello.[127]

The House had had a similar hearing two weeks before Cranston's statement and in that hearing Chester G. Atkins (D,Mass) had been equally dismissive of the administration's stance which blamed Vietnamese/PRK intransigence for the failure of the Paris conference. Atkins however, claimed Paris failed because 'the Khmer Rouge and its international backers sought to expunge from all official records any acknowledgement of their acts of genocide'.[128]

Atkins's statement also exposed another contentious issue, the Khmer Rouge's 'international backers', China. There was clearly resentment over what was considered to be the continual appeasement of the Chinese. Jim Leach explained the discomfort as follows:

We should stick persistently to principle rather than to place American foreign policy decision-making in the hands, in this case, of the Chinese – which are not very clean hands – or in the hands of Prince Sihanouk which are not all wrong but hardly pure.[129]

The real problem after the Paris failure was that certain Congressional members did not feel that the administration had either listened to their advice prior to the conference or learned from it afterwards. Senator Robert Byrd summed up their feelings in a plea that, given Bush's love of secrecy, predictably fell on deaf ears:

Surely we have learned from our experience in Vietnam, if nothing else, that if we are to succeed in a new policy toward that region, it cannot be achieved through secret policymaking, secret military programs, secret arms transfers or secret deals.[130]

The reference to arms deals was made shortly before a Senate hearing (12 June 1989) which debated proposed covert aid to the NCR and in so doing opened up another crack in the administration's reality. Even Richard Holbrooke, formerly a State Department official, was concerned about the option of aiding the NCR in this way. He agreed with both Cranston and Atkins who had argued that such a policy would be dangerous and counterproductive and a nonsensical option.[131] They believed the administration's attempt to bolster Sihanouk's position before upcoming negotiations was unrealistic because it consequentially empowered the Khmer Rouge. Stephen Solarz, however, did not refer to the negotiation process but to counterbalancing the KR. He believed that arming the NCR, indeed anybody prepared to fight the KR, was a 'moral obligation' if another 'Asian Auschwitz' was to be avoided.[132] The Solarz reality is dominated by the spectre of the Jewish holocaust and its Cambodian manifestation. The genuine political/moral tension is evident in all his statements and he can appear to move from camp to camp.

Senator Claiborne Pell (RI) put down an amendment to the legislation authorising funding for lethal aid to the NCR which urged the President to do whatever was necessary to bring the KR to justice for genocide and also encouraged Prince Sihanouk to move towards an alliance with the PRK.[133] This was another route to settlement which the US position at Paris effectively ignored.

For a short time there was a relative lull in the opposition but it resurfaced in early 1990 at another Senate hearing. In this hearing Senator Kerry repeated the claim that the US was merely appeasing China in allowing Khmer Rouge formal involvement in any negotiation. He said the reality was that the US had permitted itself to 'become the prisoner of Prince Sihanouk and the [PRC's] recalcitrant position that the Khmer Rouge have to be incorporated into a solution of the problem'.[134] The administration, in the form of David Lambertson, simply reiterated their view that the Khmer Rouge was 'an unpleasant reality' and that the administration were on 'the right track'.[135]

Lambertson gave a masterly performance allowing sufficient ambiguity in his answers to leave the way open for later policy changes. Perhaps the 'Baker shift' of July was already gestating. An obviously disturbed Alan Cranston concluded the hearing as follows:

> In the course of this extraordinary hearing, it became clear to me that our administration's policy is not only ineffective, but potentially destructive. The Bush administration continues to support a policy which includes the Khmer Rouge in a solution, and sidesteps the issue of the Chinese role as principal supplier and supporter of the genocidal Khmer Rouge. This policy must be changed immediately.[136]

As a consequence of Congressional concerns the Senate passed a Concurrent Resolution (No. 101, 7 March 90) which expressed the sense of the Senate as being *against* a quadripartite government, as legitimising the KR; *for* an enhanced UN role; *for* discussions with the Hun Sen government; and pressed the administration to encourage the PRC to stop supplying the KR.[137] Perhaps Michael Horowitz put the Congressional concerns most bluntly when he referred to a State Department report on Cambodia as bearing 'darn near no relation to reality'.[138]

It may have been this growing Congressional pressure which forced Secretary of State Baker to make his policy shift statement in July 1990. Whether it was a change, a shift, or a revision is not too important because whatever it was it demanded a reassessment of opposing views. Two days after the Baker announcement there was a further Senate hearing at which Cranston said he was 'glad that Secretary Baker ha[d] finally announced a new American policy toward Cambodia, but it was not enough'.[139] What was missing according to Cranston was direct talks with Hun Sen, pressure on China, and an end to US military assistance to the NCR. Senator Kerry went further by arguing that the highest priority for the administration should be the prevention of genocide and the 'intent of Congress [was] being violated by what [was] happening'.[140] Four days after Baker's announcement more than 60 Senators sent a letter to the President asking him to re-examine US foreign policy towards Cambodia in the light of Congressional intent.

Either due to pressure or genuine reassessment, the administration gradually incorporated the demands of Congress into their policy. The remaining issues concerned deep-rooted administration aversion to any form of legitimisation for the PRK or the Vietnamese. The House held a hearing on the economic embargo in June 1991. The chairman of the International Economic Policy and Trade Sub-committee, Congressman Gejdenson, argued that the US embargo of Vietnam no longer made any sense and that in spite of the fact that Bush had said 'that the Persian Gulf War had expunged the Vietnam War from the national psyche, he has also renewed the embargo and compelled its restrictions to be vigorously applied'.[141] Senator Murkowski (Alaska), in his capacity as Chairman of the Senate Veterans Affairs Committee, said that the veterans were in favour of lifting the embargo since it would allow them to go back to Vietnam and 'deal with the issues that have confronted them for many years'.[142] Solarz argued for a retention of the embargo until a genuine settlement had been reached.

The Congressional reality ran ahead of the presidential reality and maybe that is how the democratic process should work. As long as one partner is creative and adventurous and the other cautious it is irrelevant who takes which role. And maybe it is preferable that it should be the President who provides the caution. The *media* too can provide either a restraining or a liberating influence and in the case of Cambodia it generally tried to force the pace in a direction broadly similar to that of Congress, albeit with more emotive language. An editorial in the *Washington Post* (19 June 1992), shows how language is used to define the reality. Cambodia is, for example, that 'hapless Southeast Asian nation', and the Khmer Rouge are, of course, 'the force of communist thugs' who were also 'well-armed and unprincipled' and had indulged in 'a three-year reign of terror', while the Chinese were the ones who had done 'the most to sustain the Khmer Rouge as a pawn in their traditional rivalry with Vietnam'.

However, one of the media's more damaging accusations was that the administration still clung to the Vietnam syndrome, despite protestations to the contrary. Early in the Bush presidency the administration was criticised by Eileen Blumenthal in the *Wall Street Journal* (1 February 1989) for having a policy which 'mainly represents its feud with Vietnam. Thus the US is in the perverse positioning of punishing Cambodia for having been rescued by its enemy.' Mary McGrory summed this up as policy 'guided by Vietnamphobia'.[143] Nayan Chanda found it strange that the US had clung to its paranoia about Vietnam since 'American friends in ASEAN ha[d] dramatically increased their contacts and trade with Hanoi'.[144] Mary McGrory, again in the *Washington Post* (14 May 1989), summed up the frustration felt by the opposition when she said that, '[o]ld obsessions die hard. Anything to do with Vietnam makes US hackles rise and causes a rush to the head, which prevents clear thinking.'

The other major focus of the media was the Khmer Rouge. The media tended to see US policy as providing a certain legitimacy for the KR which they could not otherwise achieve. The *Washington Post* (12 March 1989) went so far as to suggest that the KR did not present any real military threat and could only provide any real danger through an 'internationally sanctioned settlement that would give them a political and military advantage they could not otherwise gain'. It has been argued that part of the impetus for the 'Baker shift' was a gradual realisation that comments such as those above might be true. William Shawcross believed that Baker, being a 'canny politician ... determined to avoid débâcles, realized at five minutes to midnight ... that [Washington] risked being tarred by a disaster – a Khmer Rouge victory'.[145]

However, perhaps the most significant media event of the Bush period was the night of 26 April 1990 on which ABC-TV presented two programmes on Cambodia. The first was an hour-long documentary which was followed by the second, a forum chaired by Peter Jennings. The initial programme made the accusation that the US was covertly supporting the KR both directly and indirectly, lethally and non-lethally. Largely based on hearsay and implication the programmes and their aftermath nevertheless provided what amounted to a year-long build-up of pressure by the media, in tandem with elements from the Congress. The programme was only three months before the Baker shift and may have been a factor. Richard Solomon, for example, did not emerge from the programme very well having made an elementary slip about the US supplying arms. Solomon said that he had made a mistake. The newspapers quickly picked up on this slip and Walter Goodman thought that Solomon did 'not seem to be trying hard to sound persuasive' when denying US complicity.[146]

The effect of the programme is difficult to measure but it is true that Jennings had heightened public awareness of what Goodman described as 'yet another covertly conducted war'. And the *Washington Post* also confirmed Jennings' view that US policy was due in equal parts to deference to China and a 'hesitation to look anew at Vietnam 15 years after the American defeat'.[147] As part of a pressure campaign in favour of a particular version of reality, the media clearly played a significant role.

Academia and the *NGOs* also played their part. These two communities exhibited perhaps the most extreme domestic alternatives to the administration's views. Jeremy Stone of the Federation of American Scientists (FAS) actually detailed a complete alternative view in an article entitled 'Preventing the Return of Pol Pot: Conventional Wisdom versus New Appraisal'.[148] In this parallel world the basic tenets were as follows:

- Pol Pot's Eastern Zone government rebelled and defected to Vietnam in 1978/79.
- Vietnam was faced with a 'mad dog government as a neighbour which attacked it and would not negotiate and so Vietnam responded by overthrowing the government; what [was] wrong with this?'
- American willingness to appease China and spite Vietnam and follow the ASEAN line led to a 'policy based on geopolitical rather than humanitarian interests'.
- 'Isolating the PRK only forces [them] to be more dependent on the Vietnamese.'

- 'The PRK government, contrary to the conventional wisdom, is not really very socialist.'

And finally Stone poses the following question which he believed exposed policy options ignored by the Bush administration. He asked, 'if the Thais had overthrown Pol Pot and used the Khmer Serei ... would not the world have expressed gratitude toward the Thais and the new government been seated, promptly, in the United Nations?' Such a hypothetical scenario serves as a reminder of the existence of genuinely alternative realities.

From academia Michael Haas developed another reality which is essentially conspiratorial but nevertheless plausible. He argued, for example, that Washington actually worked hard to subvert the 1989 Paris conference in order 'to preserve a strategic relationship with China, then Solomon pointed the finger at Hanoi as the obstinate party'.[149] He also contended that Sihanouk had been in close negotiations with Hun Sen for a year prior to the Paris conference of 1989 to exclude the KR and it was only at the start of the actual conference that he reneged on their dealings. When asked why he had reversed his position Sihanouk was quoted as saying that he dared not disagree with the KR. Thus for Haas 'the fiction of Sihanouk's autonomy was thereby shattered early in the conference'.[150] Haas also quoted Roland Dumas, one of the co-chairman of the PICC, as saying that the KR had been unusually difficult and this was confirmed by an unnamed ASEAN delegate who complained that the KR was intransigent. A Son Sann delegate also said that 'the Khmer Rouge came to wreck the conference'.[151] So for Haas, the failure of the Paris conference was not the fault of Hanoi and Phnom Penh, who made concessions, but of China, the Khmer Rouge and the United States whose total number of compromises 'was zero'.[152] Although the analysis by Haas was based, among other things, on a series of interviews which may or may not have been truthful, the point is they nevertheless provided evidence for the construction of a perfectly plausible reality.

In a similar vein Edmund Muskie, the former Secretary of State, returned from a trip to Cambodia convinced that dealing with the Hun Sen government presented the only viable option open to the US government. He did not see an illegitimate regime but a government which had a 'de facto acceptance that [was] palpable and who by its actions to date ha[d] certainly earned the right to be dealt with directly by foreign governments'.[153]

The common thread of the component parts of the *conglomerate view* was that the moral issue of the Khmer Rouge was predominant and non-negotiable. The positions were as predictable as were those of the administration from their pragmatic viewpoint. There was, however, one group which, while sharing the goals of this group, were definitely *not* motivated by humanitarian concerns, that was the business community. They also believed in changing US policy by lifting the trade embargoes. Gerald Warburg (Multinational Business Development Corporation) argued that developing links with Vietnam in trade, travel and telecommunications would not only encourage the liberalising trends already underway but would also create US jobs. He also pointed out that other nations, the French, British, Dutch and Japanese, for example, were already in Vietnam and the US was losing out.[154] For the Bush administration this was probably more persuasive than the moral argument.

Vietnam/PRK/Soviet Union

By the end of the Bush presidency it appeared to Hun Sen that it was the PRK and Vietnam and the Soviet Union, in that order, who had made the concessions in the ongoing peace process. As late as January 1991 the PRK government had been clinging to two 'non-negotiable' tenets, the maintenance of the State of Cambodia (SOC) and the explicit condemnation of Khmer Rouge genocide.[155] However, it became obvious that the Soviet/Vietnamese/PRK alliance was effectively the losing side and as such would be in a weak negotiating position. Their statements began to be delivered in a tone of bravura or bluff. This tone was, of course, at its strongest in 1989 prior to the withdrawal announcement.

In a Phnom Penh Home Service Radio Broadcast, Hun Sen praised the Jakarta Informal Meetings (JIM) as the only forum for solving problems but at the same time railed against Sihanouk, referring to him dismissively as 'this former King' and asking whether the lives of millions of Cambodians could be entrusted to a man 'without any sense of reality?' 'Remember,' he continued, 'we are not losers in a war who are merely awaiting orders from the victors.'[156] In a speech at the opening of JIM-II, Vietnamese foreign minister Nguyen Co Thach reiterated the need for the 'big countries' to move away from a 'state of confrontation' into a new era of 'peaceful coexistence'. However, he also dwelt heavily on the past and spent some seven paragraphs recounting the history of the decade 1979–89. During those seven paragraphs he used the term genocidal no less than eighteen times.[157] The importance of the genocidal issue to the Vietnamese reality is clear. Their later decision not to pursue it indicates the relative powerlessness of their position.

Even when the Vietnamese announced their withdrawal on 5 April 1989 (jointly with the PRK and Laos) they attempted to maintain face by also announcing that if, after the withdrawal 'foreign countries did not completely end military aid to the Kampuchean parties, especially the Pol Pot clique, and cease all interference, the People's Republic of Kampuchea would call on other countries to give assistance to the Kampucheans to defend themselves'.[158] If, as is widely accepted, one of the reasons for Vietnamese withdrawal was their economic collapse[159] then such a threat was effectively meaningless, once the Vietnamese left there could be no going back. In fact, the day after the announcement Nguyen Co Thach admitted that once Vietnam had withdrawn they would 'never return'.[160] As Michael Williams put it, Vietnam could 'no longer afford to escape a choice between its security needs and its economic needs', they desperately needed to escape what he called the 'Cambodian vortex'.[161] By late 1990 Thach was openly admitting that Vietnam 'would not allow its future to become hostage to the Cambodian parties'.[162]

According to Michael Leifer, however, the decision to withdraw earlier than planned was not a cut and run exercise but a judgement about the PRK's 'chances of military survival and an interest in influencing both the Soviet Union and China in advance of their summit in May, as well as encouraging Prince Sihanouk to come to terms with Hun Sen'.[163] It seems plausible, nevertheless, that such a judgement was more heavily influenced by a desire for it to be true than a belief that it was true. Shortly after the announcement Thach maintained his upbeat approach by claiming that he had reached firm agreements with China and Thailand to ban arms supplies to the KR and that such a deal would 'so badly demoralize them that they [might] continue to be a problem but they [would] be a skin rash not a cancer'.[164] Again this was probably either bravura or wishful thinking.

By late 1991 Hun Sen's government had officially dropped communism at a special congress of the KPRP which also changed its name to Cambodian People's Party (CPP). In a complementary action Heng Samrin was removed and replaced by the more overtly nationalist Chea Sim. The Phnom Penh government was, by that stage, primarily engaged in exercises of image enhancement – revising the national anthem, changing the national flag and amending the constitution to make Buddhism the state religion. Anything which would limit the concessions the SOC would be required to make. The PRK's reality had effectively been altered by that of the Soviet Union and, in turn, the Vietnamese. Their domestically generated change of interest had caused the PRK to face a reality which included the KR as a 'fact of life', Sino-Soviet rapprochement, US–Soviet detente and the collapse of communism, in short, a new reality. They dealt with it as best they could but they appeared to be the 'losers, awaiting orders from the victors' they had claimed not to be.

China/Khmer Rouge/ASEAN/Sihanouk/Thailand

If the PRK were the losers then this strange alliance could be considered the victors. *China* was naturally the predominant force in constructing this reality. The Chinese regional view was dominated by their traditional paranoia concerning Vietnam, a fact demonstrated by constant references to Vietnamese lack of sincerity.[165] Chinese isolationism also affected their world-view. It even manifested itself in a mild condemnation for President Bush during a visit to Beijing in February 1989. In a thinly veiled warning Premier Li Peng said there were attempts to influence China's internal affairs and if this came 'from government officials, it would throw a shadow on existing friendly relations'. Bush responded by saying that the relationship with China was 'one of the very most important relationships that we have'.[166] All this only four months before Tiananmen. The Chinese obviously knew how important they were to the US.

The Chinese also attached all the blame for the 1989 failure at Paris on Vietnamese intransigence[167] and would only accept moves towards normalisation with Vietnam when they felt confident the Vietnamese had been effectively emasculated by their economic plight and no longer posed a threat. It was only in late 1991 that the Chinese Prime Minister Li Peng admitted that 'relations between China and Vietnam [would] gradually resume towards normalization'.[168]

However, perhaps the most enlightening indication of the Chinese world-view came in an extensive article in the *Beijing Review* (11–17 December 1989). This article proposed that in the wake of the Vietnamese withdrawal the Americans were 'attempting to capitalize on the current situation and re-enter Indo-China and thereby regain US strategic interests in this region'. This idea is in direct contrast to the notion of American disentanglement. The article argued that the establishment of a non-Communist government in Kampuchea would allow the US to 'return to Indo-China'. There was also concern expressed that the detente between the Soviet Union and the US was a potential threat to China.

China's reality consisted of a threat-infested environment in which alliances were only functionally worthwhile if they dampened the threat environment. For China then, in November 1989, Thailand was a friend and Premier Chatichai Choonhaven was described as 'understanding of China's quelling of the anti-government riots in Beijing in June'.[169] However, when Chatichai hosted a visit by Hun Sen in February 1991 the Chinese were clearly unhappy and applauded the military coup which overthrew Chatichai.[170] China cherished complete sovereignty and judged others by their threats to that sovereignty and in so doing adhered to the dictum 'my enemy's enemy is my friend'. As an example, after years of confrontation with the Soviet Union they were willing in 1989 to develop a rapprochement and even issue joint statements to the effect that they both favoured a quadripartite government under Sihanouk simply because it dampened regional tension.[171]

Sihanouk himself maintained his usual mercurial existence calling for Khmer Rouge inclusion in November 1989[172] and then bemoaning their inclusion two years later when he said that 'the Cambodians were forced by the [P5] to accept the return of the Khmer Rouge'.[173] Sihanouk's brand of pragmatism was based on his apparently genuine view that what was best for the Khmer people was Sihanouk. Anything that promoted that vision was, therefore, acceptable. Perhaps Sihanouk's pragmatic viewpoint is best understood by referring to his own words:

> the Khmer Rouge have killed five of my children. They have killed 14 of my grand-children. I know what kind of people they are. Yet, I have to try to create some process of reconciliation in my country. It is my judgement it is better to have them in the process than frozen out, where I am sure they are going to make civil war.[174]

Any legitimisation of the PRK was seen by Sihanouk as a major obstacle to his eventual return to power. He could, and had, worked with the KR but he would find it more difficult to accommodate Hun Sen, and vice-versa. He was particularly unhappy with both Chatichai's welcome for Hun Sen and Baker's vacant UN seat decision, both of which Sihanouk believed conferred a degree of legitimacy on the PRK.[175] Sihanouk's attendance/non-attendance at JIM, for example, and his resignations/reinstatements from a variety of positions were merely tactical devices aimed at achieving his ultimate reinstatement as Cambodian Head of State.

For the *Khmer Rouge*, survival was their only concern. They needed to adjust in order to survive and to eventually reassume their previous position. By October 1990, for example, they had carried out an education programme in which military considerations had been 'absolutely subordinated to politics'.[176] The goal had not changed only the tactics. The KR world-view was essentially xenophobic and almost by definition paranoid. Michimi Muranushu argued that the Khmer Rouge are an archetypal example of 'dichotomous thinkers', they could only think in terms of friends and enemies with nothing in between.[177] As a result it was almost impossible for them to *genuinely* negotiate. Negotiations for the KR merely represented an alternative tactical device. During the Bush administration that tactic was to stall and wait until *all* foreign forces were out of Cambodia.

For the KR, Hun Sen fell into that category. As late as July 1992 the KR were still demanding that there 'should be no government of the State of Cambodia' in any structure erected under the Peace Agreement.[178] In their view, the four Cambodian parties should be accorded equal footing. Their concerns were confirmed, at least in their own eyes, by UNTAC which was 'too partial to the Phnom Penh government'.[179] Khmer Rouge reality was predicated upon a xenophobically generated siege mentality.

ASEAN shared a very mild version of the same mentality. It too saw a dangerous environment that had to be handled. They remained essentially passive, hoping to achieve their desired goals through diplomacy. ASEAN was extremely concerned, therefore, when the benign status quo appeared to be altered by the Baker announcement of July 1990. ASEAN unity had previously been somewhat fragile but was stiffened by the Kampuchean issue. After the Vietnamese withdrawal this cement was removed, exposing old rivalries, as did Thailand's quasi-recognition of Hun Sen. Concern over the 'Baker shift' forced ASEAN to 'close ranks around their original stand of upholding a cardinal rule of international relations: respect for national sovereignty'.[180]

The cracks which appeared in ASEAN ranks with the Vietnamese withdrawal were between those who considered Vietnam had passed the test and should be invited into the fold (Malaysia and Indochina) and those (like Singapore) who wanted Vietnam to take measures to alter its economic and political systems *before* any further detente – as the Singapore Prime Minister said, 'antagonists do not become bosom friends overnight'.[181] Despite these potentially damaging differences ASEAN managed to remain intact and retain a relatively consistent policy towards Cambodia. ASEAN's primary concern was for stability, everything was subordinated to that end.

Thailand, as ASEAN's 'front line state', was also primarily concerned with stability. Although he received Hun Sen in January 1989, Chatichai was still pledging support for the CGDK and withholding recognition of the PRK two months later in Beijing.[182] Later that year the Thai foreign minister announced that Thailand would 'reduce its role in the settlement of the Cambodian problem'.[183] Seemingly the combination of increasing domestic pressures and decreasing Vietnamese threat meant that such a retreat was acceptable.

As momentum towards the elections of 1993 gathered pace the relative influence of China, Khmer Rouge, Thailand, ASEAN and Sihanouk settled into a tactical jockeying for position; the strategic goals had been effectively won and lost, realities had been adjusted and fused, with the exception of the Khmer Rouge who rejected what appeared inevitable to the others. The other alternative realities were also seen to be aligned with what was apparently the inevitable progress towards the settlement agreed in Paris in October 1991.

AMALGAM OF REALITIES

The problem for a foreign policy based on pragmatic reactions to events lies in discerning the significance of those events. In hindsight the crucial moments of the Bush presidency, for Cambodia, were the two Paris conferences of 1989 and 1991, the Vietnamese withdrawal of 1989, and the period in which UNTAC and the Cambodian Supreme National Council (SNC) coexisted to take the country up to the elections of 1993. This was where the various realities came into direct contact.

When the Vietnamese announced their withdrawal on 5 April 1989 it included reference to the reality as they perceived it. Thus the statement said that Vietnam would withdraw 'all its troops from Kampuchea by the end of September 1989, by which time foreign interference in Kampuchea's internal affairs and all foreign military aid to all Kampuchean parties must cease'.[184] This would seem to suggest that *other* foreign interference in Kampuchea was the problem, and since that would cease then the Vietnamese could

withdraw with a job well done. Of course, an alternative interpretation was that the reduction in Soviet aid was so drastic that
continuing Vietnamese occupation was rendered untenable. Another
contributory factor may have been a genuine feeling that the PRK
had developed sufficient wherewithal to survive unsupported.

Whatever the reasons, this one event reignited the whole
Cambodian issue and encouraged all the parties to try for a settlement at the PICC of August 1989. The conference was said to have
failed. The US blamed Vietnamese intransigence and insistence upon
retaining the use of 'genocide' in any settlement; the Khmer Rouge
were blamed by Vietnam for refusing to accept genocide; the US was
blamed for using the failure of the conference to blame Vietnam who
were, of course, blameless. In truth the first conference was unlikely
to have succeeded since it was the first real opportunity that the
parties had had to confront each other openly. They had arrived at
the conference with immovable positions but it was a process that had
to be performed. It permitted the parties to depart with honour but to
contemplate how best to progress.

Progress *was* made because two years later the second PICC
succeeded. In the interim several other significant events also
occurred, not least the Baker policy shift of July 1990. Immediately
after the Paris failure Alan Cranston and Stephen Solarz joined
forces to pressure the Bush administration to rethink US policy to the
extent that Solarz also adjusted his thinking on the lethal aid issue,
now arguing to phase it out.[185] They were to make Cambodia an irritant for the administration which would demand action sooner or
later. By the time Baker had made his statement, pressure had built
inexorably and the Peter Jennings ABC-TV special was said to have
been the catalyst for Congressional unease and potential rebellion
which pushed Baker into his announcement. The Bush administration
had 'squirmed as never before, over the fallout from Jennings' documentary'.[186] Contributing to Baker's unease was the testimony of CIA
officials to the Senate Intelligence Committee that the Khmer Rouge
controlled 30 per cent of Cambodia and were advancing steadily.[187]
Although these estimates proved overly pessimistic they were
extremely worrying at the time.

The other interested parties reacted to the Baker shift predictably.
China continued 'supplying arms to the resistance, especially to the
Khmer Rouge and insisted Cambodia's seat in the UN should not be
left vacant'.[188] The Vietnamese welcomed the statement and were
'ready to negotiate with concerned countries on the Cambodian

issue'.[189] ASEAN were concerned that US decisions, made 'without advanced consultation with ASEAN may cause problems'.[190] There is little doubt, however, that the timing of the shift had much to do with averting a Congressional revolt since Baker had received a letter of condemnation, from more than 60 Senators, only four days before his statement. Baker's statement also represented an agreement with Eduard Shevardnadze to act in concert and dampened the worst excesses of media criticism.

The Baker initiative had also come amid a series of meetings among the five permanent members of the UN Security Council (P5) which in turn had resulted from the breakdown of the first PICC. By their third meeting on 12/13 March 1990 the P5 had produced a 'framework' which was subsequently published as UN Document No. A/45/167 (16 March 90). The document provided a synthesis of the ideas which had been touted over the previous six months:

> the need for the United Nations to have an enhanced role ...; a comprehensive political settlement ...; free and fair elections under the UN's direct administration; creation of a SNC which would be the unique legitimate body and source of authority in which ... national sovereignty and unity should be enshrined.

The final version of the P5 framework, produced in May 1990, included, in addition to the above, recommendations which ensured the verification of withdrawal, cessation of military assistance, a durable cease-fire, cantonment, UN peacekeepers to control the elections and the run-up to the elections.[191] A later P5 communiqué added a statement to the effect that the SNC must be 'fully functioning' in order for the PICC to be reconvened. They also reaffirmed their support for Sihanouk's election to the chair of the SNC while expressing concern that the SNC had failed to resolve the issue which had resulted in an 'inability to form a delegation to occupy Cambodia's UN seat'.[192]

The P5 also involved Indonesia, Canada, India, Laos, Malaysia, Australia and Japan and the whole process gathered pace during the last two months of 1990. By that stage the convergence of superpower interests (i.e. extrication) was forcing general agreement with the P5 framework, so much so that China was able to announce that since the signing of the framework they had not 'provided any military assistance to the resistance forces in Cambodia'.[193] In conjunction with the JIM meetings, which consisted of the four Kampuchean factions, the ASEAN states and Vietnam and Laos, the P5 meetings had laid the foundations for the second PICC which took place later in 1991.

One particularly important product of the JIM series was the emergence of the 'Australian Plan' which formed the basis of the P5 framework.[194] The initial work on the 'Red Book', as it was called, began immediately after the failure of the first PICC. Gareth Evans (the Australian foreign minister) and Stephen Solarz met in New York and formed the basis of the Australian plan. At its core was the enhanced role for the UN as a method of side-stepping the power-sharing impasse which had been a major factor in the original breakdown in Paris. Senator Evans proposed a UN involvement during a transitional period and he also suggested a change in the status of the Cambodian seat. The Australians argued, and with some justification, that it was the 'enhanced UN role' which had broken the post-Paris stalemate.[195] Although the Red Book was an extremely detailed work it was the basic ideas that counted – the enhanced UN role, the vacant UN seat and the SNC. Of course, these were only ultimately effective because the US, Soviet Union and China agreed that they should be.

The SNC did have problems, particularly its composition and leadership. It was generally agreed that Sihanouk would eventually become President but whether the SNC would have twelve, thirteeen or fourteen members and who would be vice-chairman were contentious issues. At one stage Hun Sen was insisting upon being the vice-chairman but he eventually dropped his claim in response to Sihanouk's resignation as leader of the National Government of Cambodia (NGC) when he declared that he had 'no party and no army [and was] completely neutral'.[196] The other problem was the requirement for both the SOC and the NGC governments to be dismantled and subsumed into the SNC structure. Sihanouk is credited with the breakthrough idea to make the SNC a 'super-government' which would operate as an umbrella above the SOC and NGC and would, therefore, not necessitate their demise. This device enabled the SNC to operate nominally alongside the UNTAC authorities and also enabled virtually everybody to save face.

From early 1991 until October 1991 there was a significant acceleration in the peace process due to at least three factors. First, the US/Chinese/ASEAN inspired isolation of the Phnom Penh government and its complementary sanctions against Vietnam were beginning to bite. Secondly, there was a realisation that the KR offensive had stalled and that the SOC was unlikely to suffer military defeat. There was also no real enthusiasm for any KPNLF or ANS chances of success. Thirdly, China began to realise that it had achieved all its strategic goals. Evidence had come in June 1991 at the seventh Vietnamese party congress when anti-Chinese hard-liner Nguyen Co Thach was sacrificed, possibly to open the way to Sino-Vietnamese normalisation. Coming into the second PICC every party would derive some benefit from an agreement.

As a consequence, on 23 October 1991, the warring factions signed a peace agreement which nominally ended 13 years of war. The final document of the PICC represented an elaboration of the P5 framework in addition to elements from the first session of the PICC.[197] What was not present in the final document was specific reference to 'genocide'. This represented another concession by the SOC and what must have been a particularly distressing one. At the first JIM meeting (28 July 1988) the phrase 'genocidal policies and practices of the Pol Pot regime' was used in the final communiqué. In a General Assembly resolution (3 November 1989) the phrase had been watered down to 'the universally condemned policies and practices of the recent past'. By February 1990 the Red Book spoke of 'human rights abuses of a recent past' and finally the P5 framework of 26 August 1990 mentioned 'the policies and practices of the past'. Despite SOC protestations they were forced into a series of compromises.

On 20 November 1991 the General Assembly passed Resolution 46/18 which fully supported the Paris agreement and established the UN Transitional Authority in Cambodia (UNTAC), 'the biggest and most complex operation in UN history'. From the start of UNTAC throughout 1992 there was a single obstacle that outweighed any others. It was a failure on the part of the KR to comply with virtually any aspect of the agreement that required them to diminish their power on the ground. They would not comply with cantonment, they would not disarm, they would not allow UNTAC troops into the areas they controlled. While this was continually referred to as jeopardising the peace process, as were KR attacks on ethnic Vietnamese and UNTAC personnel, it might actually have *saved* the process. *The Guardian* of 6 November 1992, for example, referred to a four-faction meeting in Beijing as a 'last-ditch attempt to save the peace accord', but at the same time a European diplomat was quoted as saying that UNTAC was 'determined to forge ahead, never excluding the Khmer Rouge but simply repeating that if you don't register, you can't vote'.[198] Even the Chinese were becoming impatient with KR intransigence. In a personal letter from Hun Sen to Jeremy Stone the

SOC premier pointed out that an election without the Khmer Rouge seemed the most likely option and he continued that it was 'also more sane and more decent as criminals and terrorists do not have the right to stand for elections in the first place'.[199]

Pressing on regardless of the Khmer Rouge may be seen as the correct course in light of the ultimate success of the election process but during 1992 there was an angry debate between the French and Australian approaches to dealing with the KR. The French advocated forcing the KR to comply. In July 1992 this disagreement culminated in the sacking of the French commander of the UN Advanced Mission in Cambodia (UNAMIC) and second-in-command of UNTAC, General Michel Loridon, by his Australian commander General Sanderson. Loridon had argued that the KR were deliberately stalling in order to expand their control prior to the elections and once they had failed to comply with Phase II they should have been forced by UNTAC either to comply or to retaliate. If they complied, he reasoned, that would be fine. If not then 'it is possible ... that [we] might lose 200 men – and that includes myself – but the Khmer Rouge problem would be solved for good'.[200] Loridon's Australian commander and, more importantly, his political boss Mr Akashi did not agree with this belligerent attitude. Loridon therefore left UNTAC after only eight months saying that he was 'frustrated by [his] inability to implement the UN mandate. Here was our chance to deal with the Khmer Rouge. But I haven't succeeded in getting my superiors to agree with me.'[201] Morally Loridon may have had a case but he was never going to win; the major powers were trying to *extricate* themselves, not become involved in a jungle war against highly competent guerrillas.

Surveying the amalgam of realities through the Bush presidency suggests that a congruence of circumstances and interests occurred which allowed the Cambodian elections of 1993 to become the unexpected success they were, although even now the long-term success of the peace process for the Cambodian people is less sure. The two most important factors in the culmination of the peace process were the ending of the Cold War, which permitted an optimism, particularly in the utility of the UN, and the general exhaustion of the combatant and non-combatant interested parties. In the first flush of this new enthusiasm there was extreme disappointment at the failure of the initial PICC. However, this generated the Australian plan and the involvement of the P5 which, in turn, overcame the natural antipathies of the internal factions, forcing them to view their own survival as more likely in collective terms. Once the P5 had committed themselves to a solution the third Indochinese war had entered its end-game, though whether this will preclude a fourth war is a moot point. It would be easy to point at specific events such as Gorbachev's accession, the end of the Cold War, Sino-Soviet rapprochement, Sino-Vietnamese rapprochement, Thai–PRK rapprochement, and media events as contributory factors, which they undoubtedly were, but it may simply have been that the conflict had run its course, that the single most important factor was exhaustion.

CONCLUSION

A succinct assessment of the Bush foreign policy was delivered by Terry Diebel when he said it displayed 'an intriguing mixture of competence and drift of tactical mastery set in a larger pattern of strategic indirection'.[202] Ironically, however, it was probably this mixture and its implied inadequacy that made it possible for Bush to preside over the final acts of the Cambodian peace process. A pragmatist, essentially disinterested in this particular issue and preoccupied with what he considered the 'real' foreign policy problems of superpower interaction was, perhaps, ideally suited to handle such a morally ambivalent situation. With the removal of what James Baker called 'the overlay of US-Soviet competition', the United States saw itself as being in a position to 'provide geopolitical balance, to be an honest broker, to reassure against uncertainty'.[203] This meant that it could take a quasi-objective, patriarchal stance requiring only reaction to specific events, since it had already provided its own overlay for the world. Not so much a 'new world order' but a reconstructed reality.

A small measure of Bush's relative disinterest in Cambodia can be inferred from the raw statistics of the count of references to Cambodia made by the President in his public statements, or rather the lack of them. In 1989 there were *two* comments both made shortly after the PICC failure. The whole of 1990 saw another *two*. In 1991 there were *none*, which, considering the success of the PICC, was astonishing. In 1992-93 combined, there were another *three*. However, it must be understood that the disinterest was relative. From August 1990 to March 1991, for example, Bush was otherwise engaged with the Gulf conflict, while in the latter stages of 1992 he had chosen to concentrate on the Somalian crisis as his parting foreign policy gesture.

Mandelbaum suggests that the ending of the Cold War meant that regional conflicts which had previously derived their importance from the superpower struggle were far less consequential for US foreign policy, and Cambodia seems to be a clear example.[204] The Bush administration probably concluded that it had limited interest in Cambodia and even less ability to be able to influence events unilaterally. Such a conclusion would automatically favour a reactive approach and, as has been stated earlier, that would have suited Bush's character. The main Bush goal was to revive stability in the area without becoming too involved. The lack of any real policy statements after the second PICC indicates the Bush administration considered it had fulfilled its limited responsibilities.

The only real issue remaining after Paris was normalisation with Vietnam and this did expose the weakness of a President without 'vision'. Bush found it extremely difficult to break the Vietnam syndrome. Perhaps this was not personal but his lack of interest allowed the 'Kissinger boys' to hold sway. In his inaugural speech Bush had called for a 'statute of limitations on Vietnam', but four years later Jim Hoagland wrote in the *Washington Post* (12 July 1992) that 'America's war in Vietnam ha[d] become an unlikely touchstone for [the Presidential] campaign'. It was further suggested that it was 'an abiding irony that the United States lost the war in a military sense, but ended up imposing a victor's terms for normalization ... perhaps a vengeful United States is wielding its economic might to inflict the defeat it failed to impose with its army'.[205] Perhaps Vietnam will always be a touchstone for US foreign policy so why should Bush be any different?

What Mervin called Bush's weakness, his 'chronic lack of consistently held beliefs and convictions'[206] was probably the 'attribute' which enabled him to shift US foreign policy towards Cambodia when the coalition of the media, congress, academia, NGOs, plus a White House lack of interest, all combined to exert enormous domestic pressure on the President. The Vietnamese withdrawal exposed a problem and the coalition provided the pressure, consequently the pragmatist provided the reaction; and, given the limited objectives, it was a successful reaction. A firm critic of US policy, Jim Leach, said as much in a Congressional hearing, 'I think the Bush administration has been largely vindicated.'[207]

Specifically he was referring to the Bush 'open-door' policy on China which Congress, including Leach, had opposed. Interestingly the President had remained resolute in the face of Congressional pressure on China but altered his position in the face of similar pressure on Cambodia. This might indicate a President prepared to be persuaded by convincing argument, or one who is more interested in superpowers than regional powers and thus more resolute on issues affecting them. What it probably most clearly demonstrates is the difficulty in predicting how a President who constructs a reality from a pragmatic world-view will act on any given issue because his reality will be so contextually rooted. Unless the analyst shares his pragmatism, or can at least empathise with it, the task will be full of apparently unexpected pitfalls.

Notwithstanding the difficulties of prediction, US foreign policy towards Cambodia was not radically different under a pragmatic president. Admittedly a major shift in the US position did occur with the Baker statement, but given the media and Congressional pressure it is impossible to prove that Reagan or Carter might not have acted in a similar manner and remained consistent with their own realities. It could be argued that with relatively unimportant issues, such as Cambodia, the pragmatic view will tend to predominate because lack of interest permits more flexibility. For example, a shift as fundamental as that made by Baker would have come under far greater scrutiny had it concerned a major policy issue. Similarly the rhetoric can be less rigorous as is shown in this chapter by some of the contradictory statements made by the administration's spokesmen. Finally, there does not appear to be anything radically different about the type of rhetoric used by the Bush policy-making team in constructing their reality when compared with those of the three previous administrations who did not share Bush's complete dedication to pragmatism. Understanding that Bush had a pragmatic world-view was neither a help nor a hindrance and permitted much the same quality of analysis as those based on more ideologically generated world-views.

Conclusion

One irrefutable conclusion of this analysis is that, throughout the four presidencies, United States foreign policy towards Cambodia was remarkably robust. The realities of each administration were well defended, at all levels of government, against the considerable pressure exerted by other realities, both political and moral. This was especially true of the foot-soldiers of the State Department. It is also clear that only issue-specific staff were in any way concerned with Cambodia. For example, the relative lack of influence of Caspar Weinberger and Harold Brown on the Cambodian issue became obvious during searches through the documentary evidence. Although both were powerful figures, other than when Cambodia threatened to involve the Department of Defence they were disinterested.

That disinterest relegated them to level three of the hierarchy and looking closely at the degree of involvement on this specific issue enabled other individuals to be accurately located. Cheney, for example, was also located at level three and quite legitimately so. Designating significant personnel, on the basis of role and issue also illustrated the functional utility of the Assistant Secretaries of State in representing the administration's policies, particularly in Congress. The performances of the Assistants in all four administrations was, incidentally, generally impressive – at least from the administration's perspective. The adoption of a simplified, three-tier, interpretation of the decision-making structure allowed detailed explanations and analyses of the 'principate' which bear comparison with other analysts' assessments.

The decision to use Cambodia as a case-study initially seemed a sound choice. The Carter administration's difficulty in accommodating an avowedly human rights oriented foreign policy in an increasingly hostile environment was well illustrated by the dilemma presented by the Vietnamese invasion of Cambodia in December 1978. Also, moral tension within the administration should have been inflamed by the Vietnamese invasion, which was presented as a confrontation between states' rights and human rights. However, as the research unfolded Cambodia was obviously not as central as had originally been assumed. While there were some interesting *philosophical* debates about Cambodia, virtually any other issue pushed

Cambodia off the agenda. Given the place of Indochina in the American psyche it was surprising that Cambodia was so peripheral; perhaps the Weinberger Doctrine, with its non-interventionist bias, had been more persuasive than was imagined. It was in making sense of this apparently surprising lack of concern that the identification of competing realities proved useful. Cambodia's significance lay in the fact that, like Vietnam, it was peripheral but given Cold War logic it had the potential to become central. Realities which still contained superpower clients inevitably generated cautious, stability driven foreign policies.

The inference of those realities from public utterances was relatively straightforward and in certain instances, such as Douglas Pike's 'bear' story,[1] virtually impossible to avoid. Here was a senior State Department official describing the Vietnamese politburo as a unitary actor to whose psychological profile he alone was privy. That he operated and formed these views on the basis of a view of reality unique to himself is an unavoidable conclusion. Also, his view of reality clearly affected his judgement and his judgement was valued by significant decision-makers. The reality, irrespective of its derivation was clearly influential. Given Pike's role as an adviser his influence might have been peripheral, but the relative lack of status accorded Cambodia meant that advisers' views were often accepted at face value. When an issue is relatively insignificant in the perception of the higher level actors, level three actors have significant influence.

The task of inferring realities was more difficult, of course, with members higher up the elite than Pike. Pike was an Indochinese specialist and thus his total world-view would contain a greater proportion of detail on South East Asia than that of the President or Secretary of State, for example. With the members of level one and two it was possible to infer a reality from their general statements but there then had to be a second order inference about Cambodia. This was primarily the result of the scarcity of comments about Cambodia. Notwithstanding this difficulty it did prove possible. President Reagan's reality, for example, could be represented as a simplistic and dichotomous relationship between good and evil, between 'good guys' and 'bad guys', between 'us' (the capitalist West) and 'them' (the Communist bloc). Thus when Reagan spoke of Cambodia it was consequently predictable. Although post-perestroika there were subtle changes they were merely in who constituted 'them' and 'us' and not in the core beliefs of the reality.

Accepting the notion of separate realities, rhetoric was a powerful factor in the maintenance of those realities and an important indicator for their analysis. Coral Bell's assertion that 'words are deeds'[2] was repeatedly proven. When a President says 'read my lips' it has consequences for his future actions and he knows that. When, for example, Bush castigated China for Tiananmen Square he was careful to avoid making specific statements of intent. Given that he saw the world as an environment to be managed, and that previous statements had signalled his view of China's importance, a contemporary analysis, based on Bush's rhetoric, could reasonably have concluded that it was unlikely that MFN status would be withdrawn. An historical analysis, armed with the knowledge that less than five weeks after Tiananmen, Bush dispatched very senior personnel to Beijing on a damage limitation exercise, would have reached much the same conclusion. Thus a certain predictive element can be legitimately claimed for this type of analysis.

Given that the general approach of this research was relevant, what did it reveal about the foreign policy of the United States towards Cambodia from 1977–1992? In February 1993 Stephen Solarz said that in his opinion 'the central thrust of [US] policy was correct in that it led to a settlement of the Cambodian issue'.[3] Given the consistency of US demands for Vietnamese withdrawal, free and fair elections, and no return to power of the Khmer Rouge, his assessment was not unreasonable. The policies developed by the various principates had achieved their stated goals despite the serious reservations of their many opponents. The realities constructed by successive administrations had served the administrations well.

The relevant element of each administration's reality was the designation of Vietnam as the regional villain. The United States' previous involvement in Indochina and the fact that Vietnam was allied for much of the period to the Soviet Union made the demonisation of Vietnam inevitable. The more surprising common feature of the realities was the relative insignificance of Indochina for American foreign policy in general. Cambodia in particular was invariably a secondary or even tertiary factor, always peripheral. It was only when other agencies, the media for example, generated sufficient interest through films and journalism that any of the administrations really responded; even then they tended to react defensively, almost passively. An example of such reactive policy-making might be argued to have occurred in 1978 when there seemed some chance of normalisation with Vietnam. When the Vietnamese invaded Cambodia,

Carter merely abandoned normalisation plans which were actually quite close to fruition. As Carter said in his memoirs, 'when the government in Hanoi decided to invade Cambodia and also began to take on the trappings of a Soviet puppet, we did not want to pursue the idea [of normalisation]'.[4] Normalisation was an issue fraught with political dangers whereas maintaining the status quo was not. This single incident simultaneously shows the significance of Indochina in the American psyche *and* the lack of importance of the issue to policy-makers. Indochina had *latent* explosiveness as an issue and as such would be dealt with only when that potential was in danger of being realised; the Baker shift was just such a moment.

Carter's statement was consistent with the predominant statist imperative at the centre of the realities of the various administrations. Any debate surrounding the tension between states' rights and human rights was invariably settled in favour of the former, although Stephen Solarz argued that choosing between the two was not necessary. When responding to the question which of the two United States' goals, Vietnamese withdrawal or the non-return of the Khmer Rouge, was the most important, he answered, 'If you ask me to choose, I would say preventing the return of the Khmer Rouge was clearly the more important; but I didn't see them by any means as mutually exclusive propositions.'[5] Notwithstanding Solarz's preference, United States policy statements generally cited the withdrawal of Vietnamese forces as the first priority and even Solarz himself admitted that US policy 'was driven *primarily* by a desire to prevent Vietnamese expansion'[6] (emphasis added); other requirements such as the emasculation of the Khmer Rouge and the self-determination of the Cambodian people were decidedly secondary.

The dilemma of states' versus human rights was not so much ignored by the decision-makers as circumvented. Cyrus Vance had said, for example, that it was sometimes necessary to 'take a position which, although essential for our national interests, is at the same time extremely distasteful'.[7] This was in reference to the vote for the DK seat in the UN, which was taken, according to Vance, as 'the only decision consistent with our overall national interests'.[8] Those national interests had come to be perceived, at least in terms of South East Asia, as coincident with those of ASEAN. The relationship with ASEAN was seen, throughout the period under review, as 'the cornerstone of US policy in the area'.[9] What is clear is that the realities of the Carter, Reagan and Bush principates included minimum US involvement with maximum US influence based on fear of a Soviet-backed

Vietnamese regional hegemony; and that very basic view remained relatively consistent throughout the various presidencies.

The confidence of each principate in its own view of the world was only challenged when significant events external to the policy elite either demanded a change for political reasons (such as the Congressional pressure during the Bush presidency), or forced the emergence of a new dominant world-view, such as the victory of the Brzezinski line during Carter's term. However, in their different ways, both 'adjustments' were understandable and perhaps even predictable given the personalities and management styles of the two Presidents. Until these events, reality seemed to be fixed and continuous; after them, reality was reviewed and reconstructed and was once more seen as fixed and continuous.

This pattern is similar to the 'punctuated equilibria' model favoured by Bob Boynton of Iowa University.[10] The mathematical model from which Boynton's model is derived states that variables interact below the level of certain constants until a state of equilibrium is attained. This equilibrium will be maintained until such time as the value of one or more of the constants alters. That alteration will set in motion the variables which will again seek a new state of equilibrium. And so the cycle would continue. In Boynton's application of the model the superpowers are the constants and the Cambodian politicians the variables. Thus while the superpower relationships remained stable the situation in Cambodia was stalemated, or in 'equilibrium' in the vernacular of the model. Boynton talks of the United States, China, Soviet Union and, in a more limited way Vietnam, as being the constants. Thus when the values of the constants changed in 1989/90, the variables (Hun Sen, Sihanouk, Son Sann, Khieu Samphan et al.) were kick-started back into motion in order to seek a new equilibrium.

This book views competing realities as 'constants' and distinguishes a hierarchical and relative significance for each one. For US foreign policy each administration's reality was in equilibrium which appeared permanent – until the moment of change. The radical shift in United States policy announced by James Baker in July 1990 was clearly a moment when the equilibrium was punctuated; however, the more significant question is, what punctuated it? The same is true of the Sino-Soviet rapprochement, the collapse of Communism, Tiananmen Square, the Vietnamese withdrawal, all represented changes in the structure of different realities. Where this analysis differs from Boynton's is that it contends that constants can also take on the characteristics of variables. Thus the passive stance of the United States allowed it to be reactive to the changes in the values of the other constants, that is, to act as a variable.

Thus, for most of the time, administrations could ignore other realities and it was only when confidence in their own realities began to evaporate that alternative realities became significant. Until the need for change was perceived from within alternatives remained peripheral, either as obstacles to be negotiated, in the case of other states' realities, or as political irritants, in the case of those constructed by the domestic media, congress or academia. The fact that changes in policy clearly do occur suggests that inferring a world-view and a static reality from public statements is not sufficient in itself to explain foreign policy, there must be some reference to the alternative realities which can, in part, generate changes. Looking at the policies towards Cambodia this seems evident. Once a reality had been accepted the attachment to that view remained until a significant event damaged the structure of the reality. At that time serious re-evaluation occurred which did, however, entail stepping outside the parameters of the administration's view of the world in its most basic sense. Thus even though Bush appeared to abandon his belief that negotiation with Vietnam was impossible without certain preconditions, the sudden reversal of that view was consistent with his basically pragmatic reality; given the pressure he was under from Congress and the media, and his own pragmatic outlook, his shift was perhaps even predictable.

This book reveals that United States foreign policy towards Cambodia had an extremely low priority. No administration was unduly concerned about events in Indochina and as such it was possible to leave the issue on the 'back-burner' until such time as sufficient additional heat was applied to demand attention. During those periods policy was effectively conducted by level three officials. When heat *was* applied, in 1990, by a variety of agents, the result was the involvement of levels one and two and the dramatic 'Baker shift'. The remarkable consistency of United States foreign policy during the period under review, through the terms of four administrations, may be argued to have been the result more of disinterest than a thoughtful appreciation and evaluation of the consequences of such policy.

This is perhaps most clearly shown by looking at the statements of two of the better known, non-administration, protagonists – Mary McGrory and Stephen Solarz. Neither held government office, although Solarz's position as Chairman of the East Asian sub-committee gave him influence, but both were immersed in the issues. Their positions are of interest because they highlight diametrically opposed interpretations of the situation – two alternative realities, in fact.

In August 1991 McGrory wrote that those 'who bother to inquire about Cambodia soon learn that the policy is based on pure spite and appeasement'.[11] McGrory's reality consisted of a duplicitous US government driven by *realpolitik* and vengeance. When asked to respond to this statement Solarz did so as follows:

> It's a cute and clever soundbite but it's a lot of crap. I knew the people involved in formulating our policy and I do not believe that our policy was driven by spite for Vietnam nor by appeasement for China. I think our policy was driven primarily by a desire to prevent Vietnamese expansion, a desire to facilitate self-determination for the Cambodian people, and a determination to try and prevent the return of the Khmer Rouge to power; based on a recognition of the *realities* we confronted.[12]

A part of Solarz's reality was a recognition of the necessity of Chinese cooperation and he argued that both China and Thailand would have had to be 'comfortable' with any settlement. He went on to assert that he did not consider that taking into account Chinese concerns was appeasement: 'I don't consider that as appeasing China, I consider it a *realistic* way of trying to advance American interests and American values by taking into account the *realities* of the situation.'[13] In answer to the question what *were* American interests, Solarz answered, 'withdrawal of Vietnamese forces, humanitarian and moral interest in preventing another genocide in Cambodia, and regional peace and stability'.[14]

Solarz's reality, then, was opposed to McGrory's and was in various instances also different from any of the administrations' versions but he genuinely believed that there *was* an objective reality which others simply failed to see. Similarly the realities constructed by each administration actually *existed* for them. The truth seems to be that all the realities existed and competed for pre-eminence; mostly, and naturally, in the domain of United States foreign policy, it was the reality created by United States administrations that was generally successful. However, when making predictions about foreign policy from inferred realities it must be recognised that occasionally the established equilibrium will be punctuated by events.

When Richard Melanson talked of foreign policy being the resultant of a 'tyranny of presidential rhetoric largely disconnected from international and domestic realities'[15] he was guilty of hyperbole. Presidential rhetoric was often ascendant but it was difficult to prove tyranny, it may have been in a state of tension with the alternative realities created by other actors but it was most certainly connected, even if only in its refutation of them. Presidential rhetoric *was* qualitatively different but not the predominant factor that the term tyranny would suggest. Each separate reality competed on its own terms but always with an eye to the claims of the others, even when not actually acknowledging them. However, while the President was clearly at the apex of the foreign policy structure in a general sense, this research shows that for issues of relative insignificance, such as Cambodia proved to be, the detail of policy, and consequently to a large extent policy itself, was effectively delegated to third level actors. As these tended to be conservative State Department regionalists, conservatism became policy. The reality inhabited by each administration was conservative and comfortable and only when it became uncomfortable was it altered. The only question was which reality provided the greatest comfort?

Epilogue, 1993–97

Since the signing of the Paris agreement in October 1991, and the subsequent UN supervised elections of May 1993, United States foreign policy towards Cambodia has primarily consisted of a commitment to promote human rights and democracy by supporting democracy assistance programmes and any efforts aimed at the establishment of a viable market economy; mostly these aims are furthered by the provision of aid. Until 1997 this low-key policy of distant involvement, which incidentally was the goal of the previous administrations, has served the Americans well. Late in 1991 the US opened a mission in Phnom Penh and shortly thereafter lifted its economic embargo. When the Royal Cambodian Government was formed in September 1993 the US resumed full diplomatic relations. From that time until quite recently there was little to concern US foreign policy-makers. The US provides sufficient aid and support such that any *direct* US involvement is as unnecessary as it is unthinkable. Given that remaining detached from Indochina had been the driving force of the administrations assessed in this book, the Clinton presidencies do not offer any analytical surprises. In fact, the battles Clinton has fought with Congress, coupled with the President's own preference for domestic issues, have predictably meant that while foreign policy has become a 'political' issue the *conduct* of foreign policy in general has tended to take a back seat. If that is true in *general* then it is clearly all the more so with a peripheral and unthreatening issue such as Cambodia.

The new driving force for America's Indochinese policy, although arguably it always has been, is trade. In August 1995 Secretary of State Warren Christopher visited Indochina and opened the first US Embassy in Hanoi. During that visit a State Department official is quoted as saying, 'In the old days we wanted to make Asia safe for democracy, these days we want to make it safe for American exports.'[1] In two short years the Clinton view that human rights and trade could be inextricably linked had given way to a recognition that the US was merely one of many nations scrambling for the expanding markets which the growing Asian economies provided. Under enormous pressure from the US business lobby Clinton had, in May 1994, reversed his stance on Most Favoured Nation (MFN) status for China and exempted them from meeting certain requirements of the

189

Jackson-Vanik Amendment much as Bush had done previously. It seems a stable business environment is more important than the need for a flourishing democratic culture. The judgement that the former will lead to the latter is still strong in the administration but more in rhetoric than in action. So the *official* communiqué of the Christopher visit reaffirmed:

> the President's and the Government's continuing commitment to Cambodia's democracy, its emerging civic organizations, and its nascent market economy. The United States continues to support efforts in Cambodia to build democratic institutions, promote human rights, foster economic development, eliminate corruption, improve security, achieve the fullest possible accounting for POW/MIAs, and to bring members of the Khmer Rouge to justice for their crimes.[2]

To date Cambodian democratic institutions have been suspended, the National Assembly not having met since January 1997, human rights are regularly abused, the economy is in dire straits, corruption is rife, security is only functioning as a result of a coup and is fragile at best, and the Khmer Rouge leadership are either dead or incorporated into the political hierarchy.[3] Not a great record of succes. Yet for the United States this lack of success is not disastrous. It enables the US to parallel the positions of the ASEAN states and parade that as policy.

ASEAN came of age politically during the period of Vietnamese occupation of Cambodia. That situation allowed the Association to exhibit a foreign policy activism for the consumption of world opinion. Since the 1993 elections, however, ASEAN had been relatively quiet on Cambodia and, until the Hun Sen putsch of July 1997, were preparing to admit Cambodia as a full member of the Association. The coup put ASEAN in an awkward position. The Association has a strict principle of non-interference in the domestic affairs of either member states or other regional nations. ASEAN reacted to the coup by postponing Cambodia's entry and confirmed that decision at the same meeting in which Laos and Myanmar were admitted. However, the difficulty of the situation was clear when the Association did not remove Cambodia's 'observer' status, which is a procedural stepping-stone to full membership. This indicated that entry was only postponed. The suspension of the membership procedure and regular attempts at negotiations were ASEAN's only possible responses to the coup. Primarily these low-level responses were designed to halt any *further* aggression by Hun Sen but their restraint also illustrated a recognition that a stable Hun Sen government might actually be preferable to the unstable coalition it had replaced. ASEAN indicated certain conditions for lifting the suspension such as the reinstallation of the coalition government, although the inclusion of Ranarridh was not part of the deal,[4] and a commitmemt to free and fair elections. With the appointment of Ung Huot (FUNCINPEC) as Ranarridh's replacement, and despite King Sihanouk's initial refusal to endorse the appointment, the first condition, of the reinstallation of the coalition, has been technically met. Hun Sen also agreed to the other condition of free and fair elections which took place in July 1998. ASEAN are thus in a position to reconsider the suspension. Hun Sen's position has been further strengthened by Chinese recognition of his regime and by the reluctance of the Americans to suspend humanitarian aid.

United States pronouncements and actions have also tended to be mostly demonstrative but they have again been confronted by the spectre of the Khmer Rouge, albeit this time by its demise. Both main parties have attempted to entice defectors from the collapsing KR to their causes. The main beneficiaries of this strategy would be Ranarridh whose military power base is weak. Thus the Americans, who have tended to favour FUNCINPEC, are again caught in the moral dilemma that the only salvation for their nominees may be the KR. Attitudes to the KR have always illustrated the tension between the Cambodian and American interpretations of the rights of the state and those of individuals. There was, for example, considerable Western unease at the amnesty for KR defectors which has been a constant plank of the Royal Government of Cambodia's (RGC) ongoing strategy to subvert and defeat the KR. The amnesty brought considerable criticism from foreign governments and human rights groups who argued that as signatories to the Geneva Convention on Humanitarian Law and the Covenants on Human Rights, the RGC clearly breached relevant articles by granting amnesty. The RGC countered that Article 5 of the Cambodian legislation which had outlawed the KR allowed an amnesty period of six months for members of a political body or those belonging to the military forces of the 'Democratic Kampuchea' group to reintegrate without being charged for offences they had caused. Hun Sen pursued a *realpolitik* policy in spite of the obvious pressures to which he was subjected and he was supported by the majority of the coalition, including Prince Ranarridh. Ultimately, this policy succeeded but led to the battle between FUNCINPEC and the CPP for the remnants of the KR when it eventually began to collapse in early 1996 and it was arguably the impending success of the negotiations between Ranarridh and Khieu Samphan (KR) which precipitated Hun Sen's coup. During the entire period when the tensions between Ranarridh and Hun Sen were building the US had virtually no input other than at local ambassadorial level and continued with its distanced approach.

They had adopted a similar position when Sirivudh and Rainsy were exiled and expelled in 1995 and when the media and the judiciary were attacked by the government. Again when the rows between Hun Sen and Ranarridh intensified in early 1997 and fights between Nhek Bun Chhay and Hun Sen's troops broke out the US watched the situation 'with interest'. When Hun Sen finally launched his coup he targeted Nhek Bun Chhay and inflicted a complete defeat on Ranarridh's forces within 48 hours. The US were forced to acknowledge what had been apparent to most Cambodia watchers since the elections of 1993. This was that since the distribution of power within the government had favoured the CPP from the outset the probability of an eventual Hun Sen take-over was high. After the elections, in which the FUNCINPEC had achieved a victory, the major ministries were handed to the CPP who had Defence, the Interior, Commerce, Finance (after Sam Rainsy was sacked) and the National Bank – all the power houses of state. When the Hun Sen take-over finally happened it presented the US foreign policy community with its first real problem on Cambodia since the elections and they reacted predictably.

As with previous analyses the reality inhabited by the administration can be assessed through the testimony of level three actors. The first detailed response to the coup was presented to the House by Deputy Assistant Secretary for East Asian and Pacific Affairs, Aurelia E. Brazeal on 6 July 1997. She outlined the five core principles which would guide US reactions to the crisis. These were:

1. The violence that overturned the results of the 1993 elections is unacceptable; fighting must stop immediately.
2. All political parties, including FUNCINPEC, must be allowed to operate freely in Cambodia.
3. There must be free and fair elections in 1998.
4. We remain opposed to any role for the leaders of the Khmer Rouge; those responsible for crimes against humanity should be brought to justice.
5. The framework of the Paris Accords must be reinstated.[5]

Effectively US foreign policy towards Cambodia was a repetition of that stated in 1991. It again ignored other realities such as the fact that Ranarridh's FUNCINPEC were once more welcoming Khmer Rouge support for a coalition against Hun Sen, just as they had during the days of the CGDK; that FUNCINPEC itself was not a united party; that FUNCINPEC was militarily incapable of resisting the CPP alone; that Sihanouk was an irrelevance; and that Hun Sen had taken over Sihanouk's mantle as the great survivor. Instead they rejected Hun Sen's overtures and declared that the Royal Cambodian Government had forfeited its legitimacy and had 'destroyed the basis for constructive relations with the US'.[6] What that meant was constructive *economic* relations. According to the statement America 'will stay engaged' but the conundrum of human rights and trade will take some handling. Even the aid agencies are advocating caution because aid accounts for nearly 50 per cent of Cambodia's budget and provides some 10 000 jobs. Since the Paris Accords the US has pumped $300 million into Cambodia, mostly through USAID but also in military assistance to clear land-mines. Some in the NGO community question whether suspending aid is the answer and indeed whether Hun Sen is likely to respond or simply pass on the suffering to the Cambodian people.

Rand Robinson, assistant country director for CARE International, was one not convinced suspension was the answer. He believed that SoS Albright missed an opportunity when she cancelled a trip to Cambodia in June 1997 because of security concerns. He argued that she should have made the visit and 'played the stern lady', a role to which she is not unaccustomed.[7] In a sense this issue encompasses a perennial foreign policy dilemma for the United States, harm the people or harm the regime. However, Cambodia is insignificant for all but a tiny section of the American people and receives proportionately minuscule attention except when forced onto the agenda by the type of violence a coup brings. Hun Sen's coup of 1997 was short and generally only page two news, at best. Such insignificance allows American policy to be long-term and low-key. It is a sign of the times that Vietnam has become a channel for American diplomacy in the region. As a recent full member of ASEAN, Vietnam had agreed with the other members to delay Cambodian entry[8] and the Americans have told them 'how important it is to our bilateral relationship that Hanoi continue to support the regional consensus and play a constructive role on Cambodia'.[9] In the new American reality, it seems, even Vietnam is not necessarily a villain.

The policy on Cambodia is clearly in line with Clinton's view that while America cannot solve every world problem they can work with others to make a difference. In concluding her statement Ms Brazeal makes just that point, 'There is no question that intense international involvement will be necessary to restore stability to Cambodia; the US is ready to play a leading role in that effort.'[10] The United States is again content to follow ASEAN's lead, despite its ambivalence, and that always means keeping open lines of communication. A troika of foreign ministers from Indonesia, Thailand and the Philippines have met with Hun Sen at least twice after he had initially rebuffed ASEAN involvement. Madeleine Albright has also dispatched missions led by Stephen Solarz and Desaix Anderson to the region and she has initiated the formation of a 'Friends of Cambodia' group similar to the 'Group of Ten' which helped monitor the implementation of the Paris Accords. The intention of the 'Friends of Cambodia' is simply to *support* ASEAN initiatives and they provided pressure in the 1997 General Assembly which led to the credentials committee refusing to recognise the Hun Sen government even though King Sihanouk had signed accreditation to enter the General Assembly. The UN, under pressure from the United States, has decided on the 'vacant seat' policy which previous American administrations had vetoed. Ironically, Stanley O. Roth (an Assistant Secretary for East Asian and Pacific Affairs) claimed the vacant seat gambit as a major American success story. He obviously has not studied the history of this topic.*

Eventual ASEAN membership for Cambodia is viewed by the State Department as a 'powerful incentive for the restoration of political stability to Cambodia',[11] and while this might be true, ASEAN's interpretation of political stability will differ greatly from that of the United States. ASEAN has its own agenda, an important element of which is to complete the membership of the Association by adding Myanmar, Laos and Cambodia, one of the bases of its constitution.[12] The ASEAN agenda has at its core one concern – trade. That is why the United States is happy to play safe with a low-profile incrementalist approach which uses ASEAN as its regional proxy. Even the US needs stability in order to trade. In a world of competing realities perhaps one is beginning to dominate: economic reality. The foreign policy of the United States towards Cambodia is now clearly rooted in that reality.

*Testimony before the Senate Foreign Relations Committee, Sub-Committee on Asia and the Pacific, 10 June 1998.

Notes

PROLOGUE

1. Sihanouk, Prince Norodom, *My War with the CIA*, London: Penguin Books, 1973, p. 79.
2. Ibid., p. 103.
3. Ibid., p. 110.
4. Kissinger, Henry, *Years of Upheaval*, London: Weidenfeld & Nicolson, 1979, p. 251.
5. Armed reconnaissance into Cambodia seeking to target Viet Cong bases.
6. Von Marschall, Walter Baron, 'The War in Cambodia: its Causes and Military Development and the Political History of the Khmer Republic 1970–1975', *Seaford House Papers, 1975*, HMSO, pp. 101–2.
7. Kissinger, *Years of Upheaval*, p. 337.
8. Ibid., p. 344.
9. This is made clear in a State Department cable (15050) sent to Ambassador Swank. The cable is quoted in Kissinger, *Years of Upheaval*, p. 1218.
10. Ibid., p. 355.
11. Ibid., p. 365.
12. *New York Times*, 12 August 1973, quoted in Chanda, Nayan, *Brother Enemy*, London: Harcourt Brace Jovanovich, 1986, pp. 38–9.
13. Ibid., p. 7.
14. Ibid., p. 22.

INTRODUCTION

1. Halle, Louis J., *American Foreign Policy: Theory and Reality*, London: George Allen and Unwin Ltd, 1960, p. viii.
2. Shapiro, M., *The Politics of Representation – Writing Practices in Biography, Photography and Political Analysis*, Madison: University of Wisconsin Press, 1988, p. 100.
3. Carter, Jimmy, 'Foreign Policy Based on America's Essential Character', Speech given at Notre Dame University, 22 May 1977, *State Department Bulletin*, 13 June 1977.
4. Quoted in Fromkin, David and Chace, James, 'What *Are* the Lessons of Vietnam?', *Foreign Affairs*, Vol. 63, 1984–85, p. 734.
5. Ibid.
6. See, for a small sample, Schlesinger, Arthur M. Jr., *The Imperial Presidency*, London: André Deutsch, 1974; Hilsman, R., *The Politics of Policy Making in Defense and Foreign Affairs: Conceptual Models and Bureaucratic Politics*, Englewood Cliffs: Prentice-Hall Inc., 1987;

Perlmutter, Amos, 'The Presidential Political Center and Foreign Policy', *World Politics*, 27 (1), October 1974.

7. Hilsman, *Politics of Policy Making*, p. 314.
8. Schlesinger, *The Imperial Presidency*.
9. Neustadt, Richard, *Presidential Power*, New York: Wiley, 1960.
10. Halperin, Morton H., 'Why Bureaucrats Play Games', *Foreign Policy*, 2, 1971.
11. Halperin, Morton H., 'The Decision to Deploy the ABM: Bureaucratic Foreign and Domestic Politics in the Johnson Administration', *World Politics*, 25 (1), October 1972, p. 90.
12. Quoted in Scheslinger, *Imperial Presidency*, p. 178.
13. Hilsman, *Politics of Policy Making*, p. 315.
14. Ibid., p. 118.
15. Rosati, Jerel A., 'Developing a Systematic Decision-Making Framework: Bureaucratic Politics in Perspective', *World Politics*, 23 (2), January 1982.
16. Hermann, Margaret G. and Hermann, Charles F., 'Who Makes Foreign Policy Decisions and How: an Empirical Inquiry', *International Studies Quarterly*, 33, 1989, p. 381. See p. 383 for tables.
17. Spear, J. and Williams, P., 'Belief Systems and Foreign Policy: the Cases of Carter and Reagan', chapter 9 in Little, R. and Smith, S. (eds.) *Belief Systems and International Relations*, Oxford: Blackwell, 1988, p. 195.
18. Jastrow, Joseph, *The Psychology of Conviction: a study of beliefs and attitudes*, Boston: Houghton, Mifflin Co., 1918.
19. Taber, Charles S., 'POLI: An Expert System Model of US Foreign Policy Belief Systems', *American Political Science Review*, 86 (1), December 1992, p. 891.
20. Shultz, George P., 'New Realities and New Ways of Thinking', *Foreign Affairs*, Spring 1985, 63 (4).
21. Muskie, Edmund, *Exploiting Cambodia: Issues and Reality in a time of Transition*, Center for National Policy Press, Washington DC, October 1990.
22. George, A. L., 'Quantitative and Qualitative Approaches to Content Analysis', in Ithiel de Sola Pool (ed.), *Trends in Content Analysis*, Urbana: University of Illinois Press, 1959, p. 7.
23. Jervis, Robert, 'The Costs of the Quantitative Study of International Relations', chapter 10 in Knorr, Klaus and Rosenau, James N. (eds.), *Contending Approaches in International Relations*, Princeton: Princeton University Press, 1969, p. 205.
24. Bull, Hedley, 'International Theory: the Case for the Classical Approach', in Knorr and Rosenau, *Contending Approaches*, p. 20.
25. Larson, D., *The Origins of Containment*, Princeton: Princeton University Press, 1985. In this book the author used Truman's speech enunciating the Truman Doctrine as an example. He argued that while the speech was originally concerned with another matter it came to represent his overall conception of the Soviet threat; in effect it *became* reality.
26. Ibid.

27. Bell, Coral, *The Reagan Paradox: American Foreign Policy in the 1980s*, Aldershot: Edward Elgar, 1989.
28. Berger, P. and Luckmann, T., *The Social Construction of Reality: a Treatise in the Sociology of Knowledge*, London: Penguin Books, 1976.
29. Carroll, John B., *Language, Thought and Reality: Selected Writings of Benjamin Lee Whorf*, New York: MIT Press, 1959, p. 57.
30. Grace, G. W., *The Linguistic Construction of Reality*, London: Croom Helm, 1987, p. 3.
31. Doty, Roxanne Lynn, 'Foreign Policy as Social Construction: a Post-Positivist Analysis of US Counterinsurgency Policy in the Philippines', *International Studies Quarterly*, 37 (3), September 1993, p. 310.
32. The use of levels is consistent with certain elements of Singer's 'levels-of-analysis approach in that it includes two of Singer's levels, the President and the immediate group surrounding him. Singer, D., 'The Levels-of-Analysis Problem', chapter in K. Knorr and R. Verba, *The International System: Theoretical Essays*, Princeton: Princeton University Press, 1961.
33. See Walker, S. G., 'The Motivational Foundation of Belief Systems: a Re-Analysis of Operational Code Construct', *International Studies Quarterly*, 27, 1983, as just one example of the legitimacy of constructing 'group' belief systems.
34. Here 'content analysis' refers to the notion that 'from the content of the decision-makers' messages, valid inference may be drawn concerning the attitudes of the speaker' (North, Holsti et al., *Content Analysis*, USA: Northwestern University Press, 1963, p. 92).

1 THE CARTER ADMINISTRATION

1. Brzezinski, Zbigniew, *Power and Principle*, London: Weidenfeld and Nicolson, 1983.
2. Moore, Raymond in chapter 4 of Abernathy, W., Hill D. and Williams, P., *The Carter Years: the President and Policy Making*, London: Francis Pinter, 1984.
3. Brzezinski, *Power and Principle*, p. 44.
4. Ibid.
5. Quoted in Moens, Alexander, *Foreign Policy Under Carter: Testing Multiple Advocacy Decision Making*, Boulder, Co.: Westview Press, 1990, p. 35.
6. For a discussion of this model see George, Alexander, 'The Case for Multiple Advocacy in Making Foreign Policy', *American Political Science Review*, September 1972, pp. 751–85; as practised under Carter, Cyrus Vance referred to it as the 'collegial approach'; Vance, Cyrus, *Hard Choices*, New York: Simon and Schuster, 1983.
7. Moens, *Foreign Policy*, p. 9.
8. See Barber, James, *The Presidential Character*, New York: Prentice-Hall, 3rd edition, 1977. Barber presents a typology of presidential character.
9. For an example of this criticism see the Williams chapter op. cit. in Abernathy et al., *The Carter Years*.

10. Carter, Jimmy, *Keeping Faith*, London: Collins, 1982, p. 54.
11. Watson, John, *National Journal*, 30 October 1976.
12. Hahn, Dan F. 'The Rhetoric of Jimmy Carter, 1976–1980', *Presidential Studies Quarterly*, 14 (2), 1984, p. 271.
13. Ibid., p. 267.
14. Quoted in ibid., p. 266.
15. *New York Times* (*NYT*), 29 January 1990, p. A12.
16. Hahn, *Rhetoric*, p. 280.
17. Jordan, Hamilton, *Crisis: the Last Year of the Carter Presidency*, London: Michael Joseph, 1982, p. 45.
18. Quoted in Brzezinski, *Power and Principle*, p. 44.
19. Ibid.
20. Ibid., p. 43.
21. Vance, Cyrus, *Hard Choices: Critical Years in America's Foreign Policy*, New York: Simon and Schuster, 1983, p. 414.
22. Brzezinski, *Power and Principle*, p. 43.
23. Jordan, *Crisis*, p. 51.
24. Ibid.
25. Brzezinski, *Power and Principle*, p. 13.
26. Ibid.
27. Jordan, *Crisis*, pp. 49–50.
28. Brzezinski, *Power and Principle*, p. 34.
29. *The Independent*, 1 May 1993, p. 14.
30. Ibid.
31. Carter, *Keeping Faith*, pp. 54–5.
32. Brzezinski, *Power and Principle*, p. 47.
33. Quoted in Chanda, Nayan, *Brother Enemy: the War After the War*, London: Harcourt Brace Jovanovich, 1986, p. 147.
34. Carter, *Keeping Faith*, p. 51.
35. Jordan, *Crisis*, p. 47.
36. Carter, *Keeping Faith*, p. 52.
37. Jordan, *Crisis*, p. 48.
38. Brzezinski, *Power and Principle*, p. 38.
39. Sullivan, William H., 'Dateline Iran: the Road Not Taken', *Foreign Policy*, No. 40, Fall 1980, p. 181.
40. Vance, *Hard Choices*, pp. 35–6.
41. Ibid., p. 114.
42. Ibid.
43. Brzezinski, Zbigniew, 'The Best National Security System: a Conversation with Zbigniew Brzezinski', *Washington Quarterly*, No. 1, 1982, p. 73.
44. Quoted in Jordan, *Crisis*, p. 48.
45. Brzezinski, 'The Best National Security System', p. 73.
46. Carter, *Keeping Faith*, p. 143.
47. Ibid.
48. Ibid., p. 142.
49. Vance, *Hard Choices*, p. 441.
50. Ibid.
51. Brzezinski, *Power and Principle*, p. 53.

52. Ibid., p. 81.
53. Ibid., p. 55.
54. Carter, *Keeping Faith*, p. 43.
55. 'Human Rights Violations in Cambodia', *Public Papers of the Presidents, Carter 1978*, 21 April 1978, p. 767. These papers are referred to hereafter by the abbreviation PPP.
56. PPP, Carter 1979 (II), remarks at the White House, 13 November 1979, p. 2112.
57. PPP, Carter 1979 (III), White House statement, 6 December 1979, p. 2197.
58. PPP, Carter 1979 (II), proclamation 4700, p. 2080.
59. Quoted in Chanda, *Brother Enemy*, p. 146.
60. 'Tragedy in Indochina: War, Refugees and Famine', Hearing before the House of Representatives Committee on Foreign Affairs, Sub-Committee on Asian and Pacific Affairs, p. 117. Hereafter referred to as the Sub-Committee on Asian and Pacific Affairs.
61. Ibid., p. 114.
62. Carter, *Keeping Faith*, p. 194.
63. PPP, Carter 1979 (I), news conference, 27 February 1979, p. 348.
64. 'American Policy and Global Change', 25 October 1977, *Congressional Record*, 1 November 1977, pH11999.
65. Quoted in Rosati, Jerel A., *The Carter Administration's Quest for Global Security*, Carolina: University of Carolina Press, 1987, p. 40.
66. *Congressional Record*, pH11999.
67. 'A Foreign Policy Based on America's Essential Character', speech delivered at Notre Dame University, 22 May 1977, *Department of State Bulletin*, 13 June 1977, p. 622.
68. *American Foreign Policy: Basic Documents, 1977–1980*, USGPO, Washington DC 1983, AFP Doc 592.
69. *Washington Post (WP)*, 4 January 1979, p. A22.
70. 'Security Issues: Korea and Thailand', Sub-Committee on East Asian and Pacific Affairs, 22 March 1979, p. 22.
71. PPP, Carter 1979 (II), remarks to the press, 26 October 1979, p. 2037.
72. PPP, Carter 1980, interview with the press, 12 April 1980, p. 674.
73. Address to newspaper editors, 10 April 1980, *State Department Bulletin*, May 1980, p. 4.
74. Vance, *Hard Choices*, p. 450.
75. Ibid., p. 123.
76. Appendix 1 in *Hard Choices* (pp. 441–62) was a 24 October 1976 memorandum entitled 'Overview of Foreign Policy Issues and Positions'. This quote is from p. 444.
77. Vance, *Hard Choices*, p. 421.
78. Ibid., p. 124.
79. ASEAN (Association of South East Asian Nations) consisted at the time of Thailand, Malaysia, Singapore, Brunei, Indonesia and the Philippines. ASEAN is a predominantly economic organisation with a constitution specifically enshrining the concept of non-intervention in internal affairs as a cardinal principle. The constitution also aims at the

eventual inclusion of the 'ten' South East Asian states which consist of the original members plus Vietnam, Laos, Burma (Myanmar) and Cambodia.

80. 'US Policy in Southeast Asia', Sub-Committee on East Asian and Pacific Affairs, July 1981, p. 1.
81. Report of Congressional Delegates at the 1979 United Nations General Assembly (April 1980), contained in House report 80-H382-15. The British Library use this codification pre-1982 and Su Doc numbers thereafter.
82. Vance, *Hard Choices*, p. 126
83. Ibid., p. 127.
84. Ibid.
85. Ibid., p. 516.
86. *UN Chronicle*, December 1980, Vol. XVII, No. 7, p. 209.
87. Ibid.
88. Telegram S/13003, quoted in *UN Chronicle*, February 1979, Vol. XVI, No. 2, p. 6.
89. Message S/13001, 31 December 1978, ibid.
90. Ibid., pp. 7/8.
91. Ibid., p. 7.
92. Ibid., p. 8.
93. Ibid.
94. Ibid., p. 9.
95. Ibid.
96. Ibid.
97. Ibid., p. 11.
98. Security Council debate 23–28 February 1979, *UN Chronicle*, March 1979, Vol. XVI, No. 3, p. 5.
99. China launched a punitive action against Vietnam which penetrated up to twelve miles into the northern provinces in February 1979. They withdrew in 1980 after an estimated 20 000 casualties of which 8000 were presumed dead.
100. General Assembly, 12 October 1980 (Credentials Committee), *UN Chronicle*, December 1980, Vol. XVII, No. 7, p. 209.
101. *UN Chronicle*, February 1979.
102. Haas, Michael, *Cambodia, Pol Pot, and the United States: the Faustian Pact*, New York: Praeger, 1991, p. 15.
103. Hearing before the Sub-Committee on International Organizations of the Committee on International Relations, House of Representatives, 95th Congress, 1st session, p. 32.
104. Ibid., p. 39.
105. Ibid., p. 46.
106. Senate Hearing, 21 August 1978 (79-S381-3), p. 24.
107. Ibid.
108. Letter placed in evidence at the Hearings before the Sub-Committees on Asian and Pacific Affairs and on International Organizations, 96th Congress, 2nd session.
109. Ibid.
110. Ibid., p. 55.

111. Vietnamese News Agency (VNA), 4 March 1979, *BBC Summary of World Broadcasts (SWB)*, FE/6059/A3/3.
112. Quoted in the New China News Agency (NCNA), 20 May 1978, *SWB*, 21 May 1978.
113. Vance, *Hard Choices*, p. 121.
114. Leighton, Marian Kirsch, 'Perspectives on the Vietnam-Cambodia Border Conflict', *Asian Survey*, May 1978, p. 456.
115. *Far Eastern Economic Review (FEER)*, 23 February 1979, p. 33.
116. Dutter, Lee E. and Kania, Raymond S., 'Explaining Recent Vietnamese Behaviour', *Asian Survey*, 20 (9), September 1980, p. 931.
117. Brzezinski, *Power and Principle*, p. 409.
118. Ibid., p. 413.
119. PPP, Carter 1979, 27 February 1979, p. 348.
120. Address at the GIT, PPP, Carter 1979, 20 February 1979, p. 303.
121. 'Asian Security', *Research Institute for Peace and Security* (2nd annual report), Tokyo, October 1980, p. 152.
122. Haas, *Faustian Pact*, p. 15.
123. Leifer, Michael, *ASEAN and the Security of South-East Asia*, London: Routledge, 1989, p. 97.
124. Veto 141, 15 January 1979, UN Document S/13027 and veto 142, 16 March 1979, S/13162.
125. Op. cit. (n. 119) *Asian Security*.
126. Chanda, *Brother Enemy*, p. 377.
127. Presidential statement entered into the record of the Sub-Committee on Asian and Pacific Affairs, 17 October 1979, p. 114.
128. Ibid., p. 123.
129. Sub-Committee on Asian and Pacific Affairs, 31 October 1979, p. 205.
130. Ibid., 18–19 December 1979.
131. Brzezinski, *Power and Principle*, p. 440.
132. Carter quoted in Jordan, *Crisis*, preface.
133. AFP Document 605, USGPO, Washington DC.
134. *UN Chronicle*, December 1980, Vol. XVII, No. 10, p. 53.
135. White House press release, quoted in Rosati, *The Carter Administration's Quest*, p. 6.
136. Ibid.
137. Stoessinger, John, *Crusaders and Pragmatists: Movers of Modern American Foreign Policy*, New York: W. W. Norton & Co., 1979, p. 284.
138. Haas, *Faustian Pact*, p. 22.
139. Jordan, *Crisis*, p. 53.
140. Smith, Gaddis, *Morality, Reason and Power: American Diplomacy in the Carter Years*, New York: Hill & Wang, 1986, p. 98.
141. Vance, *Hard Choices*, p. 409.
142. Ibid.
143. *Current Policy*, No. 106, 5 November 1979, p. 1.
144. Hoffman, Stanley, 'The Hell of Good Intentions', *Foreign Policy*, No. 29, Winter 1977–8.
145. Ibid., pp. 7–8.
146. Abernathy et al., *The Carter Years*, p. 75.
147. Quoted in Carter, *Keeping Faith*, p. 256.

148. PPP, Carter 1980, p. 964. Remarks at the first annual dinner of the Asian/Pacific American Democratic Caucus, 22 May 1980.
149. *New York Times* magazine, 4 February 1979, p. 52.

2 THE FIRST REAGAN ADMINISTRATION

1. *Holy Bible*, Matthew 12: 30.
2. Bell, C., *The Reagan Paradox: American Foreign Policy in the 1980s*, Aldershot: Edward Elgar, 1989.
3. Tucker, R. W., 'Reagan's Foreign Policy', *Foreign Affairs*, 1988/89, p. 5. Tucker uses the term 'mediocre'.
4. Quoted by Don Bonker, Chairman of the Sub-Committee on Human Rights and International Organizations at a Congressional Hearing on 15 September 1982 (83-H381-28), p. 14.
5. Hill, D., Moore, R. and Williams, P., *The Reagan Presidency: an Incomplete Revolution?* London: Macmillan, 1990, p. 9.
6. Haig, Alexander, Jr., *Caveat: Realism, Reagan, and Foreign Policy*, London: Weidenfeld and Nicolson, 1984, p. 12.
7. Kegley, Charles W. Jr. and Wittkopf, Eugene R., *American Foreign Policy: Pattern and Process*, 3rd ed., London: Macmillan, 1987, p. 360.
8. Hastedt, Glenn P. *American Foreign Policy: Past, Present, Future*, New Jersey: Prentice-Hall, 1988, p. 121.
9. *Current Policy*, No. 353, USGPO, 24 November 1981, p. 2.
10. 'The Democratic Kampuchea Seat at the United Nations and American Interests', Hearing before the Sub-Committees on Asian and Pacific Affairs and Human Rights, 15 September 1982, p. 32.
11. Melanson, Richard A., *Reconstructing Consensus: American Foreign Policy Since the Vietnam War*, New York: St Martin's Press, 1991, p. 229.
12. O'Dowd, Ann Reilly, 'What Managers Can Learn From Manager Reagan', *Fortune*, 15 September 1986, p. 26.
13. Nye, Joseph S., Jr., 'Understanding US Strength', *Foreign Policy*, No. 72, Fall 1988, p. 109.
14. Drew, E., 'A Political Journal', *New Yorker*, 20 February 1984.
15. Nye, *Understanding US Strength*.
16. Tulis, J. K., *The Rhetorical Presidency*, New Jersey: Princeton University Press, 1987.
17. Reagan quoted while employed by General Electric on the TV programme *GE Theater*. Dugger, R., *On Reagan: the Man and his Presidency*, London: McGraw-Hill, 1983, p. 351.
18. Ibid., p. 353.
19. Baker, Ross K., *The Election of 1980: Reports and Interpretations*, New Jersey: Chatham House, 1981.
20. Hill, *The Reagan Presidency*, p. 9.
21. Melanson, *Reconstructing Consensus*, p. 88.
22. Quoted in Mervin, D., *Ronald Reagan and the American Presidency*, London: Longman, 1990, p. 187.
23. This case is most clearly made in Duggan, *On Reagan*.

24. Stockman, D., *Triumph of Politics*, New York: Harper and Row, 1986, p. 95.
25. Michael Foley, chapter 2 in Hogan, J. (ed.), *The Reagan Years: the Record in Presidential Leadership*, Manchester: MUP, 1990, p. 51.
26. Kegley, *American Foreign Policy*, p. 575.
27. Ibid., p. 357.
28. Hastedt, *American Foreign Policy*, p. 144.
29. Kegley, *American Foreign Policy*, p. 359.
30. Allison, G., *The Essence of Decision*, Boston: Little, Brown and Co., 1971.
31. Quoted in Hastedt, *American Foreign Policy*, p. 275.
32. Haig, Alexander, 'American Power and American Purpose', *Current Policy*, No. 279, USGPO, 27 April 1982.
33. Bell, *The Reagan Paradox*, p. 9.
34. Hastedt, *American Foreign Policy*, p. 125.
35. *The Tower Commission Report*, New York: Bantam and Times Books, 1987, pp. 78–80.
36. Kegley, *American Foreign Policy*, p. 578.
37. Dugger, *On Reagan*, p. 357.
38. Melanson, *Reconstructing Consensus*, p. 228.
39. Bell, *The Reagan Paradox*, p. 2.
40. McMahan, J., *Reagan and the World: Imperial Policy in the New Cold War*, London: Pluto Press, 1984, p. 12.
41. Ibid., p. 13.
42. Ibid., p. 10.
43. Address to the General Assembly, 26 September 1983, quoted in the *UN Chronicle Special Supplement*, March 1984, p. 16.
44. Quoted in the *New York Times* (*NYT*), 21 February 1982, Section IV, p. 1.
45. *Current Policy*, No. 561, USGPO, 3 April 1984.
46. SWB, 20 June 1981, FE 6754/A3/1. This comment was made in response to an alleged threat by John Holdridge.
47. Michael Smith, chapter in Hogan, *The Reagan Years*, p. 267.
48. *NYT*, 3 April 1984.
49. Melanson, *Reconstructing Consensus*, p. 148.
50. Although the Reagan Doctrine was not formally enunciated until the 1985 State of the Union Address the ideas were clearly operational during the first term.
51. Dugger, *On Reagan*, p. 513.
52. Ibid., p. 350.
53. Gelb, Leslie H. and Lake, Anthony, 'Four More Years: Diplomacy Restored', *Foreign Affairs*, 63 (3), 1985, p. 466.
54. Kegley, *American Foreign Policy*, p. 74.
55. Ibid., p. 111.
56. Congressional hearing, see n. 10 above.
57. Haig, *Caveat*, p. 30.
58. Schultz, George P., 'New Realities and New Ways of Thinking', *Foreign Affairs*, Spring 1985, 63 (4), p. 711.
59. 'US Interests in Southeast Asia', *Current Policy*, No. 295, USGPO, 15 July 1981.

60. 'US Policy Towards Indochina Since Vietnam's Occupation of Kampuchea', hearing before the Sub-Committee on Asian and Pacific Affairs, 15, 21, 22 October 1982.
61. Ibid., p. 41.
62. Ibid.
63. Ibid.
64. Ibid.
65. Ibid., p. 164.
66. Ibid.
67. *Current Policy*, No. 295.
68. Hastedt, *American Foreign Policy*, p. 276.
69. Shultz quoted in *TWP*, 4 April 1984, p. A17.
70. Sub-Committee, *US Policy Toward Indochina*, n. 60, p. 164.
71. Sub-Committee, *The Democratic Kampuchea Seat*, n. 10, p. 14.
72. Ibid.
73. Ibid.
74. Ibid., p. 15.
75. Ibid., p. 23.
76. Ibid., pp. 16–17.
77. Ibid., p. 17.
78. 'Kampuchea and American Foreign Policy Interests'. Hearing before the Sub-Committee on Asian and Pacific Affairs, 23 July 1981, p. 12.
79. Op. cit. (n. 10), p. 1.
80. Sub-Committee on Asian and Pacific Affairs (84-H381-8), p. 66.
81. Haig, *Caveat*, p. 91.
82. 'Cambodia After 5 Years of Vietnamese Occupation', Sub-Committee on Asian and Pacific Affairs, 15 September 1983, p. 5.
83. Op. cit. (n. 10), p. 20.
84. Ibid., p. 2.
85. Sub-Committee on Asian and Pacific Affairs (83-H381-14), p. 58.
86. Op. cit. (n. 60), p. 1.
87. Ibid.
88. Op. cit. (n. 82), p. 5.
89. Ibid.
90. Op. cit. (n. 10), p. 17.
91. Op. cit. (n. 60), p. 165.
92. Op. cit. (n. 85), p. 5.
93. Ibid., p. 21.
94. Ibid., p. 52.
95. UN General Assembly debate, 27 October 1983, *UN Chronicle*, December 1983, Vol. XX, No. 11, p. 33.
96. Ibid.
97. Op. cit. (n. 10), p. 18.
98. Op. cit. (n. 60), p. 193.
99. Ibid., p. 165.
100. SWB, 18 June 1981, FE/6752/A1/1.
101. Ibid., p. A1/4.
102. Pike, Douglas, *Far Eastern Economic Review* (*FEER*), 11 June 1982, p. 42.

103. Haig, *Caveat*, p. 12.
104. This analysis is presented in Chanda, *Brother Enemy*.
105. Op. cit. (n. 10), p. 38.
106. Op. cit. (n. 59), *Current Policy*, No. 295, p. 3.
107. Op. cit. (n. 60), p. 269.
108. Ibid., p. 257.
109. Ibid.
110. Op. cit. (n. 10), p. 33. Moulinaka (Mouvement pour la Libération Nationale du Kampuchea) was Sihanouk's political party in 1979 and became FUNCINPEC (Front Uni Nationale pour un Cambodge Indépendent, Neutre, Pacifique et Coopératif) in 1981.
111. Ibid.
112. Op. cit. (n. 60), p. 265.
113. Op. cit. (n. 82), p. 24.
114. Op. cit. (n. 10), p. 18.
115. SWB, 28 January 1981, FE/6634/A3/7.
116. SWB, 29 January 1981, FE/6635/i.
117. SWB, 30 January 1981, FE/6636/A3/1–2.
118. SWB, 16 June 1981, FE/6750/A3/4.
119. SWB, 31 January 1984, FE/7554/A3/1.
120. SWB, 30 January 1981, FE/6636/A3/2.
121. SWB, 19 February 1982, FE/6958/A3/3.
122. SWB, 24 April 1983, FE/7319/A3/5.
123. Foreign and Commonwealth Background Brief, *ASEAN and Cambodia*, September 1982.
124. Ibid.
125. SWB, 29 January 1981, FE/6635/A1/2.
126. SWB, 13 May 1981, FE/6722/A3/5.
127. SWB, 22 September 1981, FE/6834/A3/1.
128. SWB, 1 November 1982, FE/7171/A3/3.
129. SWB, 5 February 1983, FE/7250/A3/5.
130. *UN Chronicle*, December 1983, Vol. XX, No. 11, p. 30.
131. See, for example, vetoes Nos. 141/142.
132. SWB, 5 February 1983, FE/7250/A3/5.
133. Van der Kroef, Justus M, 'Kampuchea: the Diplomatic Labyrinth', *Asian Survey*, Vol. XXII, No. 10, October 1982, p. 1023.
134. SWB, 25 March 1983, FE/7291/A3/1.
135. SWB, 17 June 1982, FE/7054/A3/5.
136. Chanda, *Brother Enemy*, p. 388.
137. *UN Chronicle*, Vol. XVIII, No. 9, September/October 1981, p. 37.
138. Ibid., p. 38.
139. UN document A/36/361.
140. *UN Chronicle*, Vol. XXVIII, No. 11, December 1981, p. 6.
141. SWB, 31 January 1981, FE/6637/ i.
142. SWB, 18 June 1981, FE/6778/A3/3.
143. Ibid., p. A3/2.
144. Ibid., p. A3/4.
145. SWB, 10 February 1982, FE/6950/ i.
146. SWB, 2 February 1982, FE/6958/A2/1–4.

147. SWB, 16 February 1982, FE/6920/A2/3.
148. SWB, 16 March 1981, FE/6674/A3/1.
149. SWB, 14 May 1981, FE/6723/A3/6.
150. SWB, 21 June 1982, FE/7057/A3/3.
151. *UN Chronicle*, Vol. XIX, No. 11, December 1982, p. 10.
152. Ibid., p. 11.
153. Ibid.
154. Solarz agreed with this interpretation when interviewed by the author.
155. Op. cit. (n. 78), p. 2.
156. Ibid., p. 3.
157. Ibid., p. 9.
158. Op. cit. (n. 60), p. 254.
159. Op. cit. (n. 10), p. 1.
160. Op. cit. (n. 82), p. 52.
161. Ibid., p. 66.
162. Ibid., p. 32.
163. Ibid., p. 33.
164. Bernard Nossiter in *NYT*, 20 September 1981.
165. Dan Oberdorfer in *TWP*, 12 July 1984.
166. Van der Kroef, Justus M., 'Kampuchea: Diplomatic Gambits and Political Realities', *Orbis*, Spring 1984, p. 161.
167. Letter to the *FEER*, 11 June 1982, from Colin Pratt, former Australian Hon. Consul General for Cambodia.
168. PPP, Reagan 1984, p. 685.
169. Chanda, Nayan, 'CIA no, US aid yes', *FEER*, 16 August 1984.
170. Ibid., p. 16.
171. *UN Chronicle*, Vol. XXI, No. 9, 1984, p. 21.
172. Bekaert, Jacques, 'Cambodia: a nasty little war', *International Defense Review*, Vol. 22, March 1989.
173. Kiernan, Ben, 'A Proposal for Peace', *Inside Asia*, February–March 1985, p. 37.
174. *UN Chronicle*, Vol. XXI, No. 8, 1984, p. 55.
175. Op. cit. (n. 82), p. 34.
176. Haig, *Caveat*, p. 3.
177. Ibid.
178. Op. cit. (n. 82), pp. 91–2.
179. PPP, Reagan 1984, p. 685.
180. *UN Chronicle*, Vol. XXI, No. 8, 1984, p. 17.
181. Hearing before the Sub-Committees on Europe and the Middle East and on Asia and Pacific Affairs, July–October 1983, p. 227.

3 THE SECOND REAGAN ADMINISTRATION

1. *The Tower Commission Report*, New York: Bantam Books, 1987.
2. Weinberger, Caspar, *Annual Report to Congress*, Fiscal Year 1987, p. 77.
3. See Hill, D., Moore, R. and Williams, P. (eds.), *The Reagan Presidency: An Incomplete Revolution?* London: Macmillan, 1990, p. 183.
4. McKeever, Robert J., 'American Myths and the Impact of the Vietnam

War: Revisionism in Foreign Policy and Popular Cinema in the 1980s', chapter 3 in Walsh and Aulich (eds.), *Vietnam Images: War and Representation*, Basingstoke: Macmillan, 1989, p. 52.

5. Bell, Coral, *The Reagan Paradox: American Foreign Policy in the 1980s*, Aldershot: Edward Elgar, 1989, p. 17.

6. Shultz, George, 'New Realities and New Ways of Thinking', *Foreign Affairs*, Spring 1985, Vol. 63, No. 4.

7. Geyelin, Philip, 'The Reagan Crisis: Dreaming Impossible Dreams', *Foreign Affairs*, 1986 Round-Up Issue, p. 457; quoting Arthur Miller's character, Willy Loman, in *Death of a Salesman*.

8. Quoted in Mervin, David, *Ronald Reagan and the American Presidency*, New York: Longman, 1990, p. 172.

9. Quoted in Tucker, Robert W., 'Reagan's Foreign Policy', *Foreign Affairs*, Winter, 1988–9, p. 9.

10. PPP, Reagan I, p. 454.

11. Mandelbaum, Michael, 'The Luck of the President', *Foreign Affairs*, 1985 Round-Up, p. 12.

12. Ibid.

13. Hill, *The Reagan Presidency*, p. 196.

14. Ibid., p. 191.

15. Smith, Michael, 'Ronald Reagan's Disintegrating World', *The World Today*, February 1987, p. 25.

16. Shultz, George, *Turmoil and Triumph: My Years as Secretary of State*, New York: Charles Scribner's and Sons, 1993, p. 274.

17. Shultz quoted in Hill, *The Reagan Presidency*, p. 181.

18. See chapter 10 in Hill, *The Reagan Presidency*, for a brief description of Weinberger's role in Defense policy-making.

19. See, for example, Speakes, L. and Pack, R., *Speaking Out: Inside the Reagan White House*, New York: Charles Scribner's and Sons, 1988.

20. Hill, *The Reagan Presidency*, p. 195.

21. Shultz, *Turmoil*, pp. 902–4, 990–1. Carlucci pushed his position in National Security Decision Directive 276.

22. Regan, Donald, *For the Record: From Wall Street to Washington*, New York: Harcourt Brace Jovanovich, 1988, pp. 218–39.

23. O'Neill, Tip with Novak, W., *Man of the House*, New York: Random House, 1987, pp. 372–3.

24. Mervin, *Ronald Reagan*, p. 160.

25. Ibid.

26. Ibid.

27. Ibid.

28. Regan, *For the Record*, p. 234.

29. Mervin, *Ronald Reagan*, p. 131.

30. Hastedt, Glenn, *American Foreign Policy: Past, Present, Future*, New Jersey: Prentice-Hall, 2nd edition, 1991, p. 116.

31. Ibid.

32. Ibid., p. 121.

33. Discrepancies in job titles/descriptions when compared with level three lists from other chapters indicates the *personal* nature of influence in the American system.

34. *Tower Commission*, pp. 79–80.
35. Brzezinski, Zbigniew, 'The NSC's Midlife Crisis', *Foreign Policy*, No. 69, Winter 1987–8.
36. Ibid., p. 92.
37. Hastedt, *American Foreign Policy*, pp. 124–5.
38. Ibid., p. 45.
39. Ibid., p. 149.
40. Mervin, *Ronald Reagan*, p. 159.
41. Geyelin, *The Reagan Crisis*, p. 454.
42. Melanson, Richard A., *Reconstructing Consensus: American Foreign Policy Since the Vietnam War*, New York: St Martin's Press, 1991, p. 148.
43. Mervin, *Ronald Reagan*, p. 131.
44. Shultz, *Turmoil*, p. 84.
45. Hill, Moore and Williams, *The Reagan Presidency*, pp. 218–19.
46. Smith, *Ronald Reagan's Disintegrating World*, p. 26.
47. Kegley, Charles W. and Wittkopf, Eugene R., *American Foreign Policy: Pattern and Process*, 3rd edition, London: Macmillan, 1987, p. 341.
48. See Barger, Harold M., *The Impossible Presidency: Illusions and Realities of Executive Power*, Glenview: Scott Foresman, 1984.
49. Shultz, *New Realities*, p. 705.
50. Shultz, George, 'Power and Diplomacy in the 1980s', *Current Policy*, No. 561, 3 April 1984.
51. Kegley, *American Foreign Policy*, p. 594.
52. *Halliwell's Film Guide*, 9th edition, London: Harper Collins, 1993, p. 981.
53. Kegley, *American Foreign Policy*, p. 450.
54. Shultz, George, 'The Meaning of Vietnam', *Department of State Bulletin*, Vol. 85, No. 2099, June 1985.
55. Acheson, Dean, *Present at the Creation: My Years at the State Department*, New York: W. W. Norton and Co., 1969, p. 528.
56. Miller, Linda, 'Innocence Abroad? Congress, the President and Foreign Policy', *The World Today*, April 1987.
57. PPP, Reagan II, p. 1546.
58. Ibid.
59. Mandelbaum, *The Luck of the President*, p. 400.
60. Geyelin, *The Reagan Crisis*, p. 451.
61. Ibid., p. 454.
62. *TWP*, 15 January 1986.
63. Shultz, *New Realities*, p. 706.
64. Anderson, Martin, *Revolution*, New York: Harcourt Brace Jovanovich, 1988, pp. 291–2.
65. Foreign Assistance and Related Programs Appropriations for 1986. Hearings before a Sub-Committee on Appropriations, House of Representatives, 27 March 1985, H181–97.
66. Ibid., p. 170.
67. Ibid., p. 171.
68. Ibid.
69. Ibid., p. 212.
70. Ibid., p. 236.

71. Ibid., pp. 236–7.
72. Ibid., p. 241.
73. Ibid., p. 242.
74. Ibid.
75. *UN Chronicle*, Vol. XXIII, No. 1, January 1986, p. 17.
76. Ibid.
77. Ibid.
78. *TWP*, 6 July 1985.
79. *TWP*, 12 July 1985.
80. Shultz, *The Meaning of Vietnam*, p. 13.
81. 'An Update – Americans Missing in Indochina', John C. Monjo, *Department of State Bulletin*, May 1986, p. 63.
82. *TWP*, 12 October 1988.
83. State Department statement in *TWP*, 11 April 1985.
84. From personal interviews conducted by the author with members of both American and British special forces it is clear that no distinction was made between the NCR and KR personnel when training and assistance were provided.
85. *TWP*, 8 July 1988.
86. Twining, Charles H., 'The Situation in Cambodia', *Current Policy*, No. 113, 29 September 1988. Walters, Vernon A. 'Efforts Towards a Cambodian Settlement', *Current Policy*, No., 1131, General Assembly address, 18 October 1988.
87. PPP, Reagan II, 1985, p. 1207.
88. PPP, Reagan I, 1986, p. 541.
89. 'US Policy Toward Anti-Communist Insurgencies', hearing before a Sub-Committee of the Committee on Appropriations, Senate Hearing 99-315, May 1985, p. 5.
90. Ibid., p. 118.
91. Ibid., p. 7.
92. Ibid.
93. Sub-Committee on Asian and Pacific Affairs (88–H381–38), p. 279.
94. 'The Implications of Establishing Reciprocal Interest Sections with Vietnam'. Hearing before the Sub-Committee on Asian and Pacific Affairs, 28 July 1988, (H381–65), p. 23.
95. Ibid., p. 2.
96. Ibid., p. 6.
97. Ibid., p. 36.
98. Ibid., p. 38.
99. Ibid., p. 47.
100. Ibid., p. 57.
101. Ibid., p. 58.
102. Ibid.
103. Ibid., p. 63.
104. Ibid.
105. *Congress Quarterly Almanac*, 1988, p. 540.
106. Hearing before the Sub-Committee on Asian and Pacific Affairs on H. J. Res 602, 30 June and 28 July 1988 (H381-64).
107. Ibid., p. 2.

108. Ibid., p. 32. This testimony was given by David Lambertson, Deputy Assistant SoS, East Asian and Pacific Affairs.
109. Ibid., p. 67.
110. Ibid., p. 73.
111. PPP, Reagan II, 1988–9, p. 1344.
112. Walters, *Current Policy*, No. 1131.
113. Solarz, Stephen J., 'When to Intervene', *Foreign Policy*, No. 63, Summer, 1986, p. 28.
114. *UN Chronicle*, No. 10/11, Vol. XXII, November/December 1985, p. 58.
115. *UN Chronicle*, No. 1, Vol. XXIII, June 1986, p. 17.
116. SWB, 2 January 1985, FE/7839/A3/4.
117. Ibid., p. A3/5.
118. SWB, 26 January 1985, FE/7863/13/2.
119. SWB, 21 January 1985, FE/7854/ i.
120. SWB, FE/8633/A3/4.
121. SWB, FE/0338/A3/2.
122. SWB, 18 December 1986, FE/8446/ i.
123. SWB, 12 March 1987, FE/8517/A2/8.
124. Sub-Committee on Asian and Pacific Affairs, 28 July 1988.
125. SWB, 9 January 1985, FE/7845/A3/4.
126. SWB, 29 January 1985, FE/7863/ i.
127. *UN Chronicle*, Vol. XXII, No. 10/11, November/December 1985.
128. SWB, 4 December 1987, FE/0018/A3/3.
129. *UN Chronicle*, Vol. XXII, No. 1, 1985, p. 11.
130. *UN Chronicle*, Vol. XXVI, No. 1, March 1989, p. 15.
131. See *UN Chronicle*, Vol. XXIV, No. 1, February 1987, p. 80.
132. SWB, 20 March 1985, FE/7905/A3/3.
133. *TWP*, 4 October 1988.
134. *UN Chronicle*, Vol. XXIII, No. 1, June 1986, p. 17.
135. *UN Chronicle*, Vol. XXIV, No. 1, February 1987, p. 80.
136. Quoted in Leifer, Michael, 'Cambodian Conflict – the Final Phase ?', *Conflict Studies*, No. 221, May 1989, p. 17.
137. *TWP*, 10 February 1985.
138. *TWP*, 13 April 1985.
139. Op. cit. (n. 105).
140. See, for example, William Branigan's report in *TWP* 10 February 1985.
141. SWB, 2 April 1985, FE/7917/A3/5.
142. SWB, 17 August 1985, FE/8032/ i.
143. SWB, 22 August 1985, FE/8037/ i.
144. Bilveer, S., *Asian Defence Journal*, May 1985, p. 34.
145. *TWP*, 12 February 1985.
146. McGregor, Charles, 'The Sino-Vietnamese Relationship and the Soviet Union', *Adelphi Paper 232*, Autumn 1988, p. 7.
147. Bach, William, 'A Chance in Cambodia', *Foreign Policy*, No. 62, Spring 1986, p. 85.
148. Duiker, William J., 'Vietnam Moves Toward Pragmatism', *Current History*, April 1987, p. 179. At the same 6th Congress, Truongh Chinh resigned from the Politburo.
149. Alagappa, Muthiah, 'Regionalism and the Quest for Security: ASEAN

and the Cambodian Conflict', *Australian Journal of International Affairs*, October 1993, p. 200.
150. Monjo, John C., *Department of State Bulletin*, May 1987, p. 30.
151. Alagappa, *Regionalism*.
152. Leifer, *Cambodian Conflict*, p. 11.
153. *UN Chronicle*, Vol. XXV, No. 2, June 1988, p. 6.
154. *UN Chronicle*, Vol. XXV, No. 4, December 1988, p. 33.
155. Ibid.
156. *TWP*, 18 June 1988.
157. *TWP*, 15 July 1988.
158. Ibid.
159. *TWP*, 8 August 1988.
160. *TWP*, 25 July 1988.
161. Chanda, Nayan, *FEER*, 27 October 1988, p. 17.
162. SWB, 17 December 1988, FE/0340/i.
163. Farewell address, 11 January 1989, *Weekly Compilation of Presidential Papers*, 25.3.53.
164. See, for example, Geyelin, *The Reagan Crisis*; Mandelbaum, *The Luck of the President*; Miller, *Innocence Abroad*.
165. Wills in Hogan, Joseph (ed.), *The Reagan Years: the Record in Presidential Leadership*, Manchester: MUP, 1990, p. 46.
166. Sharpe, Kenneth E., 'The Real Cause of Irangate', *Foreign Policy*, Fall, 1987, p. 32.
167. Bell, *The Reagan Paradox*, p. 26.

4   THE BUSH ADMINISTRATION

1. PPP, Bush, 1989, p. 5. Press conference given the day after the inaugural.
2. Quoted in Bell, Coral, *The Reagan Paradox: American Foreign Policy in the 1980s*, Aldershot: Edward Elgar, 1989, p. 134.
3. Ibid.
4. *TWP*, 9 January 1989.
5. Quoted in *TWP*, 19 January 1989.
6. Ibid.
7. Bush, George with Victor Gold, *Looking Forward*, London: Bodley Head, 1988, p. 174.
8. Hartmann, Frederick A. and Wendzel, Robert L., *America's Foreign Policy in a Changing World*, New York: Harper Collins, 1994.
9. Prados, John, *Keepers of the Keys: A History of the National Security Council from Truman to Bush*, New York: William Morrow and Co., 1991.
10. Hartmann, *America's Foreign Policy*, p. 166.
11. Kegley, Charles W. and Wittkopf, Eugene R., *American Foreign Policy: Pattern and Process*, 4th edition, New York: St Martin's Press, 1991, p. 257.
12. Ibid., p. 502.
13. Goodgame, Dan, *Time Magazine*, 22 October 1990, p. 26.

14. Kegley, *American Foreign Policy*, p. 351.
15. Bush, *Looking Forward*, p. 251.
16. Ibid., p. 252.
17. Kegley, *American Foreign Policy*, p. 554.
18. See, among others, Melanson, Richard, *Reconstructing Consensus*, New York: St Martin's Press, 1991, p. 205.
19. Bush, *Looking Forward*, p. 204.
20. Melanson, *Reconstructing Consensus*, p. 211.
21. *TWP, National Weekly Edition*, 24 February–1 March 1991, pp. 9–10.
22. Hastedt, Glenn, *American Foreign Policy: Past, Present, Future*, 2nd edition, New Jersey: Prentice-Hall, 1991, p. 114.
23. Barber, J. D., *NYT*, 19 January 1989, p. A31.
24. Stoessinger, J. G., *Crusaders and Pragmatists: Movers of Modern American Foreign Policy*, New York: Norton, 1985, p. 317.
25. *NYT*, Op-Ed, 19 September 1989.
26. Hastedt, *American Foreign Policy*, p. 219.
27. Hartmann, *America's Foreign Policy*, p. 166.
28. Deibel, Terry L., 'Bush's Foreign Policy: Mastery and Inaction', *Foreign Policy*, Fall, 1991, p. 6.
29. Hastedt, *American Foreign Policy*, p. 122.
30. Goodgame, Dan, *Time Magazine*, 7 January 1991, pp. 14–15.
31. Deibel, *Bush's Foreign Policy*, p. 9.
32. Mervin, David, *The President of the United States*, New York: Wheatsheaf, 1993, p. 234.
33. Kegley, *American Foreign Policy*, p. 502.
34. *Current Policy*, No. 1178, USGPO, 24 May 1989, speech to the Coast Guard Academy.
35. PPP, Bush 1989, 9 February 1989, p. 79. Address to a Joint Session of Congress.
36. Mervin, *The President*, p. 216.
37. Goodgame, Dan, *Time Magazine*, 22 October 1990, p. 26.
38. Deibel, *Bush's Foreign Policy*, p. 8.
39. Hastedt, *American Foreign Policy*, p. 114.
40. Melanson, *Reconstructing Consensus*, p. 205.
41. Ibid., p. 210.
42. Kegley, *American Foreign Policy*, p. 370.
43. Melanson, *Reconstructing Consensus*, p. 205.
44. Kegley, *American Foreign Policy*, p. 336.
45. Bush, *Looking Forward*, p. 173.
46. *TWP*, National Weekly Edition, April 17–23, 1989, pp. 23–4.
47. Deibel, *Bush's Foreign Policy*, p. 5.
48. The United States Information Agency produced a PR booklet (undated) in which Baker was described in this way.
49. Kegley, *American Foreign Policy*, p. 544.
50. Ibid., p. 546.
51. Edward Luttwak quoted in ibid., p. 550.
52. Quoted in ibid., p. 82.
53. See Williams, P. and Miller, C., 'The Bush Administaration's Foreign Policy Review', in Pugh, M. and Williams, P., *Superpower Politics:*

Change in the United States and the Soviet Union, Manchester: MUP, 1990.

54. Kegley, *American Foreign Policy*, p. 545.
55. Ibid., p. 549.
56. PPP, Bush 1989, 17 April, 12 May, 21 May, 23 May, 24 May.
57. 'Sino-American Relations: One year after the massacre at Tiananmen Square', hearing before the Sub-Committee on East Asian and Pacific Affairs [101–2], 6 June 1990, S381-24.
58. Ibid., p. 5.
59. Ibid., p. 6.
60. Ibid., p. 25.
61. Sullivan, Roger W., 'Discarding the China Card', *Foreign Policy*, Spring 1992, p. 11.
62. Op. cit. (n. 57), p. 15.
63. Baker, James A., III 'America in Asia: Emerging Architecture for a Pacific Community', *Foreign Affairs*, Winter 1991–2, 70(5).
64. *TWP*, 10 December 1989.
65. Ibid.
66. Ibid.
67. Ibid.
68. Baker, *America in Asia*, p. 16.
69. Ibid., p. 15.
70. US Information Service. Official text of Bush address to the UN General Assembly, 23 September 1992.
71. 'US Policy Toward Indochina', hearing before the Sub-Committee on East Asia and Pacific Affairs, 2 October 1989, pp. 11, 101–617.
72. *TWP*, 4 April 1989.
73. *TWP*, 15 January 1990.
74. *Current Policy*, No. 1281, 18 April 1990.
75. (a) 'The Paris Peace Conference on Cambodia: Implications for US Policy', hearing before the Sub-Committee on Asian and Pacific Affairs, 14 September 1989.
(b) 'US Policy Toward Indochina', hearing before the Sub-Committee on East Asia and Pacific Affairs, 2 October 1989, 101–617.
(c) 'Issues Affecting the Question of United States Relations with Vietnam', hearing before the Sub-Committees on Asian and Pacific Affairs and International Economic Policy and Trade, 17 November 1989.
76. Op. cit. (n. 75c), p. 57.
77. Op. cit. (n. 75b), p. 19.
78. Op. cit. (n. 75a), p. 50.
79. For an excellent explication of the legal aspects of Vietnam's 1979 invasion of Cambodia see Klintworth, G., *Vietnam's Intervention in Cambodia in International Law*, Canberra: Australian Government Publishing Services, 1989.
80. Op. cit. (n. 75a), p. 62.
81. Ibid., p. 10.
82. Op. cit. (n. 75b), p. 11.
83. Op. cit. (n. 75a), p. 37.

84. Ibid.
85. Ibid., p. 43.
86. Ibid.
87. Op. cit. (n. 75a), p. 10.
88. Op. cit. (n. 75b), p. 21.
89. Transcript of announcement by Baker issued by the State Department, 18 July 1990.
90. Ibid.
91. Ibid.
92. 'Cambodian Peace Negotiations: Propects for a Settlement', hearings before the Sub-Committee on East Asian and Pacific Affairs, 20 July and 19 September 1990, p. 64 (101–1118).
93. 'United States Policy Toward Cambodia: Prospects for a Negotiated Settlement', hearing before the Sub-Committee on Asian and Pacific Affairs, 12 September 1990, p. 4.
94. Ibid., p. 23.
95. *TWP*, 28 July 1990.
96. *International Herald Tribune* (*IHT*), 19 July 1990, p. 1.
97. *Independent*, 6 September 1990, p. 14.
98. ABC-TV, 26 April 1990, transcript no. 14, p. 9.
99. *Keesings*, p. 38149.
100. 'The Cambodian Peace Agreement', hearing before the Sub-Committee on Asian and Pacific Affairs, 17 October 1991.
101. Ibid., p. 4.
102. Op. cit. (n. 75c), p. 121.
103. Ibid.
104. Ibid.
105. Ibid., p. 139.
106. *NYT*, 24 October 1991, p. A16.
107. Chanda, Nayan, 'Civil War in Cambodia', *Foreign Policy*, Fall, 1989, p. 39.
108. *TWP*, 30 July 1989.
109. Quoted in a Federation of American Scientists (FAS) publication, *Sihanouk Forces Fighting in Co-operation with Khmer Rouge*, 13 February 1990.
110. Ibid.
111. *TWP*, 9 April 1989.
112. PPP, Bush I, 1989, 20 April 1989.
113. *TWP*, 28 April 1989.
114. *TWP*, 5 May 1989.
115. *TWP*, 1 June 1989.
116. *TWP*, 3 June 1989.
117. *TWP*, 16 June 1989.
118. 'Recent Developments in Cambodia', hearing before the Sub-Committee on Asian and Pacific Affairs, 10 December 1990, p. 54.
119. Op. cit. (n. 93).
120. Ibid., p. 5.
121. *TWP*, 28 February 1991.
122. *TWP*, 12 April 1991.

123. PPP, Bush I, 1989, 25 February 1989, p. 133.
124. PPP, Bush I, 1992–3, 2 January 1992, p. 27.
125. *TWP*, 9 September 1989.
126. *TWP*, 15 January 1990.
127. Op. cit. (n. 75b), p. 2.
128. Op. cit. (n. 75a), p. 5.
129. Quoted in FAS Public Interest Report, 42 (8), October 1989, p. 12.
130. *TWP*, 3 June 1989.
131. *TWP*, 13 June 1989.
132. Ibid.
133. *TWP*, 16 May 1989.
134. 'Prospects for Peace in Cambodia', hearing before the Sub-Committee on East Asian and Pacific Affairs, 28 February 1990, pp. 5, 101-600.
135. Ibid., pp. 39–40.
136. Ibid., pp. 127–8.
137. Senate Concurrent Resolution 101 (101–2), 7 March 1990.
138. Op. cit. (n. 134), p. 126.
139. Op. cit. (n. 92), p. 1.
140. Ibid., p. 79.
141. 'US Economic Embargo on Vietnam', hearing before the Sub-Committees on Asian and Pacific Affairs and International Economic Policy and Trade, 25 June 1991, p. 1.
142. Ibid., p. 10.
143. *TWP*, 4 April 1989.
144. Chanda, *Civil War in Cambodia*, p. 43.
145. *Independent*, 22 July 1990, p. 22.
146. *NYT*, 26 April 1990, p. C22.
147. *TWP*, 7 May 1990, p. A10.
148. FAS publication dated 11 March 1989.
149. Haas, Michael *Cambodia, Pol Pot, and the United States: the Faustian Pact*, New York: Praeger, 1991, p. 72.
150. Haas, Michael 'The Paris Conference on Cambodia, 1989', *Bulletin of Concerned Asian Scholars*, 23 (2), 1991, p. 46.
151. Ibid., p. 49.
152. Ibid., p. 52.
153. *TWP*, 26 November 1989.
154. Op. cit. (n. 141), p. 37.
155. Heng Samrin's New Year message reported in *Keesings*, p. 37963.
156. SWB, 15 February 1989, FE/0387/A3/1.
157. SWB, 19 February 1989, FE/0391/A3/4.
158. *UN Chronicle*, September 1989, Vol. XXVI, No. 3, p. 22.
159. Do Muoi [Chairman of Vietnam's Council of Ministers] said that, 'Vietnam needed to extricate itself from involvement in Cambodia in order to concentrate on its own development problems.' Quoted in Muskie, Edmund, *Exploiting Cambodia: Issues and Reality in a Time of Transition*, Washington DC: Center for National Policy Press, October 1990, p. 10.
160. SWB, 6 September 1989, FE/0556/ i.
161. Williams, Michael, *Vietnam at the Crossroads*, London: Chatham

House Papers, RIIA, 1992, p. 63.
162. *Independent*, 23 November 1990, p. 12.
163. Leifer, Michael, *Cambodian Conflict – the Final Phase?* Conflict Studies No 221, Institute for the Study of Conflict, May 1989, p. 26.
164. *TWP*, 1 June 1989.
165. SWB, 26 February 1989, FE/0395/ i.
166. See, for example, SWB, 23 February 1989 and 31 August 1989.
167. SWB, 21 August 1989.
168. *Independent*, 3 September 1991, p. 13.
169. *Beijing Review*, 6–12 November 1989, p. 10.
170. SWB, 25 January 1989, FE/0369/A3/2.
171. SWB, 7 February 1989, FE/0378/C2/1.
172. SWB, 29 November 1989, FE/0625/ i.
173. Keirnan, Ben, 'The Cambodian Crisis, 1990–1992: the Plan, the Khmer Rouge, and the State of Cambodia', *Bulletin of Concerned Asian Scholars*, 24(2), 1992, p. 23.
174. Op. cit. (n. 75a), p. 38.
175. *Beijing Review*, 30 July–5 August 1990.
176. Bekaert, Jacques, *Jane's Defence Weekly*, 2 March 1991.
177. Muranushi, Michini, 'Concept of Enemy: the Khmer Rouge and the World', paper presented at the ISA Conference, Vancouver, March 1991.
178. Chanda, Nayan, *FEER*, 23 July 1992, p. 8.
179. *Independent*, 14 October 1992.
180. Leifer, Michael, *International Herald Tribune*, 5 September 1990, p. 4.
181. Acharya, Amitav, 'A New Regional Order in South-East Asia: ASEAN in the Post-Cold War Era', *Adelphi Paper, 279*, August 1993, p. 43.
182. SWB, 12 March 1989, FE/0411/A3/2.
183. SWB, 16 November 1989, FE/0616/ i.
184. *UN Chronicle*, September 1989, Vol. XXVI, No. 3, p. 22.
185. *TWP*, 9 September 1989.
186. Haas, *Faustian Pact*, pp. 106–7.
187. Ibid., p. 110.
188. SWB, 20 July 1990, FE/0821/A3/1.
189. Ibid., A3/3.
190. Ibid.
191. *UN Chronicle*, December 1989, Vol. XXVI, No. 4, p. 25.
192. *UN Chronicle*, March 1991, Vol. XXVIII, No. 1, p. 65.
193. *Independent*, 23 November 1990.
194. 'Cambodia: an Australian Peace Proposal', working papers prepared for [JIM] 26–28 February 1990.
195. *Backgrounder*, Vol. 1, No. 18, 29 June 1990, Australian Foreign Affairs Record, Canberra, p. 7.
196. *Daily Telegraph*, 18 July 1991, p. 8.
197. UN Publication DPI/1180-92077, January 1992, p. 4.
198. *Independent*, 5 October 1992, p. 12.
199. Copy held by author.
200. Quoted in *FEER*, 23 July 1992, p. 9.
201. Ibid., p. 8.

202. Deibel, *Bush's Foreign Policy*, p. 3.
203. Baker, *America in Asia*, p. 5.
204. Mandelbaum, *The Bush Foreign Policy*, p. 11.
205. Editorial in *TWP*, 24 November 1991.
206. Mervin, *The President*, p. 234.
207. Op. cit. (n. 93), p. 3.

CONCLUSION

1. 'US Policy Toward Indochina Since Vietnam's Occupation of Kampuchea', hearing before the Sub-Committee on Asian and Pacific Affairs, 15/21/22 October 1982, p. 41.
2. Bell, Coral, *The Reagan Paradox: American Foreign Policy in the 1980s*, Aldershot: Edward Elgar, 1989.
3. Interview, 12 February 1993.
4. Carter, Jimmy, *Keeping Faith: Memoirs of a President*, London: Collins, 1982, p. 195.
5. Op. cit. (n. 3).
6. Ibid.
7. Vance, Cyrus, *Hard Choices: Critical Years in America's Foreign Policy*, New York: Simon and Schuster, 1983, p. 124.
8. Ibid., p. 127.
9. 'US Policy in Southeast Asia', hearing before the Sub-Committee on East Asian and Pacific Affairs, July 1981, p. 1.
10. Boynton, G. R., 'Telling the Cambodian Story: How Past is Present in Writing International Affairs', paper presented at the ISA Conference, March 1994, Washington DC.
11. *TWP*, 11 August 1991.
12. Op. cit. (n. 3).
13. Ibid.
14. Ibid.
15. Melanson, Richard A., *Writing History and Making Policy*, Lathane: University Press of America, 1983, pp. 181–2.

EPILOGUE

1. *TWP*, 9 August 1995.
2. Fact Sheet released by the Bureau of East Asian and Pacific Affairs, US Department of State, 20 June 1995.
3. Oddly, in early 1998 there was movement by the Clinton administration to engineer the arrest and show trial of Pol Pot, possibly as one of many foreign diversions from the President's personal domestic difficulties. However, even this small escapade was frustrated by Pol Pot's death on 15 April 1998, almost 23 years to the day since he entered Phnom Penh with his victorious Khmer Rouge. At the time of writing it is unclear whether the US will pursue other leaders such as Khieu Samphan, Ta Mok and Noun Chea; that decision may also have more to do with

domestic than foreign policy.

4. There is evidence that the State Department are not committed to Ranarridh. In testimony, Stanley Roth (see n. 11) made the following comment: 'Exiled parliamentarians, *ideally* including Prince Ranarridh, should be allowed to return to Cambodia safely ...' (emphasis added).

5. House International Relations Committee, Sub-Committee on East Asian and Pacific Affairs, 16 July 1997.

6. Ibid.

7. *TWP*, 16 July 1997.

8. Vietnam, along with Malaysia, originally resisted the suspension of Cambodia's entry at an emergency meeting of the foreign ministers on 10 July 1997.

9. Op. cit. (n. 4).

10. Ibid.

11. Statement on Situation in Cambodia by Stanley O. Roth, Assistant Secretary of State for East Asian and Pacific Affairs, before the Senate Committee on Foreign Relations, Sub-Committee on East Asian and Pacific Affairs, 4 September 1997.

12. ASEAN's constitution has a firm commitment to a 10-state membership.

Select Bibliography

Abernathy, W., Hill, D., and Williams, P., *The Carter Years: the President and Policy Making*, London: Weidenfeld & Nicolson, 1983.

Alagappa, Muthiah, 'Regionalism and the Quest for Security, ASEAN and the Cambodia Conflict', *Australian Journal of International Affairs*, October 1993.

Axelford, R. (ed.), *Structure and Decision: the Cognitive Maps of Political Elites*, Princeton: Princeton University Press, 1976.

Bach, William, 'A Chance in Cambodia', *Foreign Policy*, No. 62, Spring 1986.

Baker, James A. III, 'America in Asia: Emerging Architecture for a Pacific Community', *Foreign Affairs*, Winter 1991–92, Vol. 70, No. 5.

Baker, Ross K., *The Election of 1980: Reports and Interpretations*, Chatham House, 1981.

Barber, James D., *The Presidential Character*, New York: Prentice-Hall, 3rd edition, 1977.

Barger, Harold M., *The Impossible Presidency: Illusions and Realities of Executive Power*, Glenview: Scott Foresman, 1984.

Bekaert, Jacques, 'Cambodia: a nasty little war', *International Defense Review*, Vol. 22, March 1989.

Bell, Coral, *The Reagan Paradox: American Foreign Policy in the 1980s*, Aldershot: Edward Elgar, 1989.

Boynton, G. R., 'Telling the Cambodian Story: How Past is Present in International Affairs', Paper delivered at the ISA Conference in Washington DC, April 1994.

Brzezinski, Zbigniew, 'The Best National Security System: a Conversation with Zbigniew Brzezinski', *Washington Quarterly*, No. 1, 1982.

Brzezinski, Zbigniew, *Power and Principle*, London: Weidenfeld & Nicolson, 1983.

Brzezinski, Zbigniew, 'The NSC's Midlife Crisis', *Foreign Policy*, No. 69, Winter 1987–88.

Bush, George with Gold, V., *Looking Forward*, London: Bodley Head, 1988.

Carter, Hodding, III, 'Life Inside the Carter State Department', *Playboy*, February 1981, Vol. 28, No. 2.

Carter, Jimmy, 'Foreign Policy Based on America's Essential Character', Speech of Notre Dame, 22 May 1977, *State Department Bulletin*, 13 June 1997.

Carter, Jimmy, *Keeping Faith*, London: Collins, 1982.

Chanda, Nayan, *Brother Enemy*, London: Harcourt Brace Jovanovich, 1986.

Chanda, Nayan, 'Civil War in Cambodia', *Foreign Policy*, No. 77, Fall 1989.

Chandler, David P., 'Strategies for Survival in Kampuchea', *Current History*, No. 82, April 1983.

Chandler, David P., *History of Cambodia*, Boulder, Co: Westview Press, 2nd edition, 1992,

Cohen, Bernard C., *The Public's Impact on Foreign Policy*, New York: University Press of America, 1983.

Deibel, Terry L., 'Bush's Foreign Policy: Mastery and Inaction', *Foreign Policy*, Fall, 1991.

Dugger, R., *On Reagan: the Man and his Presidency*, London: McGraw-Hill, 1983.

Duiker, William J., 'Vietnam Moves toward Pragmatism', *Current History*, April 1987.

Dutter, Lee E. and Kania, R., 'Explaining Recent Vietnamese Behaviour', *Asian Survey*, Vol. 20, No. 9, Sept. 1980.

Farer, Tom J., 'Secretary for Defeat', *Foreign Policy*, No. 40, Fall, 1980.

Fromkin, David and Chace, J., 'What *Are* the Lessons of Vietnam?', *Foreign Affairs*, Vol. 63, 1984–85.

Gelb, Leslie H. and Lake, Anthony, 'Four More Years: Diplomacy Restored', *Foreign Affairs*, 63 (3), 1985.

George, Alexander L., 'The "Operational Code": a Neglected Approach to the Study of Political Leaders and Decision-Making', *International Studies Quarterly*, 13 (2), 1969.

George, Alexander L., 'The Case for Multiple Advocacy in Making Foreign Policy', *American Political Science Review*, September 1972, pp. 751–85.

George, Alexander L., *Presidential Decision-Making in Foreign Policy: the Effective Use of Information and Advice*, Boulder: Westview Press, 1980.

George A. L., 'Quantitative and Qualitative Approaches to Content Analysis', in Itheiel de Sola Pool (ed.), *Trends in Content Analysis*, Urbana: University of Illinois Press, 1959.

Geyelin, Philip, 'The Reagan Crisis: Dreaming Impossible Dreams', *Foreign Affairs*, 1986, Round-up issue.

Haas, Michael, *Basic Documents of Asian Regional Organizations*, Wy., USA: Oceania, Dobbs Ferry, 1984.

Haas, Michael, *Cambodia, Pol Pot, and the United States: the Faustian Pact*, New York: Praeger, 1991.

Haas, Michael, 'The Paris Conference on Cambodia, 1989', *Bulletin of Concerned Asian Scholars*, Vol. 23, No. 2, 1991.

Hahn, Dan F., 'The Rhetoric of Jimmy Carter 1976–1980', *Presidential Studies Quarterly*, Vol. 14, No. 2, 1984.

Haig, Alexander Jr., *Caveat: Realism, Reagan, and Foreign Policy*, London: Weidenfeld & Nicolson, 1984.

Halperin, Morton H. and Kanter, Arnold (eds.), *Readings in American Foreign Policy: A Bureaucratic Perspective*, Boston: Little, Brown & Co., 1973.

Hartmann, Frederick A. and Wendzel, Robert L., *America's Foreign Policy in a Changing World*, New York: Harper-Collins, 1994.

Hastedt, G., *American Foreign Policy: Past, Present and Future*, New Jersey: Prentice-Hall, 2nd edition, 1991.

Hermann, Margaret G. and Charles F., 'Who Makes Foreign Policy Decisions and How: an Empirical Inquiry', *International Studies Quarterly*, 33, 1989.

Hill, D., Moore R. and Williams P. (eds.), *The Reagan Presidency: An Incomplete Revolution?* London: Macmillan Press, 1990.

Hilsman, R., *The Politics of Policy Making in Defense and Foreign Affairs; Conceptual Models and Bureaucratic Politics*, New York; Englewood Cliffs: Prentice-Hall Inc., 1987.

Hoffman, S., *Gulliver's Troubles: or the Setting of American Foreign Policy*, New York: McGraw-Hill Paperbacks, 1968.

Hogan, J. (ed.), *The Reagan Years*, Manchester: Manchester University Press, 1990.

Holsti, O. R., 'The Belief System and National Image', *Conflict Resolution*, 6 October 1962.

Jackson, Karl D., 'Cambodia 1978: War, Pillage and Purge in Democratic Kampuchea', *Asian Survey*, Vol. 19, No. 1, January 1979.

Jervis, R., *Perception and Misperception in International Politics*, Princeton: Princeton University Press, 1976.

Jervis, Robert, 'The Costs of the Quantitative Study of International Relations', in Knorr, Klaus and Rosenau, James N. (eds.), *Contending Approaches in International Politics*, Princeton: Princeton University Press, 1969.

Jordan, Hamilton, *Crisis: the Last Year of the Carter Presidency*, London: Michael Joseph, 1982.

Kegley, Charles W. and Wittkopf, Eugene R., *American Foreign Policy: Pattern and Process*, New York: 3rd edition 1987, 4th edition 1991, St Martin's Press.

Kellerman, B. and Barrilleaux, R. J., *The President as a World Leader*, New York: St Martin's Press, 1991.

Kennan, George, 'Morality and Foreign Policy', *Foreign Affairs*, Vol. 64, No. 2, Winter 1985/86.

Kiernan, Ben, 'Vietnam and the Governments and People of Kampuchea', *Bulletin of Concerned Asian Scholars*, Vol. 12, No. 1, 1980.

Kiernan, Ben, 'A Proposal for Peace', *Inside Asia*, Feb.–Mar. 1985.

Kiernan, Ben, 'The Cambodian Crisis, 1990–1992: the UN Plan, the Khmer Rouge, and the State of Cambodia', *Bulletin of Concerned Asian Scholars*, Vol. 24, No. 2, 1992.

Kissinger, Henry, 'Domestic Structure and Foreign Policy', *Daedalus*, April 1966.

Kissinger, Henry, *The White House Years*, London: Weidenfeld & Nicolson, 1979.

Kissinger, Henry, *Years of Upheaval*, London: Weidenfeld & Nicolson, 1982.

Kissinger, H. and Vance C., 'Bipartisan Objectives for American Foreign Policy', *Foreign Affairs*, Vol. 66, No. 5, Summer 1988.

Klintworth, G., *Vietnam's Intervention in Cambodia in International Law*, Canberra: Australian Government Publication Services, 1989.

Kolko, G., *The Roots of American Foreign Policy: an Analysis of Power and Purpose*, Boston: Beacon Press, 1969.

Larson, D., *The Origins of Containment*, Princeton: Princeton University Press, 1985.

Leifer, Michael, 'Cambodian Conflict – The Final Phase?', *Conflict Studies*, No. 221, May 1989.

Leifer, Michael, *ASEAN and the Security of South-East Asia*, London: Routledge, 1989.

Mandelbaum, Michael, 'The Luck of the President', *Foreign Affairs*, 1985 round-up.

Mandelbaum, Michael, 'The Bush Foreign Policy', *Foreign Affairs*, America and the World 1990/91.

Mayer, J. and McManus D., *Landslide: the Unmaking of the President, 1984–88*, Boston: Houghton Mifflin, 1988.

McCormick, J. M., *American Foreign Policy and Process*, USA: F. E. Peacock, 1992.

McMahan, J., *Reagan and the World: Imperial Policy in the New Cold War*, London: Pluto Press, 1984.

Melanson, Richard A., *Writing History and Making Policy*, Lathane, Md.: University Press of America, 1983.

Melanson, Richard A., *Reconstructing Consensus: American Foreign Policy since the Vietnam War*, New York: St Martin's Press, 1991.

Mervin, David, *Ronald Reagan and the American Presidency*, New York: Longman Group, 1990.

Mervin, David, *The President of the United States*, London, Wheatsheaf, 1993.

Miller, Linda B., 'Innocence Abroad? Congress, the President and Foreign Policy', *The World Today*, April 1987.

Moens, Alexander, *Foreign Policy Under Carter: Testing Multiple Advocacy Decision-Making*, Boulder, Co.: Westview Press, 1990.

Muskie, Edmund, *Exploring Cambodia: Issues and Reality in a Time of Transition*, Washington DC: Center for National Policy Press, October 1990.

Nash, Henry T., *American Foreign Policy: A Search for Security*, Chicago: Dorsey Press, 1985.

Neustadt, Richard E., *Presidential Power*, New York: Wiley, 1960.

Nye, Joseph S. Jr., 'Understanding US Strength', *Foreign Policy*, No. 72, Fall 1988.

O'Dowd, Ann Reilly, 'What Managers Can Learn From Manager Reagan', *Fortune*, 15 Sept. 86.

O'Neill, Tip with Novak, W., *Man of the House*, New York: Random House, 1987.

Perlmutter, Amos, 'The Presidential Political Center and Foreign Policy: a Critique of the Revisionist and Bureaucratic-Political Orientations', *World Politics*, Vol. 27, No. 1, October 1974.

Prados, John, *Keepers of the Keys: a History of the National Security Council from Truman to Bush*, New York: William Morrow & Co, 1991.

Pugh, M. and Williams P., *Superpower Politics: Change in the United States and the Soviet Union*, Manchester: Manchester University Press, 1990.

Regan, Donald, *For the Record: From Wall Street to Washington*, New York: Harcourt Brace Jovanovich, 1988.

Rosati, Jerel A., 'Developing a Systematic Decision-Making Framework: Bureaucratic Politics in Perspective', *World Politics*, Vol. 23, No. 2, January 1982.

Rosati, Jerel A., *The Carter Administration's Quest for Global Community: Beliefs and their Impact on Behaviour*, University of Carolina Press, 1987.

Rosenau, J. N., *The Scientific Study of Foreign Policy*, London: Frances Pinter, 1980.

Schanberg, Sidney, 'The Death and Life of Dith Pran', *NYT Magazine*, 20 January 1981.

Schlesinger, Arthur M. Jr., *The Imperial Presidency*, London: André Deutsch, 1974.

Shapiro, M., *The Politics of Representation – Writing Practices in Biography, Photography, and Political Analysis*, Madison: University of Wisconsin Press, 1988.

Shapiro, M., Bonham, J. and Heradsveit, D., 'A Discursive Practices Approach to Collective Decision-Making', *International Studies Quarterly*, 32 (4), 1988.

Sharpe, Kenneth E., 'The Real Cause of Irangate', *Foreign Policy*, Fall, 1987.

Shawcross, William, *Sideshow: Kissinger, Nixon and the Destruction of Cambodia*, London: André Deutsch, 1979.

Shultz, George, 'Power and Diplomacy in the 1980s', *Current Policy*, No. 561, 3 April 1984.

Shultz, George, 'New Realities and New Ways of Thinking', *Foreign Affairs*, Vol. 63, No. 4, Spring 1985.

Shultz, George, *Turmoil and Triumph: My Years as Secretary of State*, New York: Charles Scribner's Sons, 1993.

Sihanouk, Prince Norodom, *My War with the CIA*, London: Penguin, 1973.

Smith, Gaddis, *Morality, Reason and Power: American Diplomacy in the Carter Years*, New York: Hill & Wang, 1986.

Smith, Michael, 'Ronald Reagan's Disintegrating World', *The World Today*, February 1987.

Solarz, Stephen J., 'When to Intervene', *Foreign Policy*, No. 63, Summer 1986.

Solarz, Stephen, 'Cambodia and the International Community', *Foreign Affairs*, Spring 1990.

Speakes, L. and Pack, R., *Speaking Out: Inside the Reagan White House*, New York: Charles Scribner's Sons, 1988.

Spear, J. and Williams P., 'Belief Systems and Foreign Policy: the Cases of Carter and Reagan', in Little, R. and Smith S. (eds.), *Belief Systems and International Relations*, Oxford: Blackwell, 1988.

Stockman, D., *Triumph of Politics*, New York: Harper & Row, 1986.

Stoessinger, John, *Crusader's and Pragmatists: Movers of Modern American Foreign Policy*, New York: W. W. Norton & Co., 1979.

Sullivan, Roger W., 'Discarding the China Card, *Foreign Policy*, Spring 1992.

Sullivan, William H., 'Dateline Iran: the Road Not Taken', *Foreign Policy*, No. 40, Fall 1980.

Sutter, Robert G., *The Cambodian Crisis and US Policy Dilemmas*, Boulder, Co.: Westview Press, 1991.

Taber, Charles S., 'POLI: an Expert System Model of US Foreign Policy Belief Systems', *American Political Science Review*, 86 (1), December 1992.

Thornton, Richard C., *The Carter Years: Towards a New Global Order*, New York: Washington Institute Press Book, 1991.

Tonelson, Alan, 'The Real National Interest', *Foreign Policy*, No. 61, Winter 1985–86.

Tower Commission Report, New York: Bantam Books, 1987.

Tucker, Robert W., 'Reagan's Foreign Policy', *Foreign Affairs*, Winter 1988/99.

Tulis, J. K., *The Rhetorical Presidency*, New Jersey: Princeton University Press, 1987.

Vance, Cyrus, 'Meeting the Challenges of a Changing World', *State Department Bulletin*, June 1979, speech in Chicago, 1 May 1979.

Vance, Cyrus, *Hard Choices: Critical Years in America's Foreign Policy*, New York: Simon & Schuster, 1983.

Vertzberger, Y., *The World in their Minds: Information Processing, Cognition, and Perception in Foreign Policy Decision-Making*, Stanford: Stanford University Press, 1990.

Walker, S. G., 'The Motivational Foundation of Belief Systems: a Re-Analysis of Operational Code Construct', *International Studies Quarterly*, Vol. 27, 1983.

Watson, John, *National Journal*, 30 October 1976.

Weinberger, Caspar, *Annual Report to the Congress*, fiscal year 1987.

Williams, Michael C., *Vietnam at the Crossroads*, London: Chatham House Papers, RIIA, 1992.

Yanklevich, I., 'Foreign Policy After the Election', *Foreign Affairs*, Vol. 71, No. 4.

Index

21889720R00142

Printed in Great Britain
by Amazon